C000139550

The Old-Fashioned Woman

Primitive Fancies about the Sex

By

Elsie Clews Parsons, Ph.D.
Author of "The Family," etc.

G. P. Putnam's Sons
New York and London
The Knickerbocker Press
1913

3

The Knickerbocker Press, New York

To

Those Who Believe in Her and to Those Who Don't

By Elsie Clews Parsons

The Family

The Old-Fashioned Woman

FOREWORD

PRIMITIVE ideas are always grave and always troublesome—until recognised. Then they become on the one hand powerless to create situations, and on the other, enlivening.

Feminism and anti-feminism are both made up of primitive ideas. That is why their unwitting exponents can be alike so dull and so exacting—if taken seriously. Not till they get some ethnological inkling of themselves will they become better company. If these papers succeed at all in giving it to them, their author hopes to be forgiven for adding, if even frivolously, to the already disproportionate bibliography on Woman.

Many of the books about women are of course a little antiquated, and indeed we suspect that among certain circles this book, too, in so far at least as it is critical, will be discounted as archaic. It is, let us confess; and let us admit we expect to be gathered up some day with the others as an exhibit in a Woman's Museum, a museum for collections of female poetry and biography and romance, of models of women's apartments, women's hotels, and women's buildings at fairs, of specimens of women's industries and arts and clothes; for collections of the first book read by Woman or the first newspaper, the first law brief or the first novel written by her, the first joke made by her, the first medical prescription signed or the first bone set by her, the first degree conferred upon her, the first ballot cast by her—exhibits which alone will be able to prove to a doubting posterity that once women were a distinct social class, the very special object of society's interest—for a variety of reasons.

CONTENTS

Contents

The Old-Fashioned Woman

I

HER CREATION

"AND Pragâpati thought, let me make an abode for him, and he created a woman."[1] "Man-never-known-on-Earth" made First Man, Kiarsidia, "Having Power-to-carry Light." "Man-never-known-on-Earth" also made a woman for the man, Kashatskohakatidise, "Bright-Shining-Woman."[2] To Hindu and Wichita Indian as well as to the Hebrew and his heirs, Eve is an after-thought.

What she is made of may be also significant of man's estimate of her. "In the beginning, when Twashtri came to the creation of woman, he found that he had exhausted his materials in the making of man, and that no solid elements were left. In this dilemma, after profound meditation, he did as follows: He took

N. B. References are given on pp. 331 ff.

the rotundity of the moon, and the curves of creepers, and the clinging of tendrils, and the trembling of grass, and the slenderness of the reed, and the bloom of flowers, and the lightness of leaves, and the tapering of the elephant's trunk, and the glances of deer, and the clustering of rows of bees, and the joyous gaiety of sunbeams, and the weeping of clouds, and the fickleness of the winds, and the timidity of the hare, and the vanity of the peacock, and the softness of the parrot's bosom, and the hardness of adamant, and the sweetness of honey, and the cruelty of the tiger, and the warm glow of fire, and the coldness of snow, and the chattering of jays, and the cooing of the *kôkila*, and the hypocrisy of the crane, and the fidelity of the *chakrawâka*, and compounding all these together, he made woman, and gave her to man."[3] As we shall note later Man proved not altogether grateful, Woman giving him so much trouble—in India.

And yet the Nusairiyeh Arabs must also think of her as very troublesome, for they hold that she was created from the sins of the satans.[4] The Arabs of Algeria say outright that she is an evil creature and a spoiljoy—because God made her out of the tail of a monkey.[5]

* Dähnhardt, Oskar. *Natursagen*, I, 120. Leipzig and Berlin,

The South Slavs also modify the better known Semitic version of her composition. According to them, a dog came along and ran off with the dislocated rib of Adam which God had for a moment laid on the ground. God chased the thief, but only succeeded in grabbing off his tail. So that the best he could do was to make Woman out of the dog's tail. In a Bulgarian variant of this myth, a snake with legs was the thief, and it left its legs behind in God's hands as matter for the making of Woman.[5] It is said that these stories are a convenience in dealing with over-bearing and self-assertive women, just as their more orthodox version has ever been.

They no doubt have also served to justify now and again a man's sense of superiority, that feeling which nowadays in our neighbourhood only the Jew and the Boy frankly express, the one in his daily prayer: "I thank Thee, Lord, for not having created me a woman"; and the other

---

1907. Referring to the Rabbis as his authority, Thomas Moore versifies:

"The old Adam was fashioned, the first of his kind,
  With a tail, like a monkey, full yard and a span,
And when nature cut off this appendage behind,
  Why, then woman was made of the tail of the man.

.   .   .   .

" Every husband remembers the original plan,
  And knowing his wife is no more than his tail,
  Why, he leaves her behind him as much as he can."

whenever you ask him if he wishes he had been born a girl. "It is such a pity," Margaret Fuller describes some one saying to the mother of four sons, "that one of your boys was not a girl." "Who would have been?" asks one of them, overhearing. "I would n't have been, Tom would n't have been, Will would n't have been, Jim would n't have been, who would have been?"

The boy who would have been is certainly rare; less rare the girl unwilling to be a boy. We have all met her, but seldom have we found her as frank as she was in one instance a century or so ago. "I thank Heaven I was *born* a woman," this maiden wrote, "I have now ᴄnly patiently to wait till some clever fellow shall take a fancy to me and place me in a situation. [As a man] I should not be content with mediocrity in anything, but as a woman I am equal to the generality of my sex, and I do not feel that great desire of fame I think I should if I was a man."*

* *A Girl's Life Eighty Years Ago*, p. 102. New York, 1887. Although in due time this girl, so "content with the way God had made her," was "fancied" and "placed," she was not to enjoy her "situation" for long. Twenty-six years old, she died of tuberculosis in the South—her husband in the North unable to leave his "business."

II

GIRL BABIES

" I AM just as glad to have a girl as a boy," says
the mother who from piety or sentimentality,
thinking she ought to be or averse perhaps to
commiseration, fails to realise how much by her
own words she gives herself away. "I suppose
you are glad it is a boy," is another remark judged
fitting to the occasion. Do I merely imagine I
discern disparagement, concern, or mockery in
the intonation of "all girls," or "only girls" in
references to a maleless progeny?

One admits to being fanciful in thinking of such
turns of speech as survivals of female infanticide.
And yet, were there survivals, they would probably be as slight. So many of the reasons for
female infanticide no longer exist. Except in
melodrama, marriage by capture has gone out of
vogue, hence from this point of view girls are no
longer a source of weakness to kindred or tribesmen. Courtship itself, to be sure, may be a

5

serious nuisance. Among the Papuans of Torres
Straits the fact that suitors kept parents from
sleeping at night and greatly hindered work in the
garden by day was given as one of the reasons for
not keeping girl babies alive.[1] Chaperoning is an
arduous activity with us too; still, one has yet
to hear of a parent, however worn out from a round
of supper parties or balls, advocating anything
quite so extreme.

Marriage by purchase was of distinct advantage
to girl babies. Nor is it as antiquated as marriage
by capture. Still, when it does occur with us, the
family does not profit from it as in more primitive
societies. The girl herself gets the bride-price.
Whereas the expense of marrying off a daughter
has become greater, if anything. Bringing a
girl out is more of a drain on the family resources
among us than among savages.

In primitive culture, bride-price aside, it is more
economical to save a boy than a girl where only a
limited number of children are wanted. The boy
works for the family longer. He also keeps the
family property intact. But both boys and girls
have long ceased to be economically rewarding
to their family. Our sons "keep up" the family
name, but in other respects modern parents seem
to expect more of a return from a daughter than a

son—"a girl is so much more companionable
when you are old."

Nor can the modern boy baby expect prefer-
ential treatment as a potential fighter—in view of
modern peace propaganda, of recent pleas for the
conscription of young women as army nurses, and
of the theory of childbearing as a patriotic duty.

/There are communities where the women are
said to kill their infant daughters from pity—fear-
ing the hard lot of women for them. But we
surely would hold that that was an exaggerated
view.)

A great many people discriminate more hu-
manely than through murder against their girl
babies. A Parsee father "recognised" the son,
but not the daughter, of a handmaid.² Among
the Zulus if the first-born is a boy, an ox is slaugh-
tered at the birth feast. If a girl, people say,
"Why should we kill an ox for a girl? She is only
a weed."³ The Sarts also slaughter a beast, a
sheep or a cow, *for a boy*, and his gratified father
gives the midwife a present.⁴ In Servia and
Montenegro there is much festivity for the birth
of a boy. No notice is taken of a girl. Although,
in Montenegro, if the disappointment her coming
brings is repeated, the threshold is replaced to take
off from the house the curse the malevolent must

necessarily have laid on it the day of the wedding.[5] In Switzerland the maiden who carries
the news of a birth to the neighbours wears a
nosegay. To announce a boy she holds another
in her hand.[6] The Arabs of Algeria celebrate the
birth of a boy with festive horse-races. To take
any notice of that of a girl is beneath an Arab's
dignity,[7] and for centuries her advent has been
anything but a pride or pleasure to an Arab .
father. "When any one of them has tidings of
a female child," writes Mahomet, "his face is
overclouded and black, and he has to keep back
his wrath. He skulks away from the people, for
the evil tidings he has heard."[8]

Boys being more desirable than girls, it is natural
that attempts should be made to determine sex.
The Chinese sometimes try to summon the unborn
spirit of a boy through a girl, naming a daughter,
"May-a-son-come" or "Call-a-little-brother."[9]
Father Jerome assures his Roman friend Laeta
that because she had given her infant daughter to
the Lord she herself would be the mother of sons.[10]
In the Nias Islands there is a marriage spirit
called Adù Lawuri who is called upon to give male
offspring.[11] "May God give you an 'arees!" a
bridegroom son, is the proper way to wish well to
a Moslem bride.[12]

But sympathetic magic is relied upon far more
than little sisters or phallic spirits for male progeny.   In the Islands of Torres Straits a boy doll
is nursed by the expectant mother.   She may also
give a party at which a penis-shaped fruit gathered
by her sister-in-law is pressed against her abdomen,
and then handed to a woman who has always borne
male children and who in turn passes it on to the
circle of women.[13]   Among the ancient Hindus a
little boy was made to sit in the bride's lap.[14]   An
Armenian bride is given a boy baby to hold with the
wish: "May you be a happy mother!"[15]   Boys
hit at a Czech bride with their caps.   A Herze-
govinian *fiancée* fastens a man's girdle around her
waist next to the skin.[16]   Roman matrons ate
cockstones;[17] the islanders in the Torres Straits,
male pigeons.[18]   Until quite recently a meat
diet was recommended to our would-be mothers
of sons.

If in spite of all charms a girl is born and, although a girl, let live, her infancy as well as her
birth is apt to differ ceremonially from a boy's.
In eastern Australia one or two joints of the little
finger of a baby girl's left hand are amputated—
to qualify her as a fisherwoman.[19]   To qualify her
for a good match, a Chinese baby has, or rather had,
her feet tight bound.   A Japanese girl baby had

to lie on the ground the first three days of her life—
a custom which "should teach a woman how
necessary it is for her in everything to yield to her
husband the first, and to be herself content with
a second place."[20] A Hindu girl is named and
presented to the sun, given a ceremonial meal and
a ceremonial haircut, like her brother, but the
rites are performed without *mantras* or prayers,—[21]
in India religion on her own account is not for
a woman. In Mecklenburg a new-born girl must
be kissed first by her mother, a boy first by his
father, else the girl will grow whiskers and the boy
be beardless.[22] To make a man of their baby son
the Hamitic Galla proceed more drastically, am-
putating his *mammæ* soon after birth in the belief
that they belong to women only and that with
them no man can become a brave warrior.[23]

The elaborate ritual of hygiene has taken the
place in our nurseries of other ceremonial, and
infant hygiene does not distinguish sex. And so,
nowadays, for a few months at the beginning of
life sex is left to itself. I forget—a boy baby's
things should be blue, a girl's, pink.

III

CLOISTERS AND HAREMS

"WHAT do we do day after day?" asked Hilary one rainy afternoon of her mother and sisters. "A little housework, a little sewing, a little walk, dinner, a little walk, an occasional caller, or call to be made, a little talk, tea, a little fancy work, a little reading, wash your hands and change your frock, high tea. . . . A little reading, a little whist, light your candles, and five bored human beings walk up to bed."[1] And so Hilary the rebellious set off to London to seek her fortune—and men. Hilary had a helpful grandmother and Hilary herself was determined. In other English or New English villages and in almost all more primitive societies, even in American summer resorts, girls unblessed with red hair and the right kind of ancestress have to get on as best they can. The boys go off to camp or club-house or boarding-school to be "made men," says the Australian, to "become manly," say we. Later they are kept away from home by economic exigencies, by

hunting or surveying, by stock-raising or com-
merce. War too, whether hunting heads or
living in barracks, means absenteeism. So does
getting or exercising power in church or state.
Even hospitality is undomestic. Strangers are
"put up" at the club, the centre for the men's
games and amusements. The club-house is of
course taboo to women. Some clubs they may
not even walk past; to "get at" even a husband
or brother inside others, an English "pub," for
example, or the Newport "Reading Room" or
Casino, or even to send a message through to
anyone, they have to lurk about door or side-
walk—and even such tempered proximity requires
temerity.

And yet, despite its desertion by the male, home
is but a *quasi* cloister. Although men may be
made to realise that they have no duties in it or
even that the women do not like to have them
"pottering around the house," they are free, except
on certain critical occasions, to return to it whenever they wish. So that wherever the theory
obtains that girls should be protected from the
world, *i. e.*, from men—or men from girls—special
precautions even in home life are necessary.
Fénelon advised parents not to let girls and boys
play together.[2] When a Leh-ta girl of Burma

passes a boy, she must not look at him.[3] In
Japanese high society, girls were taught not to
sit on a boy's mat or use his wardrobe or bath-
room. He might not hand them anything. Out
walking, they had to keep aloof from even the men
of their family, and, whatever their age, they were
never to go out at night without a light.[4] Once
a Corean girl is eight,[5] or a Chinese girl ten,[6] she
may not enter the men's quarters of her own house.
Were a lad to offer a Greenland girl anything,
even a pinch of snuff, she would be affronted.
A Thlinket Indian girl must not stir out except
after dark and then only with her mother.[7] A
Loango Bantu youth dare not speak to a girl
except before her mother.[8] Scrupulous mothers
with us also make a point of being at home to
their daughters' callers or of always sitting up
until they leave. Away from home, unable to be
at hand themselves, mothers delegate the rôle
of chaperon to maids and governesses, or, their
daughter having "come out," to an "attractive-
young-married-woman."

Outside of very modern circles, the professional
chaperon is an older woman. Her task is more
continuous, but usually less prolonged than with
us. Among the Australian Yaraibanna she has
to look after a girl steadily for six weeks, her

charge living at nubility in an isolated hut.[9] In
the Prince of Wales Island the girl's paternal aunt
takes care of her at this time.   For two months
she lies covered up with sand in a shallow hole
on the beach—an odd lengthening out of a "summer girl's" morning amusement.   In another island of Torres Straits it is her maternal aunts who
"do" for a girl during the three months she has
to spend cooped up within a high circle of bushes
in a dark corner of her home.[10]

Sometimes girls are kept longer "upstairs."
In New Ireland they are shut up in dark cages
for four or five years.[11]   Among the rich Ot Danoms of Borneo they may be kept as long as seven
years in their special hut.   Anemic and stunted,
they spend their time weaving mats, their only
company a slave maid or governess.   At their
"coming out," the sun and the earth, the water,
the trees and the flowers are ceremonially displayed to them.[12]

To the Ot Danoms "how much should a girl
know?" is plainly not a query.   It is in fact a
concern of civilisation.   It is quite modern too.
Ischomachos, an Athenian husband who had views
on educating his wife, a girl of fifteen, told Soc-
rates the greatest pains had been taken with her
by her parents that she might see as little as

possible, hear as little as possible, and ask the fewest possible questions.[13] In describing the Pythoness, Plutarch says that like a human bride she should have a minimum of experience, being "truly a virgin in her soul."[14]

This classical* idea of a bride's qualification has persisted sporadically. Erasmus tells us of a certain German nobleman who, desirous of marrying "a raw, inexperienced maid" that, like Ischomachos, he "might the more easily form her manners to his own humour," chose a seventeen year old girl who had been brought up in the country at home "to do nothing but gossip and play." Incidentally we may note the German, unlike the Athenian, bridegroom gets into difficulties. He undertakes to teach his bride literature and music and "to use her by degrees to repeat the heads of (the) sermons" she hears. But, growing "weary of this life," she rebels, and does nothing but cry and throw herself flat on the ground, beating her head "as tho' she wished for death." Her husband conceals his resentment and begs his father-in-law "to lend a helping hand to cure his daughter's disorder." "Why don't you cudgel her into a due submission?" asks her

* Among savages it does not always prevail. In fact among many savage tribes adolescent girls are without any hesitation carefully instructed about marriage and maternity.

father. "I know my own power," his son-in-law replies, "but I had much rather she should be reformed by your art or authority, than to come to these extremities." Within a day or so her father finds an occasion to tell her what a homely and disagreeable girl she was and how he had feared he would never be able to get a husband for her. And yet now she not only has a most distinguished husband but one who were he not so good-natured would scarce do her the honour to take her for a maid-servant, disobedient as she is to him. The young lady, "partly for fear, and partly convinced," falls down first at her father's then at her husband's feet, promising to be for ever after "mindful of her duty."*

To "put a difference betwixt the shirt and doublet of her husband," was all the learning a bride needed, declared Francis, Duke of Brittany, when he was engaged to Isabella, daughter of Scotland, a young lady "altogether unexperienced in the knowledge of good literature." It was a lack, the Duke asserverated, that made him "the more inamoured" of her.[15]

---

* ERASMUS, *Colloquies; The Uneasy Wife.* And she kept her promise, for nothing was too mean for her to readily and cheerfully go about, "if her husband would have it so." Yes, but "such husbands are as scarce nowadays as white crows," retorts the "uneasy" woman who has had to listen to the exemplary tale.

Counterparts of these noblemen, Frenchman and
German, have even been observed in the United
States. "A young man of very good brains was
telling me, the other day," writes Mr. Higginson,
"his dreams of his future wife. . . . 'She must
be perfectly ignorant, and a bigot; she must know
nothing, and believe everything. I should wish to
have her call to me from the adjoining room,
"My dear, what do two and two make?"' "[16]

But never has the theory that girls should be
kept innocent been as adequately stated as by
Jerome. Counselling Laeta about the baby girl
whose theogamy she was relying upon for a son,
he writes: "Leave her no power or capacity of
living without you, and let her feel frightened
when she is left to herself." Should Laeta feel
unequal to this achievement, she is advised to
send her baby as soon as she is weaned to the
nunnery of her mother and sister in Bethlehem,
where the child can readily be kept ignorant of the
world, "believing that all human beings are like
herself."[17]

Whether she is the destined bride of a man or of
a god, the realisation of this theory of bringing up
a girl is undoubtedly easier in a convent, however
cloistral her home may be. And so the convent
school has always had a deserved popularity.

It was in particularly high favour in Dahomi
and in the coast towns of the Ewes. Once a year
the priestesses of their patron python god raided
the town, kidnapping or pretending to kidnap all
the little girls they could lay hands on. A snake-
claimed maiden stayed a year or more in the god's
house, all the time, the god being thrifty, at the
charge of her parents.[18]

We do not know much about the curriculum of
these Slave Coast boarding-schools or of the similar but much smaller establishments in Sierra
Leone and Nigeria; but we may be certain that
dancing was an important part of it. It is in the
Shinto temples to which little Japanese girls are
sometimes sent by devout parents, and it was in
the temple schools of ancient Mexico. In Mexico
commoners' daughters took a one year's course
in singing and dancing for the god Tezcatlipoca.[19]
As boys were admitted to Tezcatlipoca's school,
it must have been very much like one of our own
curiously anachronistic dancing-schools.

Like ours, Tezcatlipoca's class was only a day
class. Quetzalcoatl was a more exacting god. In
his convents the daughters of the Mexican nobility
stayed continually from four until sixteen or eighteen, according to one historian,[20] for only one year
when they were thirteen or fourteen, according to

another,[21] serving him as housemaids and cooks.

Whatever the age at which their domestic service began, they were dedicated to deity at their birth. So was many a Christian baby girl. Laeta, for example, had dedicated little Paula, even before birth, to her god. (Like other first-born babies Paula had to pay a price for the distinction, her Christian mother coming naturally by the Jewish and Roman theory of first-fruits.)

To be properly cloistered, Paula had to leave Rome. In Rome for several centuries, "virgins in Christ" had to shelter themselves as best they could from the world. It was sometimes difficult, for none "ventured publicly to call herself a nun." Eustochium, "that paragon of virgins," as Jerome calls her, is one of those who has a specially hard time of it. The worldly-minded aunt with whom she lives finally decides not to put up any longer with her theogamic whims. So she "does" her hair and dresses her up, a sacrilege, however, soon rued. That very night an angel threatens the impious lady in a dream with the death of all her family and hell in the bargain for herself. "All of which came to pass in due time."[22] After this catastrophe, Eustochium goes to live with Marcella, a young widow who seems to have been very successful in starting monastic fashions among the high-born and hitherto indifferent or disdainful ladies of Rome.

Cell life was optional with Marcella and her proselytes. It was not until a later period that the more ambitious widow "professed" who took care of the Church's dependents, taught Church doctrine, and even baptised, was shut up by an ungenerous hierarchy and told that as "God's altar" it was unbecoming for her to "gad about."[23]

The widow who was distinguished because of her human relationship was also ordered by the state church into a cloister. In 691 a Spanish synod decreed that every widowed queen should straightway upon the death of her husband enter a convent, "it being intolerable, what often happens, that former queens should be insulted."[24] Imperial Chinese widows also became nuns to avoid "insult," i. e., remarriage.[25]

Lacking the conveniences of Buddhism or Christianity, royal widows are apt to be sequestered in ex-palaces or in mausolea—when they are not immolated at their lord's funeral. Sutteeism had been popular for centuries in China, but about 200 B.C., before the nun idea arose, it became a custom for the highest and most favoured ladies of the "back palace," to settle down as warders of the royal cemetery.[26] Very like the

scene in *Ariane et Barbe-Bleu*, that most poetical ?
of feminist briefs, is the picture of the African
grave watchers in the gloomy royal cemetery of
Buganda, "some sitting on their haunches rocking
to and fro, others crawling stealthily about the
place, others arranging fresh grass on the floor of the
tomb, and still others sitting mute and motionless
as mummies."[27] "It is not right for you to wed
his wives after him ever; verily that is with God a
serious thing," decrees Mahomet for his prospective
widows.[28] The widows of his imitative viceroys
are to-day sequestered in superfluous palaces.[29]

Outside of royal circles, widows are generally
kept at home,—house-mates cannot afford to part
with them; but in deference to the dead they are
kept apart from the living as much as possible.
They are expected not to dine out or go to "parties" or even out of doors. Indoors they may not be
allowed to talk to visitors or to talk at all, or they
may have to keep themselves so dirty or shabby or
dreary looking that none will want to talk to them.

The cloistering of royal widows in convent or
mausoleum, and the segregation at home of those
of humbler rank is a corollary of marital pro-
prietorship and of the conviction that life goes on
after death along the usual lines. Wife-cloistering
is always a *desideratum* in the proprietary family.

It is of course a luxury, like polygyny or sometimes even monogamy, ill afforded by the humble. Well done, as in the palaces of China, Turkey, ancient Mexico, or Dahomi, it is very costly. It means great buildings and hordes of servants, an outlay within the income of the mighty only. But, like polygyny too, it can be so modified as to bring it within the means of all. Among the Kaya-Kaya of Dutch New Guinea there are separate houses for men and women (as well as a bachelors' club-house outside the village), and the men may not enter the women's houses nor the women the men's.[30] A Bedouin tent is divided into two parts and a man seen entering the women's part loses his reputation.[31] The Greek house was also divided, the inner apartments of the women being under lock and key. In early English houses the women were likewise locked into their own quarters at night. In America, house architecture is determined more by the extent of the lot or the size of one's income than by the need of segregating the sexes; but, given enough space or money, *boudoir* and "study," drawing-room and smoking-room assert themselves.

It is fitting that the American house should be less sexually differentiated than, for example, the Greek. The life in it is. The Greek wife did not come to the table at all when there were guests. The American sits there for a certain time. Like the Greek husband, the American is away from home most of the time, but the American wife herself does not stay at home as much as the Greek.

When she did go out, the Greek matron was never alone. The American does not go out alone on the streets at night, but she does in the daytime. Again, unlike the American, the Greek matron seems to have entertained her friends very little. She never gave women's lunch parties or afternoon teas. Nor did she "make calls."

In the performance of these "social duties" the American lady is said to resemble most the Turkish. In fact I have been told by those who have been "in" both, that New York "society," with its men "down-town" or at their clubs in the daytime, and its women at lunch or "bridge" party, at afternoon lecture or concert, with its evening parties made up of tired or bored husbands, of wives taking more pains than the occasion seems to demand, and of a few nondescript persons, "interesting" men being unavailable, that this "society" was a fair replica of the high life of Constantinople. But that was before the escape of the *désenchantées* to Paris and the triumph of the Young Turk.

IV

IN certain circles of our society a rigid line is
drawn in a girl's life at a certain moment
between the ages of seventeen and nineteen.
It determines her dressing, her hygiene, her
occupations, her friends, her name, her behaviour,
her point of view. As she steps across it she
leaves the nursery for the world.

"Coming-out" is a custom not peculiar to civilisation. Our *débutantes* are apt to be older to be
sure than those elsewhere. Instead of a year or two
"abroad" or in a "finishing school," savage girls
usually spend but a few weeks or months in a
lonely hut or in a bed or hammock or cage in a corner of the house or on the roof. But once "out,"
a *débutante's* life is everywhere much the same.
Everywhere at this time particular attention is paid
to a girl's looks. Her *coiffure* is very important.
Her hair is curled or puffed or "put up." She begins to add to it or to wear things in it. Chinese
girls "assume the hairpin."[1] In Thackeray's day

24

"Lincoln green toxophilite" hats and feathers, whatever they may have been, were assumed.[2] The *débutante's* skin is generally "improved." Sometimes it is tattooed or cicatrised. Sometimes it is painted, sometimes merely powdered. Veils are worn. Girls are quite commonly protected against the sun, if for different reasons. Fasting or banting is often required of the girl—with us for the sake of her figure, with others for reasons more obscure. Nose-, lip-, or ear-rings are generally hung at this time. Sennar girls have a tooth knocked out.[3] I have heard of New York girls putting belladonna into their eyes before sallying from the dressing-room into the ball-room. Ball-dresses of course and in fact an entirely fresh wardrobe are requisite, or it may be that now for the first time stays or high heels, jewelry or furs, petticoats or clothes of any kind are worn.

A great deal of dancing is in order for the *débutante*. First there is the coming-out ball. Warrau girls go to theirs with their hair cut and their head and arms and thighs set off with pearls and feather-down. In Peru the ball for Conibo *débutantes* lasts twenty-four hours. They are expected by their chaperons to dance the whole time. Fortunately they are not dependent on partners, but to keep going they do have to resort to the same support as our early morning dancers.   In California a *débutante* dance lasts even longer — nine nights, — although the young lady herself is not present until the last. To the great coming-out ball of the Wintun tribe of California, guests from the entire country-side are invited.   At the close of the party the chief takes the *débutante* by the hand and dances with her down the line of guests, ◄—something like a cotillion figure with the most popular cotillion leader of the season as partner.

There are other ways of course of introducing a girl to society besides balls.   On both the East and West Coast of Africa a street parade seems popular.   Among the Swahili of Zanzibar the young person is dressed up, her face painted and her hair frizzled, to be marched through the town, teased by her friends *en route*.   All the family finery is put on a Tshi *débutante*.   Instead of the ordinary cotton petticoat, she wears a piece of silk carefully draped over a kind of bustle held in place by a belt of beads.   Her hair is covered with gold ornaments.   Necklaces, bracelets, and anklets of gold and aggry beads engirdle her.   Her neck and bosom are stencilled with white clay. Made thus presentable through family heirlooms and the contents of the attic's trunks, she, too, is

paraded through the streets, her escort holding
an umbrella over her and singing songs in her
honour.[5] Outside of Africa, *débutantes* are also
paraded, although somewhat less ceremonially or
distinctively. They are merely expected to be at
hand at fashionable hours on fashionable roads,
beaches, or lawns.

Almost everywhere in North America a coming-
out reception is in fashion. Among the Thlinkets
of the North-west the *débutante* was led out by her
mother and girl friends and mounted on a box at
a great potlatch. She wore a new calico dress, a
costly Chilkat blanket, a conical hat with totemic
designs, silver and abalone-shell nose-rings, silver
bracelets from wrist to elbow, rows and rows of
bead anklets, and embroidered moccasins. "Con-
scious of looking her best, she met without flinch-
ing the gaze of the curious."[6] Among the prairie
Indians a girl stands in gala dress next to her
mother and welcomes the arriving guests with
presents.[7] Women guests among the Musquakie
themselves bring presents. Men also come to the
reception, but they take no notice of their hostess
beyond grunting out their acceptance of the good
things she hands them to eat.[8]

Wherever people are on intimate terms with
their gods they naturally invite them to coming-

out festivities. The Tshis set out for them a
present of yam and palm oil;[9] the Patagonians
sacrifice a horse; the Caffres, from seven to ten
head of cattle.[10]   In accordance with the tendency
of civilisation to draw a line everywhere between
the sacred and the secular, the Christian church
has its own distinctive coming-out ceremony—
"confirmation." It is a quiet and modest affair,
but it too is celebrated with new dresses and
"parties." Candles are burned in honor of patron saints, and the girls themselves receive little
presents.

Among the Swahili, and in the South Sea Islands,
as well as among Catholic Christians and prairie
Indians, *débutantes* receive presents. I surmise
that the flower-loving Polynesians give their "bud"
floral tributes just as we fill the drawing-room with
flowers for ours—bedecking it for her quite as rit-
ualistically as we do when she marries or dies.

A girl usually makes her *début* in a set. This
set expresses its solidarity in different ways. In
the United States it shows itself through girls'
lunches or "sewing circles" or "teas," where the
"buds" "receive" with or "assist" one another.
They have too their own passwords and pet
phrases, their own standards and ways of "getting
on together." On the Congo and elsewhere on

the West Coast they are still more formally organised into secret societies.[11]

In them, incidentally, they take new names to
symbolise their rebirth. The girls of Nias and of
Sierra Leone also change their names.[12] Our
girls, now referred to as "young ladies,"* begin
to attach importance to their family rather than to
their baptismal name, and with the tag of "Miss"
their name appears for the first time on their
mother's visiting-card.

They are supposed to accompany their mother
when they "leave" these cards. We hear of
Ewe *débutantes* paying calls too[13]; but as a rule
girls merely stay at home to receive them. Among
the Hottentots, for example, a girl's friends and
relatives come to her house to congratulate her
and give her a party—a kind of "surprise" party.
For eight successive nights a Makololo girl's
acquaintances come to sing and dance in her courtyard. They keep it going until a very late hour.
Among the Mandingoes such parties keep up for
two months, but in this tribe a girl's friends invite
her out too. During this round of gaiety no work

* Zulu *débutantes* are called *intonjane* [Macdonald, J., *Manners,
Customs, Superstitions, and Religions of South African Tribes,
Jour. Anthropological Institute*, xx (1890–1), 117]; Kikuyu *débutantes, moi-rě'-tu* (Routledge, W. S. and K., *With a Prehistoric
People*, p. 141. London, 1910). I have been unable to learn
the status name of *débutantes* elsewhere.

is required of her,[14] and she is no doubt encouraged to get up as late in the morning as she likes.

We should consider two months a very inadequate period to come-out in. After a "gay" winter in town, when "respectable" parents "take up their carpets, set their houses topsy-turvy, and spend a fifth of their year's income in ball suppers and iced champagne,"* "house-parties" and a "season" at a "smart" summer resort are due. So that the status of our *débutantes* lasts at least one year—giving each more time to accumulate cotillion favours and earn the name of being the prettiest, or the best dancer, of all the "new girls."

More primitive *débutantes* also seek the reputation of being a *belle*—sometimes in ways more convincing and consequential than ours; but whatever their plan, they are unable to devote much time to it because they invariably do what is expected of them and—get married. Realising that the object of their coming-out, of their finery and "make-up," of their dancing, parading, and visiting is to advertise themselves as marriageable and to allure suitors, they know better than to linger on in that limbo of the "older girls" in which impatient parents and a disappointed public find it so difficult to take an interest.

* *Vanity Fair*, ch. III.

V

ENGAGEMENTS AND HONEYMOONS

THE betrothal customs of many peoples would undoubtedly trouble those of us in the habit of saying we do not believe in long engagements. Frequently children are betrothed in infancy, at birth, or even before. Vittoria Colonna was betrothed at three to the Marquis of Pescara. As soon as an Eskimo girl is born, a boy suitor is likely to present himself to her father.[1] In Melanesia the father of every new-born boy is on the watch for the birth of a suitable girl.[2] Every Arunta woman is made *tualcha mura* with some man, *i. e.*, she is designated his mother-in-law, her eldest daughter to become his wife; and so foresighted is the Australian that this *tualcha mura* relationship is established between little boys and girls.[3]

Evidently betrothal is not always for the same purpose as we understand it—getting acquainted. That in fact seems to be almost everywhere the last thing in mind, for the betrothed have usually

to avoid one another.   In Sardinia they could communicate with each other only from a balcony and
then only in sign language.[4]   In Victoria a Blackfellow was allowed to gaze at his future bride, but
he was forbidden to speak to her, although she was
sent to live for a time with his mother.[5]   In the
Malay islands of Buru, Ceram, and Luang Sermata,
a suitor did not even look at a girl.[6]   After their
mothers have exchanged calls, a Musquakie is free
to dog his ladylove's footsteps whenever she goes
out; but he may not speak to her or follow her
indoors.   Even when she finally smiles at him,
he is restricted for the next three months to serenading her.[7]   In China, betrothals are negotiated
by a professional go-between, and until the marriage presents have been received there is no communication whatsoever between the betrothed.[8]
Should a New Guinea *fiancée* meet her young
man on the road, she has to hide behind a tree
until he passes.[9]   An engaged Dorah couple
may not refer to each other by name.[10]   The
Kumaun bridegroom never sees his bride until he
joins hands with her at the wedding; the Persian
and the Egyptian, until they have consummated
the marriage.[11]

On the other hand, where getting acquainted
is the aim of a pre-matrimonial relationship, it is

sometimes carried out very thoroughly. In the New Hebrides a girl betrothed in infancy is brought up in the house of her future father-in-law, her boy *fiancé* often thinking that she is his sister.[12] A Thompson River Indian may court a girl by quietly lying down for four successive nights on the edge of her blanket. If on the fourth night she puts her hand on the outside of the blanket, she becomes from that moment a wife,[13]—a method of courting not unlike the "bundling" or "tarrying" of colonial New York and New England. A Dyak girl often marries her lover *after* she has conceived,[14] a sequence customary in many places outside of Borneo. In Scotland before the Reformation, men and girls would agree at the public fairs to live together for a year. At the end of this "handfasting" they were free either to marry or to part.[15]

With us an engaged couple may dine together or go to the play unchaperoned. In a company they are seated next to each other at the table, nor is one asked to a party without the other. In fact, on every occasion they are conspicuously left alone together—except on their wedding-day, when they are expected to meet for the first time that day at the altar.

One sometimes questions whether this pecul-

iar kind of social ostracism makes after all
for mutual sympathy or fellowship.—A girl just
engaged once gravely asked me what engaged
people talked about.—One result it does have,
however, a result that all types of betrothal plan
for in some way or another. Trespassers are
effectively warned off.

There are several ways of serving notice upon
trespassers. In New Britain the very word
"betrothed," *webat*, means "forbidden to any
one else." Once Swahili parents receive the
betrothal gift they are obliged to close their doors
to all other suitors.[16]   A betrothed South Arabian
girl may not go abroad unveiled. An Abyssinian
is kept indoors during the three or four months of
her engagement. A Wataveta negress is also kept
out of other men's sight while her engagement
lasts—perhaps for years.[17]   When a Chinese girl
is engaged, "unless there be some great occasion,
no male enters the door" of her apartment.[18]
With us no formal notice is served upon a girl's
other "followers." It is made so unnecessary
by engagement etiquette that girls in fact quite
often refuse to "announce" their engagement—
"an engaged girl has such a poor time." In her
fear of being shunned, she may even forego wearing an engagement ring.

And yet she is free to go "out"—until a few days before her wedding. "After the marriage invitations are issued, the *fiancée* does not appear in public," writes the author of *Sensible Etiquette.*[19] Special precautions are, I suppose, necessary at this time, for it is difficult to "break an engagement" after the wedding cards have gone out.

It is trying, for that matter, to break it at any time after it has been announced. People ask so many questions to find out "whose fault" it is,—however "gentlemanly" a man may be in letting the girl take all the responsibility for it. And then people will take sides,—even when they say of the disengaged couple "it is well they found out before it was too late."

What it is they may find out, their critics do not specify. In fact it is accounted caddish—for the man at least—to tell, a reserve which in separating after marriage is not even allowed, because, I suppose, the idea of disqualifying a *divorcée* for remarriage is not entertained.

But in many communities, including the lower circles of our own, engagements like marriages may be broken with impunity only for cause. In Anglo-Saxon law, "if a man buy a woman and the gifta or tradition take not place, let him [the woman's guardian] give the money back [to the bridegroom], pay as much more as penalty, and recompense the betrothal sureties in as much as the breach of their pledge is worth."[20] Among Russian peasants, once the parties of the bride and groom have shaken hands in the betrothal ceremonial, breaking the contract also involves a breach of promise suit in which the village court awards pecuniary compensation for the dishonour suffered. If it is the girl who has been repudiated, the damages are heavier because her market value has been impaired.[21] If a Hindu, who has promised his daughter, "does not deliver her afterwards, he shall be punished by the King like a thief, in case the suitor be faultless." On the other hand, a plighted suitor who abandons a "faultless maiden" shall "be fined and shall marry the maiden, even against his will."[22]

Among the Hindus, or, in fact, wherever the proprietary family is well developed, the most serious "fault" in a girl is a lack of virginity, and on this ground a bride may always be returned to her family—as damaged goods, not according to contract. Even in our disintegrated family type the most successful defence to a breach of promise suit is the allegation that the plaintiff has had a "past."

In breaking an engagement, the betrothal or

marriage gifts or the bride-price have naturally
to be returned—from either a pecuniary or a
sentimental motive, or sometimes perhaps, as in
the matter of a diamond engagement ring, from
both.

It is difficult at times to distinguish between
betrothal gifts and wedding gifts or bride-price.
Betrothal gifts may be merely a means of identi-
fying the two personalities—to this end, for example, Wetar and Amboina lovers exchange clothes
and locks of hair, a Timor-laut man gives his
sweetheart his belt.[23] An American treasures her
glove or handkerchief, or gives her his secret
society pin or a button from his military coat, or,
like the Genoese of the sixteenth century,[24] an
unmistakable type of bouquet. On the other
hand, betrothal gifts may really be the bride-price
in installments, and the main object of betrothal
itself is sometimes to allow time to get the bride-
price together, a matter perchance requiring the
co-operation of kindred and friends. In fact if
there is no engagement, there may be no bride-
price or wedding gifts at all, one of the advantages
or disadvantages of informality in marrying.

Elopement or *quasi*-elopement is not always
entirely unconventional. In many places marriage by capture is an institution, and even

where there are more deliberate ways of getting married elopers may be more or less coun-
tenanced.   In New Guinea, in Bali, and
elsewhere an eloping bridegroom is regularly called
upon in due time to pay a compensation price
to his parents-in-law.[25]   The proper amount
of "head money" having been paid, a Yoruba
girl may be escorted in bridal procession to her
bridegroom's house, or, if her suitor is disapproved
of by her parents, she may run away with him
quite without fear of consequences.[26]   A Thompson River couple may be pursued, like elopers to
Gretna Green, by an outraged father, but even
if he catch them he has to deliver his daughter up
to the man who has already become her husband,
a Thompson River Indian having but to "touch"
a girl's breast or heel to marry her.   Disinclined
for a runaway match, more formal minded natives
can get married by "placing down" at a public
gathering a number of wedding presents and paying
no end of family visits.*   The ancient Hindus had

* Teit, pp. 322-5.   A round of visits quite like the calls of con-
gratulation once customary in the United States.   "The *fiancé*,"
writes the author of *Sensible Etiquette*, "is introduced by the family
of the *fiancée* to their connections and most intimate friends, and
his family in return introduce her to relatives and acquaintances.
The simplest way of bringing this about is by the parents
leaving the cards of the betrothed with their own, upon all families on their visiting list whom they wish to have the betrothed
pair visit" (p. 66).

as many nuptial rites as the Thompson River
Indians. The repeating of sacred texts, the making
of presents (a dress, a bull, and a cow to the bride's
father), and the paying of an out and out bride-
price for the most part differentiated these rites.
For one of the less esteemed ways of marrying, however, there were no formalities at all,
merely "the union of a willing maiden with her
lover."[27]

Such curtailments of betrothal or marriage ceremonial are apt to be detrimental to the woman.
In several tribes of California the children of a
woman for whom no price is paid are no better off
than bastards.[28] Only the Hindu husband who
weds his bride with sacred texts, is guaranteed to
give a woman happiness "both in season and out
of season, in this world and in the next."[29] With
betrothal rites or a marriage contract, a Chinese[30] or a Baylonian[31] girl became a wife, without them, a concubine. In Greece and Rome a
like distinction was made by the marriage portion.[32]
Only the woman who had been married with the
khan mak ceremony inherited a Siamese man's
property.[33] Anglo-Saxon "common law" marriages have caused no end of legal embarrassments
in the inheritance of property, and the social
position of a "common law" wife has often been

questionable.　Even a civil marriage or in fact even shirking an engagement may entail "criticism."　Feeling somehow slighted, either on its own account or vicariously, the public asks questions which are a little malicious, or offers explanations still more so.　"If they are not engaged, they ought to be," or "I suppose her family objected," or "How can she feel she is married?" comments Mrs. Grundy.

Nor does that lady—or gentleman—like to be cheated out of a honeymoon.　It is pleasant to top off interest in the wedding-dress with interest in the "going-away" dress, to play jokes with rice and slippers and tags, to speculate about the bridal journey and destination, to whisper that the bride's mother at any rate knows where they have gone, or to offer them one's own cottage or bungalow.

Theoretically no one must know where the bride and groom are going*—until they get there, and then everybody there at least knows, and takes an interest.　For to take or even show a marked

*Or escaping to, as the ethnologist, intent on rape symbols, puts it.　But the author of *Sensible Etiquette* informs us that "it is no longer *de rigueur* to maintain any secrecy when "the newly married depart upon a tour" (p. 344).　One notices, in fact, a custom growing up in this country of seeing them off on their train or steamer—an influence perhaps of peasant Europe.

interest* in a bride and groom is quite customary
—as long as they are on their honeymoon.

This period varies, being in fact sometimes more
and sometimes less than the lunar month. Among
the Minahassas and the Ceram-laut, bride and
groom are secluded at home for three days, in
the Aru Islands for four, [34] in Bulgaria [35] for seven,
in Luzon for ten, among the Bedui for forty. [36]
"When a man hath taken a new wife he shall not
go out to war," the Hebrews were told, "neither
shall he be charged with any business: but he
shall be free at home one year, and shall cheer up
his wife which he hath taken." [37] Among the
Copts a bride may not go out, even to see her
parents, until her first child is born or until the
end of the year. During this period a Tartar
bride may not speak above a whisper even with
her parents. An Armenian speaks only with her
husband and only when she is alone with him.
With the rest of the household she must communicate in pantomime. She never goes out,
except at Easter and Christmas to church. If a
stranger enter garden or house, she runs away and
hides. [38] For a year or more Wataveta brides
have no household chores. They are pampered

*In primitive circles it is expressed at times, when there is no
bridal tour, in escorting them ceremoniously to their bedroom,
or in putting them to bed or in serenading them in bed.

and dressed up; but they see no man except their husbands, a common honeymoon restriction.[39] After the Australian woman of Powell's Creek is captured or purchased, she is "generally taken away to a distance and kept more or less isolated with her husband for some months, until she contentedly settles down to the new order of things."[40]

With us a bride and groom give notice that they are about to "settle down" through their "at home" cards, a kind of assurance to the public that the difficult task it has set itself, the institutionalising of their personal relationship is well under way, and that thanks to the discipline they have just been under they are now prepared to put this relationship to the severest tests.

VI

OLD MAIDS AND WEDDING RINGS

THE old maid is a fleeting phenomenon. She is unknown in savagery and not suffered in early civilisation. "When a woman does not wed a husband it amounts to a sin worthy of death," held the Parsee.[1] So reprehensible was the Hindu father who did not give his daughter in marriage as soon as she was nubile, that he was made to forfeit her nuptial fee when she married— a bridegroom of her own choosing.[2] Among the Jews in the Russian pale a girl's family, to the most distant relatives, will strain every nerve to ward off the calamity of celibacy, contributing to her dowry, hiding her defects from the marriage broker, praying and fasting to move God to send her a husband.[3] In early England an old maid was "looked on as the most calamitous creature in nature."[4] "What's more monstrous than an old maid?"[5] cried the Dutchman who so much enjoyed being kissed by the young maids of England.

Erasmus must have known one or two of her,

43

but as a category she is strictly a product of the nineteenth century. Although one may still catch a glimpse of her in *pensions* or in hotel dining-rooms, she really belongs so exclusively to the past that, like so many other social facts, she is likely to be forgotten before she is understood.

Outside of nineteenth-century civilisation there have been of course unmarried women. The code of Hammurabi in its extraordinary liberality to women scrupulously guarantees property rights to certain classes of unmarried devotees.[6] For thirty years the Vestal Virgins had to hold office, and even when they came out into the world they rarely married—"from religious fears and scruples."[7] Dismissed from the provincial houses of the Inca, the Peruvian women who since childhood had been awaiting his pleasure were never allowed to marry. The inmates of the houses of the Sun were never dismissed, and no man ever entered their convents. "For it was said that the women of the Sun should not be made common by being seen of any."[8] To put an end to scandal and libel, the virgins professed of Christendom were also cloistered and their vows made irrevocable.

But Babylonian votaries, Roman Vestals, Peruvian Sun-brides, or Christian nuns were hardly old maids. They were all, except perhaps* the Romans, married—to deity. Their African prototypes, West Coast priestesses and Baganda princesses, are still given to the gods.

Such theogamies are an important means of keeping the gods content and well disposed, always a heavy responsibility. It is quite natural that the king-priest should sometimes meet it with the help of his daughters. Through them he cements an alliance with his god just as he would with a human colleague. Subsequently, ambitious hierarchies encourage commoners to imitate the royal rite.

But besides serving as a gracious bond between the gods and men, sacerdotal brides have other functions. The Peruvian Sun-brides wove fine clothes for their husband, the Sun. His son and proxy, the Inca, wore them. They also baked bread and brewed liquor for the Sun's great festivals. They had to be most careful in keeping up his sacred fire. They must have become skilful polishers of metal as they had a "garden of trees and plants and herbs and birds and beasts" which would have delighted the gold-loving heart

* Before the Vestal Virgins became the handmaids of the Mother Goddess, they may have been given by their chiefly father to his sun god. The evidence for this theory, however, is slight.

of Midas, not to speak of their pots and pans and jars.[9] Christian nuns also wove fine garments— not always for others. They were of course noted needle-women, embroidering ecclesiastical hangings and vestments and altar pieces. In the days of their highest prestige they were also very learned ladies. They wrote verses, treatises, and plays, and illuminated them. Hildegard of Bingen compiled a *materia medica*, Herrad of Elsass, a history of the world. Moreover, the lady abbess held property and managed great estates. Shirking none of her feudal responsibilities, playing her part with scholars and men of affairs, a social organiser, a politician, and a traveller, she was naturally a distinguished personage. Like the Sun-brides of Cuzco, she was of course a woman of high birth, and her nunnery was an aristocratic school and workshop,—until in later centuries it became an almshouse or a hospital.[10]

When in the sixteenth century the English nunnery was doomed, what became of the English nun? Did she return to her family averse to matrimony, repining over the well-ordered life of her nunnery, and taking on airs of superiority over women without a mission in life—like the homing college girl to-day?

The college girl can marry whenever she wants

to, we are told—statistically, but it is likely that the
sixteenth-century ex-nun could not.   Then as now
in monogamous and adventuring England there
were not husbands enough to go round. Competition for them must have grown more lively with
the disappearance of the nunnery and—to the men
at least—more demoralising.   Its bad effects on
the Englishman are still marked, effects which, in
spite of the married women's property acts of the
eighties and of what the suffragette is doing for
him to-day, may not wear off for some time.)

Celibate though she was, the medieval nun did
not have to forego either male society or respectability.   The passing of the nunnery, however,
compelled a choice.   Towards the close of the
eighteenth century it was evaded, to be sure, by a
few favoured ladies, like Mistress Carter and
Hannah More, women in whom the wittiest
analyst the Lady has ever had sees foreshadowed
the unabashed spinster of another period.*   But
the *quasi*-independence and prestige of the Blue-
Stocking was short-lived even within her own
narrow circle, and by the time the nineteenth
century was well started the surplus Englishwoman was either a prostitute or an old maid.†

---

* Putnam, *The Lady*, p. 281.
† A classification of course that has existed outside of England—

In either rôle she was more or less of an <u>outcast</u>.
The old maid was of course far less nominally
outcasted than her more wayward sister. Her
status was supposed to be more involuntary,
hence she was a greater object of pity and more
readily excused. Then, too, she was "protected"
by her family; she did their chores, was subject
to their whims, or bickered with them. But she
was in fact cut off from many normal interests
and sympathies, and like the "fallen" was constantly discounted as a failure. Sometimes she
turned and was herself the bully of the family,
sometimes she mothered it into affection for her;
but tyrant or fairy godmother at home, to out-
siders she was always a dependent, a woman who
had to make the best of things, an anomaly for
jest.

Finally, however, she, too, if for different reasons, began to set loose from her family. From
"taking up things," gardening, "charity," handi-
crafts, teaching, "writing," the ladylike pastimes
inherited from the nunnery, from pathetic flings

---

with modifications and for reasons other than numerical disparity.
There was the Dupont family in France (Brieux, *Les Trois Filles
de M. Dupont*), for example. For a certain period in this country
the girl who "did n't want to get married" felt that she had to
choose between leading "a forlorn life" and playing the rôle of
professional beauty or charmer, of *demi-vierge*.

for freedom as governess or "companion," she betook herself to the forum or the market-place, and after some floundering succeeded in making herself count in public affairs or in merging herself with the wage-earner, the girl who had to support herself or others, but who always expected and was expected eventually to marry.

To be sure, as time passes and she does not marry, the world notices the fact a little, at least to the extent of undertaking an explanation. And its favourite and self-satisfying explanation continues to be a disappointment in love, a jilting, or a lover dead. The theory that its unexpected spinster was loath either to risk losing her job or to return to family segregation, by marrying, it still declines to entertain.

Nevertheless, to-day it is the married woman who is set apart, who has taken the place left empty by the old maid. She is forced either into idleness or into fictitious jobs * by the pride of her family or by the nature of our economic organisation, there being no place in it, outside of depressed industries, for a half-time worker. She is "protected" at home. She is discounted, excused, and

* "Parce qu'on dit, sans savoir pourquoi, qu'il est honnête aux femmes de travailler; mais souvent ce ne sera qu'une contenance, et elle ne s'accoutumera point à un travail suivi." (Fénelon, De l'Éducation des Filles, ch. 11).

4

sometimes pitied,* abroad.   Her wedding-ring is a token of inadequacy as well as of "respectability."

There are married women, of course, to whom the historical symbolism of the wedding-ring does not appeal, or to whom all labels, except on cans or in railway stations, are snobbishness, or who, like married men, do not feel called upon to give themselves away.   These ladies may go ring-less, but as yet no woman has found any escape from being addressed, at least by servants and shopkeepers, as "Mrs.," or from the past tense— "who was she before she was married?" as we say—or from the requirement of using another person's name as her signature, or from the liability of being asked at sight, in eighteenth-century circles and by public school boards, if she is mar-ried.   Elsewhere, of course, the question is not considered well-bred.

* See, for example, Schnitzler's play *Anatol* (*Weihnachts-Einkäufe*).

VII

ONE

A FEW years ago Washington society was highly diverted by an incident at a state dinner at the White House. As the guests were going in to dinner the White House *aide* noticed that two couples stayed behind. They were a Western senator, his wife, and their dinner partners. "I find," said the Senator to the *aide*, "that I am not taking my wife in to dinner. I married my wife to take her in to dinner, and unless I can do so to-night we are going home." Presumably the youthful *aide* was unable to controvert this view of conjugality, for it was said that the Senator and his wife sat side by side at the dinner table, the President after dinner clapping the Senator on the back and saying, "Bully for you, old fellow, I wish there were more like you."*

* It was also said that the wife of this Senator, a millionaire, got her carfare from him as she needed it, and that to win his consent to a new dress required considerable manœuvring.

In Washington and in our Eastern States such proximity *is* unconventional. "It will never do for you to sit next to your husband," your un-preordaining hostess exclaims. "I am on this side, so you must be on the other," says, in pass-ing, the spouse first to find his or her seat at the dinner-table. Dinner-table manners also require a certain amount of conjugal obliviousness. It is at least bad form for a wife to listen with any sign of enjoyment to her husband's stories or to laugh at his jokes. It is too much like laughing at her own.

On the other hand, the view that "a man who respects himself will not go to a house where his wife is not asked" persists throughout the coun-try, even if in certain circles a man no longer "forces" a dinner invitation for his wife by remark-ing upon her existence when he himself is asked out to dinner. Ladies, too, feel bound to decline a dinner invitation their husbands cannot accept. If reinvited as they occasionally are, with a "come-anyway," their "Do-you-really-want-me-without-him?" calls for a more or less elaborate reassurance from their would-be hostess.

Then, too, no man, once a popular bachelor, can fail to notice that as soon as he is married his invitations fall off, or that when his wife goes into the country or to Europe their curve is apt to rise again, or that he seems to know an unusual number of hostesses whose need of "filling a place" is chronic.

Although in many societies eating together is by no means a requirement in marriage—in fact a taboo on commensality is far more general— the Senator's underlying theory of conjugal identification is widespread and very old. "He that loveth his wife loveth himself," says the Jew.[1] So indivisible in Anglo-Saxon law were husband and wife that she could neither sue nor be sued without him.[2] The Hindu holds that a wife assumes her husband's qualities, whatever they may be, "like a river united with the ocean."[3] Half his body, she shares equally the result of his good or wicked deeds;[4] and wives and slaves remain "impure" as long as their lord.[5] Hindu salutations being regulated according to age, married women are saluted according to the comparative ages of their husbands.[6] With us, too, "precedence" is somewhat determined by age, although not vicariously. And yet in Washington, the wife, however young, of a senator or cabinet officer precedes the wife, however old, of a representative or general. "*Les femmes n'ont pas de rang.*"

Nor, sometimes, any allegiances, Napoleon might have added. In feudal Japan a woman was told that she had no particular lord. "She must look to her husband as her lord." Nor was she to "selfishly think first of her own parents, and only secondly of her husband's."[7] While the Russian bridegroom is leading his bride home, he hits her lightly from time to time with a whip, saying at each stroke: "Forget the manners of thine own family, and learn those of mine."[8] A Bengal bride has only to eat and drink ceremonially with her bridegroom to be transferred to his clan; a New Guinea bride has only to be smeared with his blood.[9] The seventeenth-century Englishwoman was bound not only to "follow the quality" of her husband, but his "Country, Family and Habitation." She was "bound to accompany him in all things, in his Journeys, his Banishment, his Imprisonment, yea although he be condemned to be a wandering Person, a Vagabond and a Fugitive."[10] In the United States an alien woman has only to marry a citizen to become one herself, and an American husband has the right to fix the "matrimonial domicile" where he pleases.[11]

Ideas of conjugal identity are often expressed in primitive therapeutics. Among the Cherokees neither husband nor wife may send for the doctor

for the other, for neither may pay him his fee of
deerskin or moccasins—an offering to the disease
spirit or a cover to protect the hand of the shaman
engaged in pulling out the sickness from the
patient's body. In consequence of this rule a
shaman may not treat his own wife.[12] In South
Australia a Blackfellow wife spits blood from her
gums on to a leaf as medicine for an ill husband.[13]
Warramunga and Tjingilli tribesmen wear their
wives' head-rings for headache, believing that the
pain will pass off into the ring.[14] The Romans
had just the same cure for headaches.[15] The
Chiquito of Brazil perhaps carry belief in a wife's
influence to an extreme. Always holding her responsible for her husband's illness, they kill her
to enable him to recover.[16]

Against such wifely devotion or self-sacrifice,
at critical times women often receive marked
marital attentions. In pregnancy, for example.
Although conjugal intimacy is frequently taboo
at this time, and although it is the time when a
man is apt to take a second wife—legitimately
or illegitimately according to what happens to be
the law of his land—nevertheless, he is called upon
to be particularly considerate, in certain respects,
of his first. Among the Transcaucasian Pshaves
he stays away, together with his wife, from all

public festivities.[17]   In Malacca he never goes out
of her sight or, in the New Britain islands, out of
doors.[18]   Should an Atjeh of Sumatra have to leave
his wife alone at this time, he has at least to remove some of the rungs of the house ladder—to
mislead the malicious spirits who are hanging
about.[19]   An Arunta husband must keep from
killing large game in order not to add to his wife's
sickness or suffering.[20]   A man of Mowat, New
Guinea, must not spear turtle or dugong[21]—
whether for his wife's sake or his own or the quarry's
we are not told.   Were a Caffre husband to bathe
at this time, he would pay the price himself—by
drowning.[22]   A Chinaman is very careful not to
disturb the earth spirits, lest his wife miscarry.
Towards the end of her pregnancy he will displace
nothing heavy inside his house, for it is well
known that things too heavy to be easily moved
are favourite spirit haunts.[23]   A Bageshu husband
may not climb a tree or rocks or go on the roof of
a house or take any violent exercise lest he should
slip or tire himself, and so himself cause his wife
to miscarry.[24]   In many other places an expectant father must keep from taking personal risks
or from hard work.   Again, he may not cut his
hair or work with tools or shed blood.   He has
still more commonly to fast or diet himself.[25]

It is probable that much of this *régime* of his is primarily for the sake of the unborn child, still, its mother is naturally involved.

In civilisation a man has fewer chances of this kind to show his wife sympathy, although his unwillingness to "leave her alone," she being more or less secluded at this time, sometimes appears to be somewhat ceremonial — when, for example, it gets a man out of an unenticing dinner engagement or frees him from jury duty.

In child-birth a sympathetic husband has also a greater number of conventional opportunities in savage than in civilised life. He it is who must exorcise or fool the spirits who are hanging about with evil intent. He can also shorten a difficult labour, assure a safe delivery, and hasten convalescence. In the Philippines, an anxious husband patrols his house all night, fighting off the birth demons with a drawn sword.[16] If an Arunta woman is having a hard time, her husband's hair girdle is tied tightly around her body, and if that does not work, he himself parades past her quarters in the women's camp to lure the unborn child after him. He is said rarely to fail.[17] In the islands of Torres Straits, a sympathetic husband had to stand in the sea until his legs were cold, when the child surely would be born, or to keep diving until it was born, sometimes for hours.[28]　In Samoa, a husband is held responsible for all his wife's labour pains,—"probably he has been running after other women,"[29]—but we are not told whether or not he tries to alleviate her distress.　A Thompson River Indian husband helps his wife to give birth quickly by himself taking a ceremonial bath and run.[30]　The Nias husband pulls out nails for her,[31] the Watubella[32] or German[33] has her lie on his clothes or wear them; the Serua prays for her—[34] like many another husband elsewhere whose prayers are perhaps only less set.

In Kamchatka a husband must keep from working on his wife's account during her convalescence from child-birth.[35]　A Maori New Zealander takes part in a rite to enable his wife to secrete more milk.[36]　In many other places he does more than that.　On the Congo, throughout South America, in the Malay Archipelago, in Southern India, among a primitive tribe of China, among the Basques, he actually simulates convalescent conditions.　He diets, takes a holiday from work, or even betakes himself to bed or hammock. Whatever may be the meaning of this custom,— the couvade, as it is called,—it plainly either directly or indirectly makes for conjugal identity.

The Miaos of China even say that the husband goes to bed—and among them he lies in for forty days—because he should bear the same hardships as his wife [37]; and the Erukala-Vandlu of Southern India, who put on their wives' clothes and cover themselves up in bed in a dark room as soon as labour begins, [38] are said to be actually attempting to trick the malevolent birth spirits into taking husband for wife.

Lydia Darrah, the Philadelphia Quakeress, had undoubtedly never heard of the couvade but she justified her lie to General Howe through analogous reasoning. Suspicious that his plan to surprise Washington at White Marsh had been betrayed, the British general asked his Quaker hostess if any of her family were up, contrary to his expressed wish, the night he met his "friends" in her house. "No," answered Lydia, without hesitation, and asked afterwards how she could say they were all abed when she herself was eavesdropping, she replied, "Husband and wife are one, and that one is the husband, and my husband was in bed." [39]

Conjugal sympathy may be harmful as well as helpful—at least to those who believe that womanly weakness is infectious. And so in many societies fishermen and huntsmen, planters, warriors and ritualists must keep away from their wives on the eve of or during their undertakings. In Australia, conjugal separation is necessary to rain-making and to a good crop of grass; [40] at Panai in the Torres Straits, to a plentiful fruit harvest; [41] in New Guinea, to the reproduction of turtles. [42] It ensures success in bird hunting in the Marshall Islands; in fishing, in the Toaripi district of New Guinea and in the Carolines; in whaling, in Madagascar and in Nootka Sound; in trapping, among the Bangala of the Upper Congo; in sowing, among the ancient Mexicans and Nicaraguans; in fighting, in New Caledonia, the Kei Islands, New Zealand, South Africa, South-east New Guinea, among Malays and North American Indians. [43] It is an indispensable mourning observance in New Caledonia, Sierra Leone, British Columbia, ancient Peru and Egypt, Japan and China, and among the Ewes, Baganda, Mälers, Nagas, and Hindus. [44] It qualifies for "curing" among the Nukahivahs, the Akikuyus and Nandi of Africa, and the Huichols of Mexico; and for the performance of other religious rites in Hawaii, among the Ewes, Fjorts, and Bahima, among the Eskimo, Tsimshian, Zuñi, and Hopi, among the ancient Mexicans, Nicaraguans, Hondurans, and Peruvians, among the tribesmen of the Rajmahal and

Nilgiri Hills and of Assam, among the ancient
Egyptians, Greeks, and Romans, among Brahmans, Gainas, Buddhists, Moslems, Jews, and
Christians. [45]

But conjugal separation does not always free
hunter or forager or warrior or priest from his
wife's influence. If a Hottentot woman lets the
fire go out, her husband's hunt will be unlucky. [46]
While her husband is out hunting a Wagogo
must not let anyone pass behind her or stand in
front of her as she sits. She must lie on her face
in bed. [47] Were the wife of a Laos man to cut
her hair or oil her body while he is out after
elephants, the beasts would burst the toils or
slip through them. [48] Among the Kayans and
Kenyahs of Sarawak, should a wife touch a comb
while her husband is away collecting camphor,
the spaces in the tree fibres where you would expect camphor will turn out to be as empty as
those between the teeth of a comb. [49] A Tcham
wife must not scold or quarrel while her husband
is out looking for eagle-wood lest he be torn to
pieces by bears or tigers. [50] When a Dyak is
head-hunting his wife must wear a sword day and
night to make him ever mindful of his own weapons. She may not sleep during the day or go
to bed before two in the morning, to keep her

husband from being surprised by the enemy in
his sleep.[51]   Wives of Tshi warriors in a campaign
paint themselves white, wear beads and charms,
and march daily through the town calling upon
the gods to protect their husbands.[52]   During
war the wives of Malay warriors may not cut
their hair.[53]   In the Babar Islands they have to
fast,[54] and among the Yuki Indians, to dance.[55]
The Galla wife of a pilgrim to the *abba-mudá*,
a high priest, must eat only of a special kind of
bread baked in ashes.[55]   A Tsimshian Indian
can compel the gods to grant his prayer by
fasting and conjugal abstinence for four or seven
days—providing his wife is faithful to him.[56]
Lyngstrand, the Norwegian sculptor, felt that if
there were a devoted woman somewhere thinking
of him, his work would be a success.*   "No woman
without piety in her heart is fit to be the companion
of any man," writes Timothy Titcomb, for "a man
who has the prayers of a pious wife, and knows he
has them . . . can rarely become a very bad man.
A daily prayer from the heart of a pure and pious
wife, for a husband engrossed in the pursuits of
wealth or fame, is a chain of golden words that links
his name every day with the name of God."†—

* *The Lady from the Sea*, Act IV.
† *Letters to Young People*, p. 30.   New York, 1860.

Evidently among many communities a faithful wife is a "great help" or "inspiration" to a man.

Although prayer is sometimes rendered ineffectual by conjugality, nevertheless a priest's wife—when he has one at all—appears to be peculiarly related to his office. She is often necessary to his sanctity; a tie between him and his god. Often she is his god's mouthpiece; sometimes his mistress. Her children might even be imputed to the god. Distinguished Pelew Island priests prophesied only through the women they shared conjugally with their gods.[57] Along the West Coast and elsewhere in Africa priest and god have a like partnership, and the fetich wife helps her priest-husband in his rites.[58] Egyptian priests kept harems of sacred concubines.[59] In Greece, the wife of the *Archon Basileus*, the *Basilissa*, performed state sacrifices and every spring took part in a "sacred marriage" with Dionysus.[60] In Rome, the presence of the *Flaminica*, the wife of the *Flamen Dialis*, was necessary at many of the rites.[61] Early Christian heresiarchs sometimes worked so intimately with women that the orthodox, at least, had no doubt as to the meaning of the collaboration. At one time their *agapetæ* lay the orthodox priests themselves open to suspicion.[62]

As a rule, however, a wife-priestess had to be a woman without a past, and her conduct in marriage impeccable. The wife of the *Archon Basileus*, of the *Flamen Dialis*, and of the Jewish high priest[63] had to be a virgin.   No Jewish or Christian priest could marry a *divorcée* or a courtesan. To the Christian, servants and actresses were also taboo and even widows were ineligible.[64] The Christian husband of a straying wife could not be ordained, and were he already in the priesthood, he had forthwith to divorce her, she rendering him unfit for office.[65]   The wives of deacons had, moreover, to be "grave, not slanderers, sober, faithful in all things."[66]

The time came when a great part of the Christian church freed itself altogether from the vexing questions inevitably brought up by limiting clerical conjugality; but in some of its minor communions, in the Greek and Anglican, a wife has been more or less of a qualification for ecclesiastical office.   And her behaviour continues to be closely scrutinised.   As among the Cherokees, the wife of a modern physician is not "attended" by her husband—it is in fact contrary to professional etiquette,—but who ever heard of a minister's wife not going to her husband's church, and must not his wife be a very unscrupulous woman to call in question even in a drawing-room any dogma he teaches?

Very long before the split in the theory of ecclesiastical marriage in Christendom there had come to be a still more important change in the general theory of the priesthood. It meant that the original priest-chief was to be differentiated into priest and king, that despite occasional back eddies the temporal was to be separated from the spiritual power. But the cleavage was not always clear cut. Divinity and sacerdotal functions continued to attach to many an early king. And their wives had a share in such survivals. If the Inca of Peru still represented his father, the Sun, the Ccoya represented her mother, the Moon.[67] The Queen of Egypt was married to Ammon-Ra as well as to the Pharaoh.[68] In many an Asiatic kingdom queens bore the ceremonial name of the goddess mate of the god of their king. A queen was part of an Oriental king's ceremonial equipment.

In modern Europe, kings also depend on queens to perform adequately what is expected of them. Do not Republicans too like their presidents to be married men? Do not the wives of English candidates for office campaign for their husbands and, although this English form of conjugal

5

co-operation is still considered bad style in the
United States, are not American candidates
always photographed in family groups?

Now, just as it would be highly unconventional
for the wife of a Presbyterian clergyman to be a
professing Episcopalian or Agnostic, it would
be very awkward for the Queen of England to be
an outspoken Socialist, or the Empress of Germany
an Anarchist, or Mrs. Taft a Democrat.　Would
it not get their husbands into trouble?　Indeed,
"tact" is expected of even the wives of diplomats,
of cabinet officers, or of government officials still
humbler.

If the political views of queens have to be those
of their kings, if diplomats and statesmen are held
responsible for the indiscretions of their wives,
why should not the wives of ordinary subjects or
citizens belong at least to the same political party
as their husbands?　In fact, are not the anti-
suffragist arguments that husbands ought to represent and do represent their wives, entitled
to consideration?　At any rate, the suffragist
should admit that she is precluded from political
"rights" thanks not to Modern but to Early Man
and to the status of the very priestess or queen
she sometimes cites as precedent for her claim to
independence.

The representative character attaching to husbands must have always caused them anxiety. In Costa Rica deaths are attributed to the "infectious" nature of pregnancy and the husband of a woman pregnant for the first time has to pay the doctor and undertaker bills of the community. [69] In East Central Africa if a husband eat food salted by an adulterous wife, he will die. So in order always to be on the safe side, he employs a little girl to regularly salt his food. [70] Under like circumstances it is death to the Acaxee Indian to taste salt, however handled, so he feels compelled to forego it altogether—when he is away from home. [71] Saxo Grammaticus tells us that once in Upsala there lived a priest of Odin whose wife Frigga was so greedy and licentious, so "unworthy to be the consort of a god," that her priest-husband had to go into exile until she died. [72] If a Hindu wife drinks spirits, in accordance with the mathematics of Hindu conjugality, "half the body" of her husband "falls." [73] American husbands appear at times to have something of the feeling this downfall must cause over wives who smoke or show their ankles or "get into" *Town Topics*.

Indeed, since the rise of our "new woman" marital representativeness has come to be so beset with dangers that some day husbands are likely to disown it *in toto*. Years ago in fact they rebelled, and with more or less success, against being held responsible—legally—for a wife's misdemeanours or debts. They even advertised their independence in the newspapers. That particular form of grumbling against a wife's extravagance has gone out of fashion, but does it not suggest a practical way of meeting other marital difficulties, of dealing with a wife's opinions, for example, so much more injurious to her husband's reputation than her bills?

The following form would be, I am told, from a legal point of view, correct:

To Whom It May Concern

" The Undersigned hereby gives notice that he will not be responsible for any opinions held or expressed by his wife, Mary Doe, in her or his name, all proper provision (of opinions) for said Mary Doe having been made by the undersigned.

"Dated. . . . . ."

A formal notice of this kind would be particularly advantageous to politicians—and to their wives. As it is, although wifely heterodoxy is awkward, calling for constant explanation, it is not nearly as serious as a husband's agreement with his wife's views, a situation which can never be explained. In no calling or profession, but in public life least of all, can a man afford to be accounted the exponent or champion of his wife's ideas or interests.

VIII

THE INSIGNIFICANT PARENT

THERE seems to be a tendency of the mind not only to want to know but to want to complicate knowledge. Until modern science stepped in, conception was one of the many facts of life which apparently could be explained too simply to satisfy. "Where does a baby come from?" ask both Child and Savage, and the answers for both are oddly elaborate. From cabbage patch or rose bush, stork-brought, in the doctor's bag, believes the Child and, with but a trifling modification, the Savage—or any other childlike speculator. The latter, unlike the Child, can not overlook pregnancy, to be sure, but as to how the child spirit first reaches its mother he feels quite free to theorise.

No Australian woman will approach certain well-known boulders unless she wants a baby; for boulders are the haunts of innumerable spirits eager for incarnation. An inhospitable woman also keeps out of the way, if she can, of a whirl-wind, for it too harbours a spirit child in search of a mother.[1] The mother of Hiawatha was said to be quickened by the West Wind. So was the ancestress of the Minahassas of Celebes. Sumatrans believe that the neighbouring island of Engano is populated by the mistresses of the Wind. There is a Moslem tradition of a pre-Adamite race of women who conceived daughters and daughters only by the Wind.[2]

In some places women have more reason than men to be afraid of snakes. Dahoman girls were let down into a great ditch to meet the snake representative of their serpent god, and some-times, to conceive by him.[3] Basuto maidens go through a like experience in a river bed.[4] Among the Ibibio of Nigeria, secret society men have compelled women to marry a member of their society on pain of marrying the Great Snake.[5] Alexander the Great was snake-begotten—at least his juridical father seemed sufficiently persuaded of it to divorce Olympias, his mother.[6] Scipio was also popularly believed to have been begotten by the serpent who haunted the chamber of his mother.[7]

Women need protection not only against snakes and winds. They have to be shielded, above all,

from the Sun. Great is his phallic power. He
looks down upon a Tonga princess asleep on the
sea beach and begets a son.[8] A certain Samoan
maiden had merely to look up at him to conceive.[9]
So devoted to him was the daughter of a Zuñi
priest-chief that her jealous people killed her.
Dying, she gave birth to twin sons.[10] The Sun
also gets the virgin princesses of Greece into no
end of trouble. Incarnate in the Pharaoh he more
legitimately begets the rulers of Egypt[11] and, in
what form I do not know, the emperors of China.[12]
In Greece, in Peru, in Babylonia, special women
are espoused to him—perhaps to dissuade him
from trespass with the wives of men. In India,
on the other hand, his attentions are ritually
solicited. A bride is ceremonially exposed to him
and her human bridegroom formally invites him
to impregnate her.[13]

Sometimes the Sun's priests serve as his proxies
in his human marriages. Priests in general are
credited with either direct or indirect phallic
facility. Barren women visit the hot-air vents of
the Syrian Baths of Solomon and the paternity
of subsequent offspring is imputed to Abu Rabah,
the saint of the baths.[14] Turkish women who
felt that they had conceived during their Friday
or Easter visits to the mosque, called their infant

a son of the Holy Ghost.[15] In the Chinese province of Koeang-Si stood a Buddhist cloister
containing *The Hall of the Children and Grand-
children*. In its cells would-be mothers were
directed to spend a night in prayer. The next
morning they generally reported that in a dream
Buddha or one of his eighteen disciples had
embraced them.[16] A Brahman virgin widow was
once taken by her father to call on his *guru*,
Rāmānand. Rāmānand graciously but thought-
lessly greeted her with the wish that she might
bear a son. And she did.[17] Elisha promises a
son to his Shunammite hostess.[18] In Queensland
pregnancy may also result from the mere wish of a
medicine-man.[19]

Very persistent is this doctor's bag theory.
Gaina and Buddhist monks are forbidden, to be
sure, to practise "the low art of making a woman
fruitful,"[20] but Christian saints or hermits, Saint
Hilarion, Simeon Stylites, and many another
have ever felt at liberty to guarantee offspring
to the faithful. Nicholas II, I have read, decreed the canonisation of the prelate to whose
prayers devout Russians believed the birth of his
heir was due.

We might infer from these impregnation beliefs,
and a great many others—conception from rain,

from fire, from smells, from endless kinds of food
or tastes or drink—that by the credulous paternity
would be entirely disregarded, but people are seldom thoroughly logical. In this case the theory
of fictitious or juridical paternity precludes any
awkwardness that magical conception or divine
or human poaching might cause a proprietary
husband. Let us recall the theory as stated by
Manu: "Those who, having no property in a
field, but possessing seed-corn, sow it in another's
soil, do indeed not receive the grain of the crop
which may spring up. . . . Thus men who have
no marital property in women, but sow their seed
in the soil of others, benefit the owner of the
woman; but the giver of the seed reaps no advantage. . . . The receptacle is more important
than the seed. . . . Even if the seed is carried by
water or wind, the crop belongs to the owner of
the   field."[21]

Indeed, in many ways this theory of paternity
is preferable, given the proprietary family_ or
survivals of it, to any theory that might be based
on actual fatherhood. It allows all the responsibility of parenthood to be put upon the mother,—
when a man does not wish to assume it. It
justifies a *défense de chercher la paternité*, as the
Code Napoleon puts it, or, the fact of paternity

proved, but a trifling charge—$500 in Illinois,[22] for example—for the support of the illegitimate child. The theory also puts all responsibility of childlessness upon the woman and justifies divorcing her for barrenness or for bearing ill-fated infants or only girls.

It may go even further. Father of nine daughters, a Bulgarian peasant cries out to their mother:

> "Ist das zehnte auch ein Mädchen,
> Schneid' ich ab dir deine Füsse
> Deine Füsse in den Knieen
> Deine Arme an den Schultern
> Steche aus dir deine Augen
> Ungestalt und blind wirst werden,
> Schönes Weibchen, junges Frauchen!"[23]

Under such circumstances paternal desperation would not vent itself with us in quite the same way; nor is barrenness recognised in our law as a cause for divorce. But may not the reluctance of our lawmakers to require medical certificates at marriage, or to penalise the married for communicating the diseases which cause barrenness, be perhaps partly due to a lingering notion of the insignificance of physical paternity?

IX

PREGNANCY TABOOS

HAVING a baby has never been as easy as it might be—even for savage women. And yet we think of it as much less trying for them than for our civilised women. In making this comparison we entirely overlook all the social complications of the function, greater in savagery even than in civilisation.

In primitive thought a woman is supposed to be able to influence the looks, health, character, and career of her unborn child in no end of ways. Consequently, great circumspection and self-deprivation are required of her. Diet is particularly important. Australians believe that congenital deformities are caused by the eating of forbidden things during pregnancy. A boy once told Roth that he was humpbacked because before his birth his mother had eaten porcupine.[1] In the Islands of Torres Straits should an expectant mother eat *at*, a flat fish, or *gib*, a red fish, her baby would have poor eyes and an unshapely nose or be wrinkled like a dotard. To give him a good voice and lusty lungs she must eat certain kinds of shell-fish which make a hissing sound while roasting. If he is born with a dark complexion, it means that his mother has been too lazy to roast the peculiar kind of earth eaten by women in pregnancy.[2] In the Admiralty Islands a woman does not eat yams, lest her child be lanky, or taro bulbs, lest it be dumpy. Were she to eat pork, it would have bristles in place of hair.[3] A Caffre woman does not eat buck or the underlip of a pig, lest her baby should be ugly or have a large underlip.[4] Nor does a Thompson River Indian eat hare, lest he have a harelip. If a Thompson River woman ate or even touched with her hand porcupine or anything killed by an eagle or hawk, the child would look and act like them. If she ate fool-hen or squirrel the child would be foolish or a cry-baby.[5] Among the Kabuis, a pregnant woman may not eat any animal that has died with young. In Servia, if she eat pork or fish, her child will be cross-eyed or slow to talk.[6]

In the islands of Amboina and Uliase, a pregnant woman is expected to restrain her appetite in general, otherwise her child will be greedy.[7] In other ways maternal conduct is often too of serious

sympathetic import to the unborn.   It is quite
commonly believed, for example, that to ensure
a safe delivery a woman should avoid all knots or
ties or bands.   Hence in some of the islands of the
Malay Archipelago, she may not weave cloth or
plait mats; nor, in parts of Germany, pass under
a clothes-line or spin or reel or twist anything.
In the Uliase islands a woman is careful not to
lean against a cooking-pot, otherwise her child
will be black.   In Saxony, if she kick a pig or hit
a dog or a cat, the child will have bristles on
its back or hair on its face.   The superstitious
Berliner believes that if she has a tooth pulled,
her child will be born a cripple.[8]   Elsewhere in
Germany a pregnant woman must beware of
entering a court of justice or of taking an oath,
otherwise her child will be involved for life in
legal troubles.   Should she pilfer, her child could
not keep from stealing.   Should she wear a soiled
apron, touch dirty water, or pin on a nosegay, her
child would be a coward or have ugly hands or
a foul breath.[9]

Likewise credulous of prenatal influences, many
of our own countrywomen practise sympathetic
magic for the good of an expected child.   They
surround themselves with beautiful objects that
the child may have a love for the beautiful.

They read poetry, listen to music, or look at pictures to endow the child with an "artistic temperament" or with poetical or musical tastes. One expectant mother I knew of hung a picture of a beautiful child where her eyes would often fall upon it in order that her own child might be beautiful.*

On the other hand, disfigurements or birthmarks are very commonly accounted for through "maternal impressions." Unwonted contacts with animals are often thought to be the cause of these experiences. We remember of course the necklace-hidden mark on the neck of Elsie Venner, and how she was supposed to have come by her serpent nature. Not far from the house chosen by Holmes for his heroine lives a man whose face was marked at birth with a great mole, from which now grows in the midst of his black beard an inch or more of grey hair, and his old mother says that when she was carrying him she was once hit in the same part of her face by a dead mouse flung out of the barn as she was passing.

During pregnancy a woman is peculiarly subject to devils or to black magic. She must therefore be on her guard. In some of the islands of the

* I have lately learned that the notion was not original with her. "Some mothers cannot fix their eyes on certain Pictures without leaving the complexion or some marks in their Infants." (*Decency in Conversation amongst Women*, p. 165. London, 1664.)

Malay Archipelago she never leaves the house
without a knife to frighten away evil spirits.
In northern Celebes she must never go about with
her hair down—flowing hair is ever a favourite
lodging-place for spirits.[10] Basuto women wear a
skin apron and Wataveta women, veils, to protect
themselves against pregnancy witchcraft.[11] The
Esthonian peasant should be careful to wear a
different pair of shoes each week, to throw the
devil off her track. The nereids of Greece are
malevolent to pregnant women. So women are
expected to avoid their haunts, not to sit under
plantains or poplars, not to linger near springs or
streams. The Gipsy woman of Siebenburgen is
careful to cover her mouth with her hand when
she yawns, to keep the evil spirits from slipping
down her throat[12]—perhaps the original reason for this "form of politeness" under other
circumstances.

Continence taboos during pregnancy are widespread. They are generally for the sake of the
child. But they are sometimes for the sake of
the woman and sometimes for her husband's
sake. Her husband may be still further safeguarded. In the Caroline Islands his pregnant
wife may not eat with him; in Fiji, she may not
wait upon him.[13] The Chinese husband did not

see his wife at all during the latter part of her pregnancy. He sent twice a day to ask for her, to be sure, but "if he were moved and came himself to ask about her, she did not presume to see him."[14] I have known American husbands who during this time were loath to accompany their wives in public places, and if they went out walking with them at all, preferred to go after dark.

A pregnant woman has not only to think of herself and her family, it behooves her to be very conscientious in her relations to society at large. She can do so much harm if she is not careful. Among the Mosquito Indians, should she enter the hut in which an ill man is sometimes segregated, he would never recover.[15] In Guiana if she eats game caught by hounds, they will never be able to hunt again. On the Amazon if she partakes of meat eaten by a domestic animal or by a man, the animal will die and the man will never be able to shoot that kind of game again.[16] Among the Yakuts she causes the bullets of the hunter to miss fire and the skill of the artisan to deteriorate.[17] German peasants believe that were she to pass through field or garden bed, nothing would grow in them for several years, or their products would spoil. Were she to enter a brewery, the beer would turn; a wine-cellar, the

6

wine would sour; a bakery, the bread would spoil.[18]

Considering the dangers she is herself subject to and to which she subjects others, a pregnant woman is naturally more or less secluded.   Among the Atjehs, should she have a visitor, she must take the precaution of not receiving him at once—to mislead the malicious spirits likely to have followed him into the house.   Among the Gipsies it is not visitors, but moonlight, to which she must not be exposed.   The Jewess of Bosnia or of Herzegovina never goes out alone at night.   In the islands of the Malay Archipelago, a pregnant woman does not go out at night at all, or, in Celebes, in the rain.   The Yakuts do not allow her to eat at the table with others.   Among the South Slavs, she may not attend public dances, and among the Pshaves she is excluded from all kinds of festivities.   When a pregnant Wanderobbo woman goes visiting, she streaks her forehead with white clay.   Out of doors the Jekri woman warns people off with a bell.   In Central Africa, during her pregnancy a woman stays constantly indoors.   Among some of the tribes of the West Coast, on the other hand, during the last three weeks of her pregnancy, she has to leave the village and live entirely by herself.[19]

My grandmother tells me that in her day* women not uncommonly attempted to conceal their condition by lacing, and that in the latter part of pregnancy they rarely left the house, except perhaps for a short walk in the evening. Nowadays, fortunately, women are able to wear, if they wish, a disguise of loose instead of tight clothes, and they seem to take more exercise and to be more out of doors, but they are still apt not to receive guests or to "go into society." Their presence is supposed to be embarrassing to boys and girls and they are therefore expected to keep away from "young" parties. But there are many circles in this country in which they would also cause discomfiture to persons of any age. A woman whose husband had been in our diplomatic service in Europe once told me that having been in the habit abroad of dining out as long as she felt well, on her return to Washington she accepted a dinner invitation "without thinking." The result was so embarrassing to the other guests and consequently to herself that she dined thereafter at home. On a recent canoe trip on the upper Connecticut we stopped one mid-day at a farmhouse to buy eggs. All our overtures had to

* And before. "Many Gentlewomen—all the time of their going with child—wear long bellied, and strait laced garments." (*Decency in Conversation amongst Women*, p. 86.)

be carried on through a crack in the door, for, until the men in our party sauntered away, the mother of the six children playing around us and of an expected seventh was averse to meeting us.

X

UNFRUITFUL

PERHAPS one of the chief functions of the novelist is to make familiarities compel attention, so to polish up the dulled or tarnished, either by use or disuse, that it catches the high-lights again. He may do this even for the institutions of the past, reviving some ancient habit or theory by putting it into a new setting, and so making it appear personal and incidental, a mere chance. We have a recent instance of this kind of ethnological plagiarism.* The scene is modern Rome; the subject juridical parenthood. It is an ancient theme treated in a modern—or perhaps *quasi*-modern manner. And it does succeed in raising questions.

Wherever progeny are of economic value, to either the living or the dead, barrenness is more or less of a curse. There are innumerable ways of "curing" it—by all kinds of concoctions of food and drink, by ointments and baths, by the wearing

* Hichens, Robert. *The Fruitful Vine.* New York, 1911.

or carrying of amulets or charms, by pilgrimage, prayer, and sacrifice. Among the South Slavs a childless woman will eat the grass and carry about in her belt earth from the grave of a woman dying in pregnancy.[1] A Chinaman will entice the spirit of a son to be born into the family by adopting a little girl as a bride for him.[2] Roman matrons were switched naked in the streets with thongs of goat hide.[3] The Hebrews promised their first-born to Jahveh, and in the case at least of Hannah and of Anna we know that the bribe was acceptable. In Tibet, in India, and on the West Coast of Africa, the gods are still open to the same influence.

The gods' representatives also work phallic miracles. Their passes, potions, and spells have been held again and again to be effective. A Thompson River shaman has only to paint on a woman's face a pattern he has seen in a dream and make her promise to name the child to his fancy.[4] We recall the phallic achievements of the Hindu *yogi*, the Australian medicine-man, and the Hebrew prophet. Jerome tells us how a certain woman of Eleutheropolis who was despised by her husband pursued St. Hilarion into his wilderness and teased him into praying for a son for her.[5] As a rule, Christianity ran down the

value of offspring, but the crowned heads of Europe,
conservatives as they are, still have prayers offered
up for heirs to their thrones. In the United States
"quacks" advertise cures for barrenness in the
newspapers.

Supernatural devices failing, a practical way
out was sometimes found for the childless woman.
The child of another might be mothered on her.
We remember, for example, how maternity was imputed to Rachel and to Leah. So too a Babylonian woman could give her husband a handmaid
to keep him from taking a concubine, [6]—in Babylonian eyes a distinction with a difference. Juridical parenthood was far more commonly imputed,
however, to men than to women. But through
juridical fatherhood the barren wife might also
profit. A kinsman or priest took the husband's
place. "On failure of issue, a woman who has
been authorised may obtain the desired offspring
by a brother-in-law or *sapinda*," writes Manu[7]
of the *niyoga*, as this old and orthodox Brahmanic
custom is called. Brahmanic sectaries, Sakti-wor-
shippers, sent their barren wives to saintly men
for impregnation.[8] Eskimo husbands pay their
angekok for the same purpose.[9]

In the proprietary family, the family type in
which offspring are at a premium, parenthood

sometimes precludes divorce and barrenness is almost invariably cause for it.   A childless Basuto woman takes her divorce for granted.[10] So does a Baganda woman—if only because she prevents her husband's garden from bearing fruit.[11]   An Aztec could divorce his head wife if she was spiteful, dirty, or barren.[12]   One of the first recorded divorces* in Rome was for barrenness.   Divorce costs a Chinaman eighty blows unless his wife is lascivious, inattentive to his parents, thievish, ill-tempered, infirm, a chatterbox, or barren.[13] A barren Hindu wife could ̄be superseded in the eighth year; one whose children all died, in the tenth; one who bore only daughters, in the eleventh.   Should a Hindu husband "show love" to a childless wife or the mother of daughters only, he himself became "censurable."[14]

In these cases it is, we notice, the husband who gets the divorce.   In the unmodified proprietary family, divorce is a male prerogative.   Moreover, the view that failure of issue is not always the fault of the woman is comparatively modern.

Nowadays, whether husband or wife be responsible, childlessness may still be a cause of polygyny— or polyandry—but, outside of Napoleonic minds, it is not a cause for divorce, nor, despite White House

* By Carvilius Ruga.

or pulpit endeavour to revive an archaic point of view, does any social stigma attach to it. The reason is plain. Children are no longer economic assets, either in this world or the next, to their parents. In fact, from a utilitarian standpoint they are too costly to be desirable at all by the individual, and that they have value from other individualistic points of view is a comparatively new idea.

The idea of their value to the community is much older; but the modern state has as yet acted up to this idea but faint-heartedly. It has only begun to take care of its existent "future citizen"; to his production it gives little or no encouragement. In a few European states a maternity insurance fund has been established, and there are laws against women working before and after childbirth, measures our pioneer government, in its concern over young industries and its bonuses to farmer and banker and shipbuilder, has not found time to consider. Some day it will be free of course to turn its attention to more modern matters. Meanwhile, is it asking too much to suggest that the rational regulation of child-bearing be no longer accounted a crime, and that society at large welcome the women engaged in "doing their duty" by it—instead of ostracising them?

As soon as society does become more convincing on the subject of "race-suicide," and as soon as the effects upon personality of having children are more clearly appreciated, it is likely that new race-suicide questions will arise, questions which hitherto have not even been suggested, the general topic being monopolised as yet by scatterbrains or fossils.

Even now there are many women and some men, married and unmarried, who long beyond and without words for children. Their craving is sometimes a veritable obsession. As their number increases and they become aware of it, taking courage from their solidarity, they may rebel against those conventions and traditions which thwart the satisfaction of their paramount desire. Will they, like Dolores Cannynge, return to the institutions of an earlier culture, or, aided by the modern science of eugenics, will they work out some new solution?

XI

IN QUARANTINE

TO many high enterprises, to war, to the chase, to prayer to the gods, women are often held to be a handicap; but during their character- istic physiological processes, when they are most women, they are at all times a very menace. Should a Mabuiag Island father see his daughter at nubility he knows he would soon come to grief; his canoe would probably be smashed up within a few days.[1] If a Unalit Eskimo approaches a girl at this time, he becomes visible, he thinks, to every animal he hunts.[2] In Costa Rica a woman preg- nant for the first time so infects the neighbour- hood that every death is attributed to her.[3] A Basuto who sees his wife after her delivery and before her "purification" feels sure to die.[4]

But it is during menstruation that a woman is most generally considered dangerous. In Western Victoria any one touching food touched by her at this time becomes "weak." Once a Blackfellow, enraged at his wife for lying unseasonably on his blanket, killed her, and then died himself of terror within a fortnight.[5] The Bushmen think that at a glance from a menstruous woman a man becomes at once transfixed and turned into a tree which talks.[6] If a Quayquirie Indian of the Orinoco treads upon the place where she has passed, his legs immediately swell up.[7] An Indian school-teacher tells me that once one of her Sioux pupils developed a tumour on the neck, and that his father took him out of school on the theory that the tumour was caused by contact with teachers who observed no monthly taboos. If a Pueblo Indian touches a menstruous woman, or, if a Chippeway uses her fire, he is bound to fall ill. The lips of any Omaha who ate with her would dry up and his blood turn black.[8] A Thompson River Indian would be attacked fiercely by bears.[9] Manu declares that the wisdom, energy, strength, sight, and vitality of a man who approaches a menstruous woman "utterly perish," whereas if he avoids one, these powers increase unto him.[10] According to the Talmud, if a woman at the beginning of her period passes between two men, she kills one of them; if towards the end of it, she only throws them into a violent quarrel.[11]

Under these circumstances quarantine is but a

proper precaution; and it is in fact almost universally observed, more or less. At this time Australian women may not walk on any path frequented, or touch anything used, by men.[12] A Persian woman could not talk to any man. A Dravidian Bhuiyâr woman has to use a special entrance, and she has to creep through this on her hands and knees to avoid touching the house thatch.[13] The Kharwars keep their women in the outer verandah of the house for eight days, and will not let them enter the kitchen or the cowhouse.[14] A Sioux Indian agent tells me that once a month she had temporarily to release the Indian women prisoners, so great was the men's objection to staying in prison with them at that time. A Vedah woman of Travancore is secluded for five days in a hut, a quarter of a mile away.[15] A Tshi woman has to leave her village altogether.[16] In fact, a special district or hut or room is almost everywhere set aside for women at this time. Even in her seclusion hut a Kolosh woman has to wear a hat, that she "may not defile heaven with a look."[17]

Besides seclusion all kinds of monthly taboos fall upon women. Thompson River women may not make or mend a man's clothes or moccasins.[18] Arunta women may not gather the Irriakura

bulb, a food staple, lest the supply fail.[19] Aru
Island women may not plant, cook, or prepare
food.[20] As in primitive as well as in modern
theory contagion is held to be very readily con-
veyed through food, food taboos fall upon menstruous women in many other places. Among the
Maoris the taboo against eating anything cooked
by them is catching; the eater becomes himself
taboo—"an inch thick." At this time a Chippeway woman may not eat with her husband,[21] nor
a Ewe woman fetch water—an argument to the
husband for polygyny.[22] Persian women may
not touch bread or a vessel of water with their bare
hands. Their drinking-vessel must be of lead and
but half-filled. They may not look at fire or at
the sun, or sit in the sun or in water.[23] Like the
Persian, the Hindu woman had to be particular
about her drinking-water. She had to drink it
out of a large copper vessel or out of her joined
hands. Moreover, she was not to eat meat, not
to apply collyrium to her eyes, not to anoint herself, not to bathe in water, not to sleep in the
daytime, not to touch fire, not to clean her teeth,
not to do housework, not to run, not to look at the
planets, not to smile.[24]

Roman women must have been almost as much
restricted as Hindus if they scrupled about the

damage they might cause. Pliny says that rue and ivy, standing corn, grasses and young vines wilt away at their touch. Buds wither as they pass them by. The fruit-tree they sit under lets drop its fruit. The mirror which reflects them becomes dim. In their vicinity, wine sours, ivory loses its color, and tools, their edge. Metals rust and bees die in their hives.[25] The European peasant to-day believes that if a woman at this time enters a brewery the beer will turn sour; if she touches beer, wine, vinegar, or milk, it will go bad; if she makes jam, it will not keep; if she climbs a cherry tree, it will die; if she mounts a mare, it will miscarry; if she enters a boat, a storm will brew.[26]

In many cases neither taboo nor damage is left to inference. An Australian woman may not eat fish or approach water lest the fish be frightened away or die, or the water dry up. Galela women may not walk over a tobacco field or Minangkabau women a rice field, lest the crop fail. In South Africa, women at this time may not drink milk, lest the cattle die. An Omaha woman may not approach a horse for fear of causing it harm. Should a Thompson River woman smoke out of another person's pipe, it would from then on be hot to smoke. Chippeway women may not walk on the ice of rivers or lakes or near where beaver are being hunted or a fishing-net is set for fear of spoiling the hunt or catch. Similarly, Lapp women are forbidden to walk on the shore where fishermen set out their nets. [27]

During the catamenia, women seem to be particularly repugnant to the gods and their representatives. Among the Tshis, they may not touch anything in a house sheltering a *boshum* or god. [28] Among the Ewes, they may not visit a priest. [29] Among the Niger Coast tribes, they may not take the regular path past a *juju* house. [30] Once the sacred king of Ashanti was met on his return from a journey by some of his over-impetuous wives. Hearing of their condition, he fell into a rage and had them cut to pieces. [31] Angoy natives believe they were formerly ruled over by queens, but that once the reigning queen was prevented by her monthly "purification" from conducting an important religious ceremony, and so the sovereignty passed on to her son, [32]—an explanation of an African Salic law which is also offered in civilisation by opponents to office-holding by women. The assistant of the Toda dairyman priest may not pass a village where there is a woman in the seclusion hut, on pain of demotion. [33] The *Veda* student may not go

directly from a menstruous woman to his sacred
book. He must in between, see a Brahman.[34]
The Jewish woman might not herself handle a
holy book. Nor might she name her god.[35] The
Persian woman might not look at a *Mindáshú*, a
celestial man;[36] the Hindu woman might not even
think of the gods.[37] Menstruous women may
not enter a dwelling where there is anything sacred
or a church—among the Tshis, the Cheyennes, and
the Nicaraguans, among the Jews, the Shintoists,
and the early Christians.[38]

Latter-day Christians have kept up the "church-
ing" of women after childbirth—a disinfection
rite, but because of their "uncleanness" they no
longer keep women away from church at other
times.

There are other places in civilisation from which,
however, they are banished. In the great sugar
refineries in the north of France, women are forbidden to enter the factory while the sugar is
boiling or cooling, because the presence of a menstruous woman would blacken the sugar. Nor
is any woman employed in opium manufacture
at the French colony of Saigon lest, for the same
reason, the opium should turn bitter. It is said
in England that meat cured by a menstruous
woman is tainted, but whether or not this belief

7

affects the wage-earning woman as well as the
housewife, I do not know.[39] Once, if we may
surmise from an old couplet, her pernicious influence must have spread beyond meat.

"Oh! menstruating woman thou 'rt a fiend*
From whom all nature should be closely screened."[40]

In spite of these beliefs, unlike the Australian
woman who has not only to leave camp, but to
encircle her mouth with red ochre and to warn
off any young man who comes near her,[41] unlike
the negress of Surinam who has to call out "*Mi
Kay! Mi Kay!*", "I am unclean! I am unclean!"
to any one approaching her,[42] a modern woman is
supposed *not* to keep to herself if she thereby betrays
her condition. She must be altogether secretive,
and the better to deceive she must act normally
in every way. To this end a girl will often endure
extraordinary discomfort or pain or run grave
risks of health. Again and again one hears a
girl say, "I would rather die than let any one
know about it," and, realising that there are even
mothers who will not mention the subject to a
daughter,[43] one almost believes the girl.

If she is loath after all to sacrifice either life or

* The function was itself personified as a fiend by the Persians.
(*Sacred Books of the East*, v, 283.)

health, she will jeopardise her reputation. Evasive or prevaricating on one point, she spreads the impression of being generally unreliable and unaccountably fickle, of being even more uncertain and changeable than she is—thanks perhaps to the very periodicity she is at such pains to conceal. "You never *can* depend upon a girl," grumbles the boy who twenty years later will be saying "*souvent femme varie*,"—with or without bitterness according to his fortune or his temper, but still in the dark and still disconcerted.

Australians believe that the catamenia comes from dreaming of a scratching bandicoot. When a Chiriguana girl first menstruates, old women run about her hut with sticks, "striking at the snake which has wounded her."[44] Because Mä'näbŭsh, the culture hero of the Menomini Indians, killed the Bear and threw a clot of his blood at his grandmother, the Bear's wife, "the aunts of Mä'näbŭsh" "have trouble every moon."[45] Once the god Indra slew a learned Brahman and then ran to the women for protection. Because they took upon themselves a third part of his guilt, he guaranteed them offspring and their husband's affection. Evidence of their part of the bargain appears each month.[46] Sincere "believers in" *Genesis* are apt to hold that the catamenia are part of the curse laid upon Eve, women's practical way of making reparation for the Original Sin. In Siam, the "wound" is believed to be made by certain spirits of the air.[47] In the Western Islands of Torres Straits, it is the Moon-man who is held responsible, and for his sake earthly men keep out of the way.[48]

We no longer have to consider the feelings of animals or spirits in this connection. Our relations with them are not as close as they once were. As for our own feelings about menstruation, they are apparently so deep-seated that we have not even begun to explain them or to explain away or justify the misunderstandings they provoke.

XII

WIDOWS

A WIDOW has always been reputed dangerous
company—if by different persons for different reasons. When she is still thought of as the
property of the deceased, marriage with her before
his claim is cancelled is naturally imprudent.
At Agweh on the Gold Coast her foolhardy suitor
is doomed to miscarry in all his undertakings,
to be drowned or to be killed in battle.[1] The
Kamchadale suitor of a widow runs the risk of
dying the same death as her husband.[2] A Bantu
Yao or a Lillooet Indian also marries a widow at
the peril of his life.[3] Once a Hudson Bay Eskimo
fell very ill soon after his marriage to a widow, and
the shaman declared that because of the jealousy
of the marital ghost divorce was necessary to
convalescence,[4] an instance of ecclesiastical inter-
ference between husband and wife unusual among
savages. In 1881 the deceased paramount chief

of the Duke of York Island effected a separation between his widows and the brother who had appropriated them, by inflicting the inconsiderate man with a very bad cold.[5]   In the Chinese province of Fuhkein, the marital ghost gets the second husband's clan, as well as the man himself, into trouble.[6]

A widow has to be careful on her own account too.   In Australia if an Unmatjera or a Kaitish widow does not smear herself properly with her mourning ashes, the conjugal ghost will kill her and strip her to the bones.[7]   In the Islands of Torres Straits an aggrieved marital ghost is said to have once burned down the house of his frivolous widow.[8]   The Matse, a Ewe tribe, believe that if a widow is negligent, Aho, the Spirit of Mourning,* will waste her away.[9]   A deceased Ama-Zulu husband can force his widow, pregnant by another, to miscarry.   Ama-Zulu ghosts have also been known to harass their faithless widows into

* Individual Matse ghosts appear to act through a representative spirit.   A like delegation of functions took place in Christendom.   "When God takes away the mate of your Bosome, and reduces you to Solitariness," writes the author of *The Whole Duty of a Woman*, when he addresses himself to widows, "he sounds you a Retreat from the Gayeties and lighter jollities of the World, that with your closer Mourning, you may put on a more retired Temper of Mind, a stricter and soberer Behaviour, not to be cast off with your Vail, but to be the constant Adornment of your Widowhood." (p. 93).

Zulu/ Virginia

leaving a second husband and returning to the
dead man's village.[10] Fearful of her dead husband's opinion of her, Barbara Pomfret of Virginia broke off her engagement and restored her
wedding-ring to her finger.* A Yao husband can
frighten his widow as much as he likes—by appearing to her as a serpent.[11] The illness of a widow-
bride in certain Hindu castes is supposed to be
caused by her first husband.[12]

The living as well as the dead require a widow to
be conscientious. Wherever sutteeism brings distinction to a family, many a widow has undoubtedly
chosen suicide as an alternative to the opprobrium
of kindred. Kindred may be very high-handed
in other ways too. If a brother-in-law met an
Arunta widow out in the bush acting as if
nothing had happened, hunting for "yams, "for example, he would be quite justified in spearing her.[13]
Once an unscrupulous Californian Nīshinam widow
went out to gather clover before it was proper,
and her brother-in-law, urged on by her father-in-
law, killed her.[14] With us, aggrieved or reproachful relatives are not so drastic or compelling,
but I have known a mother-in-law complain of
her widowed daughter-in-law having color in her
dressing-gown, and one suspects that a widow's

* Rives, Amelie. *The Quick or the Dead?*

qualms over remarriage may sometimes be intensified by a watchful family-in-law.

In view of all this supervision, it behooves widows to mourn circumspectly and convincingly. And as a rule they do. Australian widows crop or burn their hair close to their head.[15] When Lord Roehampton died, Myra cut off her long chestnut locks and tied them around his neck in his coffin.* In India the vernacular for widow is *shorn head,*[16] and in many another place widows have to shave their hair. Often, however, they may neither cut nor comb it. Washing, too, is quite generally taboo. For eight months or a year the Malagasy widow might wash only the tips of her fingers. The Bantu Fjort and the pre-Moslem Arab widow went quite unwashed for one year.[17] Caffre widows have been known to do so for three.[18] Niger Delta widows deliberately soil their faces,[19] and mud or ashes or coal are rubbed on the head or body in many places. In California, the Maidu widow covered herself with fine pitch and charcoal; the Yokaia widow mixed her pitch with marital ashes.[20] Bangala and New Guinea widows go naked, the better to bemud themselves,[21] but as a rule clothes are torn or soiled, or only ragged or old or plain clothes are worn. Ornaments

* Disraeli, *Endymion*, Ch. lxxxv.

are put away. Hindu widows may not paint their foreheads. [22] (I have never heard of a European or American with the habit of rouging when married, giving it up when widowed; but their jewelry they do lay aside.) Pearls are excepted; in fact, black pearls are considered particularly suitable. So is jet. All their outer garments are black.—Greek and Roman widows also wore black.—Crape is the only appropriate trimming, and a long crape veil attached to a small flat bonnet and falling over the face when the death is recent, thrown back when it is not, is customary.

Australian and New Guinea widows also go veiled, and Peruvian widows wore a rope of sedge around their heads. [23] The Australian widow's veil is more correctly speaking a chaplet. It is made up of small bones, hair, and feathers hanging over the face. What civilised widows do with their discarded veils, I do not know. Australian widows bury theirs in the grave. At the same time they rub off the pipe clay which has been smeared on their hair, face, and breast, leaving only a narrow white band on the forehead. But such half mourning is optional. [24] Sometimes in Victoria, when a widow is going out of mourning, she paints two stripes, first of pale brown and later of red, across her nose and under her eyes. [25]

In the Islands of Torres Straits, widows wear
frayed sago-palm leaf petticoats and necklaces,
armlets and leglets. [26]   In San Cristoval, one of the
Solomon Islands, they wear large tassels of grey
shell ear-rings.   In the Banks' Islands they wear
a rope around their neck. [27]   In Borneo a special
net garment has to be worn until it wears out and
falls off by itself. [28]

But even greater evidences of grief than "weeds"
are required of widows.   Sioux widows cut off
a finger joint to hang on the grave tree, [29] and
scarification is a common practice.   Fasting and
seclusion are still commoner.   Tshi widows are
shut up to sit on the floor in a conventional posture
and to fast for eight days. [30]   A Ewe widow is
supposed to stay housed for forty days.   Having
to go out of doors, she must hang her head, cast
down her eyes, and cross her arms over her breast. [31]
Until the annual death feast a Maidu widow can
go out only after dark. [32]   A Pima widow has to
stay home for four years. [33]   Toda widows neither
eat rice nor drink milk.   On the day of the week
their husband died, only one meal is eaten. [34]
Hindu widows never eat more than one meal a
day, and twice a month they forego it. [35]

Levity on the part of a Quakeolth Indian widow
would render her an outcast forever. [36]   The

presence of a Hindu widow at any festivity would
be ill-omened.[37] The home-staying Malagasy
widow may not speak to any one coming into the
house.[38] A Nīshinam widow speaks only in a
whisper,[39] a Central Australian does not speak
at all.[40] Civilised widows are also supposed to
be grave and unsociable. Their black-bordered
cards and writing paper preclude their being
invited to festivities—"black" is a "great protection," I have often heard them say,—and they
are apt to keep away from playhouses and places
of public amusement—at least until they have
discarded their crape veil. Laughter behind it
would appear indecorous, and to wear it at a
wedding would doubtless be considered in poor
taste. A widow recently told me that she was
unable to march in a suffrage parade because of
her mourning.

Mourning doubtless precludes widows everywhere from engagements it would not be easy
to enumerate unless one had oneself been a
widow. Sheer idleness may even be expected
of widows, but as a rule they are supposed to
work for, or be of some service to, the dead.
The Victorian widow visits the grave daily before
sunrise. She sweeps the ground and builds up
the fire lit for the comfort of the ghost.[41] Among

the Wataveta it is the duty of the eldest widow
to guard the grave from stray hyenas. She lives
near by.[42] Periodic visits to the grave or settle-
ment upon it or near by are very commonly expected of the widow. She has to keep it in good
repair, and make it look attractive. The chief
widow of the king of Tonga and her women cut
the grass from his grave, swept away the leaves, and
made a garden of sweet-scented plants for him.[43]
A certain Chinese widow is recorded as having
planted several hundred grave trees* with her own
hands.[44] The Tolkotin widow had to weed out
the marital grave with her bare fingers.[45] Civilised widows also feel responsible for the care of
the grave and visit it sporadically or on anniver-
saries. They plant flowers or leave cut flowers on
it. At home they frequently place flowers around
the picture of the deceased. The other day one
read of an American widow scattering flowers on
the sea where her husband had been shipwrecked.

Christian widows have to be content with these
flower rites, for Christianity, like the other historical religions, is antagonistic to the older ghost
cults. Where a maturer religion does not inter-

* Widowed, Diane de Poitiers displayed as her device an ever-
green tree springing from a tomb, with the words: " Left alone
she lives in him." (de Maulde la Clavière, R. *The Women of
the Renaissance*, p. 131. London and New York, 1901.)

vene, however, grave rites tend to be more elaborate. Food and drink are set out on the grave for
the ghost and ceremonial wailing is carried on
there for his satisfaction. Memorial death feasts
are also held in his honour; at them as well as at
the funeral a greater or less amount of the property
of the deceased or of his family is either set aside
for his ghost or destroyed. Under the historical
religions the only equivalent satisfactions for
widows are the burning of candles or the saying of
masses, pilgrimages or prayers, commemorative
tablets or buildings or endowments.

There are still more intimate ways of remem-
bering the deceased. A New Zealand widow had
his head dried and always slept with it by her
side.[46] Quakeolth and Taculli widows carry
his ashes on their persons.[47] Mosquito Coast
widows exhume his year-old corpse and carry his
bones.[48] The Victorian widow hangs a bag of
his calcined bones around her neck.[49] His dried
soles and palms and tongue make a necklace for
the Torres Straits widow; his lower jaw-bones for
the New Guinean.[50] One occasionally hears of a
widow in civilisation who cherishes the ashes of a
cremated husband, or keeps his embalmed corpse
close at hand, but carrying a piece of his hair
in a locket or wearing a miniature of him on a

medallion brooch is a much more common practice. Often she has his picture painted or his bust modelled.

When the deceased wants to communicate with the living, his widow is naturally his medium. Once a Fiji chieftainess, mistress of a deceased king, reported that during her nightly vigil he would appear to her in a dream to warn her against conspiracy against his heir and to encourage her to go on caring for his grave.[51] The head wife of Bambarré, a deceased king of Urua, Central Africa, enjoyed unbroken communications with her husband. On all important occasions Bambarré's reigning son sent one of his priests to her for advice.[52] Until our psychical research societies do more for us, our widows will be restricted to writing the biography or editing the letters or manuscripts of the deceased. Lady Burton, we remember, declined even that responsibility.

Widows' rites always last until all fear of ghostly infection is past. In primitive thought ghosts are believed to linger for quite a while about their old haunts. During this time they want much the same care and attention they had in life. Their interests too are much the same, and their conjugal relations are likely to be just as close. They have been known to beget offspring, and

women who do not want posthumous children sometimes take special precautions. Such
ghostly importunity does not subside of itself.
At a proper time notice has almost always to be
given the ghost to begone. His widow is then
carefully disinfected or purified. In Australia on
the Narran, she has to sleep three nights beside
a smouldering fire. She is then plunged into the
stream and smoked again over the fire.[53] The
Tshi widow is marched to the seashore and all
her clothes thrown into the water. Formerly
she was herself submerged. Now her escorts
only cry out to the ghost to leave her.[54] Matamba
widows are ducked repeatedly in order to drown
off clinging marital ghosts.[55]

We do not believe to any extent in ghost-walk-
ing, so that ghostly exorcisms are no longer necessary, and widows do not undergo purification.
Nevertheless, mourning is still prescribed for
them for a minimum period. Should one remarry
within it, it is I think two years, she would quite
generally be condemned as lacking in proper
respect for the dead or even as heartless or
unfeeling.

All the foregoing widow rites or taboos are more
or less characteristic of every type of family.
The developed patriarchal type is distinguished

by the suicide or lifelong sequestration of widows of position. Evidence of a man's wealth or rank during his lifetime, his widow is expected to add to his comfort or prestige in ghost-land. Recalcitrant widows are badly off. They are berated and abused and sometimes ostracised. Remarrying, their bride-price has to be returned to the family of the deceased by their family or by their second husband. They commonly have to forfeit their own dower rights.

In societies where the patriarchate is either undeveloped or, like our own, degenerate, a widow may also have to choose between matrimonial property and remarriage. In our case the marital motive in pre-arranging these alternatives for her is not quite clear. As there is no marriage in heaven, her husband cannot have been intriguing for a future meeting. Tertullian made this plain once for all. "Think not that it is to preserve thy body untouched for myself," he writes forehandedly to his wife, "that I am even now instilling the advice to remain a widow, suspicious because of the pain of being slighted. No debasing pleasure shall then be resumed between us. For God promiseth not to his people things so vain, so impure."[56] Nor does either Tertullian or any other Christian husband ever count upon such immediate intimacy with his surviving widow as the primitive marital ghost enjoyed.

Without any present or future claim upon the person of a widow, why then have Tertullian and other husbands wished to make digamy difficult for her? The Manichean suggests that it is because her deceased husband should continue in possession of her mind, entitled to her unceasing devotion. Is it to ensure such devotion, or, as I once heard an American husband suggest, to "protect" his Penelope against fortune-hunting, that a modern husband wills his property away from her if she remarry?

8

XIII

A MAN'S MAN

THE time seems to come for every boy when he is told directly or indirectly that he must stop playing with girls or hanging to his mother's apron strings.   In Australia a boy gets his notice ceremonially.   In one tribe he is sent by his mother into the circle of the men who are dancing before them.   In another, he and his mother sprinkle each other with water, and in another he throws his boomerang towards her spirit camp,[1] in both cases to show her that, no longer manageable, "it is time for his father to take him in hand."*   An Arunta boy of ten or twelve is warned by his tribal elders to no longer play or camp with the women or girls.[2]   If the tooth of a Kurnai initiate is not readily dislodged in the tooth knocking-out ceremony, its owner is said to have been too much with women and girls,[3]

* An undertaking shared in Australia, however, by all the older men.

just as we explain a youth's "freshness" or "effeminacy" by saying that he was "brought up at home" or that he was "a mother's darling," a "mollycoddle," or a "milksop."

Attached as he may be to his mother and sisters, the time also comes for a boy when expression of his affection is bad form. Precautions against showing it are sometimes elaborate. "Civilised" boys will take no little trouble to preclude a maternal kiss—at least in public, but often the savage boy may not even speak to or look at his mother. He turns his back, ceremonially, when she approaches; he must communicate with her through a third person. With his sisters he is "shy" too. Fiji brothers and sisters may not even speak to each other. The very name of their relation is *ngane*, "one who shuns the other."[4] In Leper's Island and Pentecost, if they recognise each other's footprints in the sand, they must turn off the track. Should the two meet on a path, the girl runs away or hides.[5] A Navaho lad can take nothing out of his sister's hand. She has to put things on the ground for him to pick them up. A Batta would consider it shocking to escort his sister to an evening party. In the New Hebrides, if he happened on one where she was, she kept him at a distance and turned her back on him, [6] — eliminating any question of introducing partners to her.

There are special periods when it is particularly offensive or even dangerous for a boy to have anything to do with women. Should he eat with one during his initiation, a Narrinyeri lad would become ugly or grey.[7] Should he touch one, a Kurnai initiate would fall sick. Were he to let a woman make bread for him or her shadow fall upon him, he would surely become thin, lazy, and dull.[8] Among the Lower Murray tribes the very sight of a woman for three months after the initiate's teeth have been knocked out, would bring numberless misfortunes upon him—blindness, the withering up of his limbs, decrepitude in general.[9] "Boys and girls from the ages of fourteen to eighteen should not recite in the same class-room, nor meet in the same study hall," declared President Porter of Yale. "The natural feelings of rightly trained boys and girls are offended by social intercourse of the sort, so frequent, so free, and so unceremonious."[10]

Such taboos or "ceremonial avoidance," as it is called, would of course be difficult to observe consistently in the same dwelling, but as a rule boys leave home for clubhouse or school. In New Caledonia, a boy leaves his mother when he is

three.[11] The Bassa Komo boys of Nigeria go to
the men's part of the village at four;[12] the Bororo
boys of Brazil go to the men's house at five;[13]
English boys go to a public school when they
are nine or ten; Americans, to boarding-school
at thirteen or fourteen.

Mothers and even sisters visit our boys' boarding-schools or colleges, sometimes ceremonially, as
at "Commencement" or for a ball game, sometimes just to see how Jack or Harry is getting on.
There is a "ladies' day" in most men's clubs and
sometimes even a restaurant for ladies. Saloons
sometimes have back rooms for women. More
primitive seminaries or clubs are as a rule less
self-indulgent or less magnanimous. Sometimes a
savage mother goes on cooking for her son after
he has left home, but she must put her vessels
down at his club doorsill, as surreptitiously as
an American mother smuggles cake or candy to
her schoolboy. Women may never enter the
bachelor's hall of the Kaya-Kaya of New Guinea,
although when they pass near it, the men inside
make a loud noise to attract their attention.[14]
When Fiji boys are initiated, women are admitted,
to be sure, into the *Nanga,* but they must look
discreetly in front of them—on pain of insanity.[15]
Should a woman at any time pry into the rotunda

of the Creeks, she would be killed.[16] Trespassing
women are threatened with death by clubmen in
many other places.

Sometimes they are merely subject to viola-
tion. They run this risk in the New Hebrides,
if they eavesdrop at the singing of the *Qatu* men
during an initiation in the secret precincts.[17]
With us staring in at a club window or greeting a
man sitting in one is less rash; it subjects a lady
only to a disparaging verbal classification.

Should a woman in East Africa intrude in the
men's house she is kept there for three years.[18]
It is said in New Mexico that an indiscreet field
worker of the American Bureau of Ethnology
was imprisoned three days in the *estuva* of Isleta,
at the mercy of its members.

There are clubs elsewhere in which over-night
visits by girls are institutionalised; but once
this form of promiscuity goes out of fashion,
the "mixed" club becomes unpopular. It seems
to involve too many restrictions. "I could n't
put my feet on the mantelpiece with women
around," says the New York clubman, ignoring
the fact that the architecture of most New
York clubs has made that feat at any rate
unusual. "Nor could I smoke or sit around,"
he probably adds, again ignoring the fact that

he has never been told by an acquaintance
that she minded his pipe or cigarette, and also
failing to realise that a place where a woman
did n't have to constantly say "don't get up" or
"do sit down" might be a comfort to her.

Be that as it may, it is important, we cannot
deny, for a man to feel at ease in his club. He
spends so much of his time in it, day and night.
Even married men do not always sleep at home.
It is very unconventional for a Fiji husband, for
example, to spend the night outside of his *bures*
or public house.[19] New Caledonian and New
Guinea husbands have private sleeping quarters[20]
and in American cities husbands are in the habit
of rooming during the summer at their clubs.
But even when they sleep at home, men make
their club their headquarters for exercise, for
drinking and gaming, for the entertainment of
foreigners, for politics and ritual, for gossip and
lounging. Englishmen are said to use it to
sulk in.

But whether a man goes to his club like an
Englishman for privacy, or like an American and
the rest of male kind for sociability, there are
times when it is no longer alluring, when a "mixed"
company or a *tête-à-tête* seems more desirable.
And yet feminine society is hard to come by,

burdened with conditions and beset with dangers
as it is. A dinner is "such a lottery"; a dance
is overpaid for the next day; one's own tastes in
exercise, in games, in shows, have to be so utterly
sacrificed. The occasion is flat or the background
"out." Then one rarely sees a woman unham-
pered by bores. With a girl, there is the chaperon
to whom one must be polite; with a married
woman, there are her husband or children, to
envy or pity,—both trying emotions. As for
widows, there is almost always a marital ghost to
be more or less considered, and it is particularly
hard to be civil to a ghost.

On the other hand, freedom from chaperon
or husband, however pleasant, is full of risk. It
is trying to be suspected as a potential suitor or
co-respondent, and before one knows it, one is.
Lord Rufford had only to lend a young lady a horse
and drive home alone with her in a postchaise, to
quite involuntarily commit himself.* A Thompson River Indian who loosens the lacing of a
maiden's dress or lounges near her is also considered to have serious intentions. For him to be
"touched" by a girl at a dance is just as serious.²¹
Farther south, in parts of the United States,
if a man dances with or calls upon a girl more

* Trollope, Anthony. *The American Senator*, II, Ch. xviii.

than once at one ball or in the same month, he is liable to be called very "attentive" or "devoted." In New England, early in the nineteenth century, to walk arm in arm was tantamount to announcing an engagement.[22] "If a gentleman looks at you at meeting, you are suspected," writes Eliza Southgate in 1802, "if he dances with you at the assembly it must be true, and if he *rides* with you"—[23] Even now, to walk home from church with a girl two or three Sundays or, in more fashionable circles, to habitually crank her motor for her, arouses expectations in the public mind—if not in hers.

As for a married woman, it is not "proper" for a Tartar to shake hands with her,[24] for a Hindu to touch her dress or give her a present or call out to her or wink or smile at her,[25] for a Beni-Mzab or a Leti, Moa or Lakor Islander to speak to her in the street or away from her husband,[26] for a Ewe to pay her a compliment,[27] for a Gilbert Islander to pass her on the road,[28] for a Californian Indian to stroll with her in the woods, for a Creek to drink out of her pitcher,[29] for an Anglo-Saxon American to take her to a play or a tropical island.

Moreover, the consequences of such indiscretions are apt to be far from pleasant—fines, flogging, or horse-whipping, loss of ears or hands

or penis, branding, exile, being haunted, death,
braving an "explanation coat,"[30] newspaper
notoriety. Nor does a gentleman care to subject
a lady to death or disfigurement, to the loss of
her ears or of her lips or nose or hair, to beating
or burning, to ghostly visitations, to ostracism.
He is also loath to so damage her reputation as
to disqualify her for marriage, still more perhaps
to force her into marriage with himself—the com-
monest way of "saving a woman's character."

Evidently caution is necessary—and I have
seen it exhibited even at the dinner-table. And
yet dining out is an attempt, however bungling,
to bring men and women together. It expresses
a comparatively modern point of view. Unless a
Uripiv man eats with men only, he must face a mys-
terious death.[31] Whatever his reason, you cannot
make a Warua let a woman see him drink.[32] The
Hawaiian woman who left her dining-room for
the men's was killed.[33] There is in New York
City a so-called suffragette restaurant in which
men and women may not eat together—"even
if they are married," adds my informant. These
instances are somewhat extreme, but as a rule
men and women do not feast together, and it is
quite often bad form for a man to eat with his
wife.

Her companionship is out of the question at
other times too. A Hindu was not only not to
eat with his wife, he was not to look at her when
she ate, or when she sneezed, yawned, or sat at
her ease.[34] A Californian Indian never enters his
wife's wigwam except in the dark.[35] Nor does
a Kaffa husband, like many a New Yorker, ever
see his wife except at night.[36] Even at night
the New Yorker may not see his wife except
in company, and then he is less with her than
the others. It would be bad form for him to sit
next to her at the play or talk to her at the opera*
or dance with her at parties† or take her out to
supper.

There is a certain valley in Loango husband
and wife may not cross side by side on pain
of childlessness. He must take the lead.[37] In
Zululand, a man and his wife walk nowhere to-

---

* "Avoid conversing in society with the members of your own
family," urges the author of *Sensible Etiquette* (p. 402).

† The author of *Sensible Etiquette* admits it is "not customary
for married persons to dance together in society," but she urges
men "who wish to show their wives the compliment of such an
unusual attention" to be independent enough to brave Mrs.
Grundy (p. 219). I had always supposed it was the wife who
was averse to conjugal companionship in public, discouraging
such "compliments" from fear of the appearance of having no
other partners or admirers.

gether even if they are both bound for the same place.[38] Nor does a Moslem ever walk abroad for pleasure with his wife. If they are necessarily out together, she must keep a long distance behind him.[39] In the high society of London, Paris, or New York, husband and wife have separate carriages or motors. In that of China, until she was seventy, a wife "did not presume to hang up anything on the pegs or stand of her husband; nor to put anything in his boxes or satchels; nor to share his bathing-house."[40] In modern English seaside resorts, also, husband and wife may not bathe together, and instances are even on record of married persons in England who have never seen each other clotheless,[41]—a taboo laid formally upon the Brahman householder.[42]

Outside of modern civilisation rarely may men and women work together, so strict is the distribution of occupations according to sex, or play games or go to the play together.

They may not even go to church together. Should an Australian show his bull-roarer or sacred stick to a woman, both he and she would be killed by the medicine-man, or he and the women of his family would automatically drop dead.[43] Torres Island women are not allowed to see the *zogo lu*, the image of Waiet and his

sacred things, and during his month-long ceremonial the women are kept apart on the north-west
side of his island. [44] A Japanese woman was
exhorted to go "but sparingly" to the temples
until she was forty. [45] Mahomet urged women
to pray at home, and from Moslem mosques they
are either wholly excluded or admitted only when
men are absent. [46] In the early Christian churches
women had a separate door, and inside, a separate
place. [47] To-day in the Greek churches they
stand apart from the men in a gallery called the
gynaikonitis. It is entered by an outside stair-
case. [48] In New England, as late as 1800, we read
of a town voting that the second and third pews
in the women's side of the gallery (the unattached
women sat in the right-hand gallery, the unattached men in the left-hand) be allotted to a
girls' boarding-school and that to these pews the
school-mistress be allowed to put doors with
locks. [49] Even in our modern churches men and
women form separate church societies, and in the
country the men stay together around the church
door as long as they can.

In Nigeria, on the first day of *its* week, the
men could not approach the women's quarters
at all. [50] At Santa Cruz there is no pushing by
women in a crowd. When a crowd collects the

women have to keep together and aloof from the centre of attraction.[51] In 1849 Elizabeth Blackwell refused to walk with her graduating class at the Commencement exercises, being the only woman, "it would n't be ladylike," she demurred.[52] Formerly in Seoul, women were allowed on the streets from eight P.M. to three A.M., and a man caught out during those hours was severely punished.[53] At Nufilole, one of the Swallow Islands, men and women are never out of doors together. In the morning the men go out first. After their return the women go and fetch water. Then the men go out again.[54] In Manhattan Island, where economic exigencies do not allow of such a definite alternation in the movements of the sexes, park benches, ferry-boats, and cars are merely labelled "men" or "women." Men are not expected to sit on the women's benches, but they may go on the women's side of the ferry-boat. Women, on the other hand, may sit on the unlabelled benches, but they may not go on the men's side of the boat. The sexed cars are of too recent a date for the development of an etiquette; but I understand that they are counted upon to introduce order into the present very unsettled ceremonial of giving up seats to women in "mixed" cars.

Against the vexations such uncertainty involves the American railway has tried for years
to protect the public by providing smoking-cars
for men and differentiated waiting-rooms,—the
problems of the lower berth it has shirked, to be
sure,—and American hotels with their "lobbies"
for men and parlors for "ladies" have made a like
attempt. Latterly, hotel promoters or managers
have taken an even more decided stand in separating the sexes, setting aside a whole floor for
women or even running hotels exclusively for one
sex.

We have noted how in times of physiological
crises the separation of the sexes is also everywhere very rigid—at puberty, during the catamenia,
at marriage, during pregnancy. It is strict too
at birth, and even at death. In many communities
no man is allowed to be near a woman during her
labour or for set periods after her delivery. In
serious illness no woman outside of the household
is allowed near a Cherokee patient, and it is likely
that formerly he himself was segregated in an outhouse to preclude contact with any woman. [55]
"A man does not expire in the hands of women,
nor a woman in the hands of men," [56] is a Chinese
maxim.

Such taboos in conduct or sympathy also in-

volve taboos of speech. Among the exogamous
tribes of Victoria, husband and wife may learn
and understand, but may not speak, each other's
dialect.[57] For two moons after marriage they
may not speak to each other at all and if communication is necessary, it has to be carried
on through a third person. Among the Wabemba
a husband has to give a young wife a present
to untie her tongue. The observation of her re-
spectful silence is called *kusimbila*, the present,
kusikula.[58] In Madagascar, propriety requires
women to address men in different terms from
those they use to one another.[59] To deceive
the men, Bornese women have invented a kind
of inverted speech for themselves, transposing
or adding syllables.[60] "As if the two sexes had
been in a state of war," writes Mistress Carter
of an eighteenth-century party, "the gentlemen
ranged themselves on one side of the room, where
they talked their own talk, and left us poor ladies
to twirl our shuttles and amuse each other by
conversing as we could."[61] The conversation of
these gentlemen was about the old English poets,
a subject Mrs. Carter thought for her part not
"so much beyond a female capacity."—But then
Mrs. Carter was a notorious Blue-Stocking.

Several years later a poet himself—Lord Byron

—declared that women ought not to read poetry—or politics. "I wuddent talk to me wife about vottin' any more than she 'd talk to me about thrimmin' a hat," said Mr. Hennessy, a point of view which in this country only Mr. Dooley and a few others have hitherto seriously questioned.

Poetry, American women do read; but as American men read only politics, neither poetry nor politics affords a "mixed" company much conversation. Moreover, taking little or no part in men's callings or games, the ladies are apt to be inattentive listeners when "business" or "shop" or "sport" are under discussion. No wonder a man is given to saying there are so few things you can talk to a woman about.

Nor can a man even lose his temper in the presence of a woman. In Central Australia, if men do get to quarrelling and shed blood in her sight, so strong is the feeling against women seeing men's blood, that the man who has been first blooded has to perform a conciliatory totemic ceremony.[62] On the Island of Leti a woman has only to throw her sarong into a mêlée to end it.[63] The duels of our ancestors were always fought behind the backs of the ladies. Even to provoke a duel in their presence was bad form. To-day no gentleman will "insult" another—at least not very openly—

9

before a lady.   He cannot even swear at another man—or in fact at anything—with a woman around.

Cut off at so many turns, ceremonially and practically, from the company of women, pursued by their representatives, inhibited in conversation with them or in one's temper before them, is it surprising that a man contents himself with the formula, "I never could understand a woman," that he puts up with the monotony or gracelessness of his club for the sake of its protection, that also for prudence' sake he even cherishes a reputation for misogyny or at any rate of being a man's man—particularly as he knows that he is thereby qualifying for getting from most women all they have to give?

XIV

WORK AND PLAY BOUNDARIES

IN this day of social plasticity there is but one
place where the occupation boundaries of
sex are still quite undisturbed—the nursery.
"Girls can't play soldier"; "boys don't know
how to cook," "Whoever heard of a boy keeping
house?" "You can't be the doctor, you 're a girl,"
our children go on saying to one another, oblivious
of such rarities as Dahoman Amazons, French
chefs, Asiatic "boys," English butlers, or female
graduates of John Hopkins or Cornell.

Savages are almost as disregardful of and
opposed to exceptions as children. Hunting,
fishing, trapping, raiding, and fighting are so
much the affair of the men that frequently intimacy
with a woman or even her mere presence would
endanger their success. Hence, New Zealand,
New Guinean, Zulu,¹ and many other warriors
keep away from women before starting on a campaign. Iroquois Indians do not marry until they

stop fighting.[2] (General Kitchener is said to
have a strong prejudice against married soldiers).
Alaskan and Malagasy whalers avoid women a
week before their expeditions.[3] Bangala trappers
likewise avoid them from the time they make or
set up their trap until the quarry is caught or
eaten.[4]

Eskimos are said to take their wives hunting,[5]
and civilised "sports" sometimes take theirs;
but whether because women "never can learn
to handle a gun," or because "you have to shave
with them around," or because your aim would be
less certain or your trap less enticing, it is plain
that as a rule out camping or shooting women are
only in the way, "decidedly a bore."

As an outcome of hunting and trapping, herding
is a masculine occupation. Toda women may
not even approach the buffalo dairies except at
set hours and by set paths. Nor do they ever
trespass at home on that part of the floor set aside
for churning.[6] An African herder usually believes that his cattle will sicken if a woman has
anything to do with them, so that in most pastoral
Negro tribes the milking has to be done by the
men.[7] Among the agricultural Bechuana the
men have also to plough.[8] Clearing and getting
ready the soil are commonly done by men; but

to a large extent planting, as a development from
their digging of roots or their gathering of berries
or seeds, is in the hands of the women. Bakongo
women would ridicule the man who undertook
to help them in the fields. Orinoco women
monopolised the tribal planting. "We do not
know as much as they do," said their husbands
in the belief that reproduction whether of children
or of corn needed the same kind of skill.[9]

Besides agriculture, marketing and transportation, clothes and pottery, children and household
chores are the business of the women. In many
places a man would no doubt meet with difficulties
in shops, but in Nicaragua if he even looks into
one, he risks a beating,[10] and in Abyssinia,
infamy.[11] It would take as much courage for
a man in Samoa to make cloth[12] as for a man
in London or New York to knit on a park bench
or do plain sewing in the drawing-room. It is
so scandalous for an Eskimo to touch a woman's
job that even to drag ashore the seal he has
killed would degrade him.[13] Once in British
Guiana some men had perforce to bake and they
were always pointed at afterwards as no better
than old women.[14] For a New Caledonian to do
any chores about the house or village would be
"undignified."[15] Pueblo Indians would laugh at

a man who undertook to plaster his house. Among
the Caffres, if a big boy showed any interest in a
baby, the other boys would call him a girl,[16] and
a solicitous Caffre father would be far more
ridiculed than the American who walks the floor at
night or wheels the baby carriage around the park.

The woman who does *not* wheel her baby carriage
is also likely to be snubbed. Should she venture
upon masculine pursuits, she is condemned
primarily because she is supposed to have left
her own. Dr. Longshore, the first woman to
practise medicine in Philadelphia, was told by
a druggist, refusing to fill her prescription, to go
home "to look after her house and darn her
husband's stockings."[17] In his opinion denying
a woman admission to the bar of her state, Mr.
Justice Bradley took occasion to say that "the
constitution of the family organisation which is
founded in the divine ordinance as well as in the
nature of things, indicates the domestic sphere
as that which properly belongs to the domain and
functions of womankind."[18] "Can you cook an
egg?" I heard a bystander on Fifth Avenue ask
one of last year's suffrage paraders. The London
heckler also depends for much of his humour upon
his theory of the essential undomesticity of the
suffragette.

" L'un me brule mon rôt, en lisant quelque histoire;
L'autre rêve à des vers, quand je demande à boire."[19]

In her biographies of married women, Maria
Child remarks of one of them, Mrs. Lucy Hutchinson, wife of the Roundhead Colonel, that although
she was possessed of extraordinary talent and
learning for a lady of her day, "she performed
all the duties of a woman in a most exemplary
manner."[20] Biography of wives or, in fact,
female biography in general is not as fashionable
as it once was, but the admirer of any notable
woman still tells you that in spite of her achievements she is very domestic; and champions of
woman-in-modern-industry urge in her support
that after all she is only doing what woman has
always done, statistics showing she has merely
followed her old-time jobs from the home to the
factory.

There are variations of course, in the economic
alignments of sex. Among the Yahgan, the men
never go out fishing.[21] Fire-making among the
Wataveta is a man's secret.[22] In East Central
Africa, sewing is done by the men of the family, and
a woman can divorce her husband for a rent in
her petticoat.[23] A Beni-Harith would rather
die of hunger than eat at the hands of a woman,
and Warua and Uripiv men have to cook for

themselves or run the risk of a supernatural mishap.[24] In Abyssinia, although he cannot carry water, all of the household wash must be done by the man of the family.[25] Nicaraguans do the housework to leave their wives free to trade. The Egyptians did the household weaving, Herodotus tells us, for the same end.[26] To gratify the American housewife's peculiar love of shopping her husband sometimes stays home to mind the house and commonly does more than a man's stint of work. The American tells you he is superior to the European because, among other reasons, American women never work like European women in the fields. There are also places in the United States where a man lets a girl row or paddle his boat or canoe only under protest, and throughout the country it reflects on a man to have a girl who is walking with him carry even her own coat.

Peculiarly feminine appointments like a parasol or a fan either girl or man is free to carry when together; to an unaccompanied man they are taboo. And a man is always expected to make it plain that he is carrying a woman's things from gallantry, not subservience. As Robert Burton once pointed out, there "is no greater misery to a man" than to be his wife's "packhorse," to have to bear with her when she says:

"Here take my muff, and do you hear, good man;
Now give me Pearl, and carry you my fan."[27]

A great many other things besides personal
equipments are sex property too. In Australia
a woman may not carry a shield, nor a man,
a digging-stick. In the Marquesas a man may
not even touch *tapa* and a woman meddling with
a canoe would be killed.[28] A Caffre woman
would not dare to help herself out of the milk-
sack.[29] An Eskimo would not think of rowing in
an *umiak*, the large boat used by the women.
The Californian Indian who chooses the "woman-
stick" in preference to the bow when they are
ceremonially offered to him, has to work with the
women the rest of his life.[30] Among the Thompson River Indians, women's implements, the
basket, the kettle, the root-digger, the packing-
line, even become their individual totem or guar-
dian spirit.[31] A Nâga who touched a woman's
pottery or weaving tool would be punished.[32]
Among the Bongos stools are used only by women.
Men forego them as effeminate.[33] "A spinning-
wheel is a woman's weapon," pleaded the un-
fortunate German abbot who to his dismay
found himself engaged in an argument with one
of the learned ladies of the sixteenth century.[34]
Reading newspapers at the breakfast-table is so

peculiar to men that a recently patented table rack
was quite appropriately advertised as a Christmas present suitable for Father or Husband.

Sex property is particularly well recognised in
the nursery. Toys are generally sexed. Is a boy
ever given a doll-house or toy kitchen or laundry,
or a girl, a toy pistol or railway or stable?

In the play of the child which does not ape
work, sex property and sex lines are also obser-
vable. Balls and bats, marbles, kites and tops
belong to boys; skipping-ropes and hoops to girls.
A girl plays baseball or marbles against the heavy
odds of being either disparaged or patronised. A
boy snatches away a girl's skipping-rope only to
tease her or to "show off," and what boy is willing
to ride a girl's bicycle or wear a girl's skates?

Again, savages like children are apt to have
separate pastimes for the sexes. Games in which
weapons are used in fun as in archery or putting
the shot or casting spears or darts are naturally
not played by women. Nor do they take part
in sports which have to do with cattle or horses.
A Toda woman would never join in catching the
sacred buffalo at the funeral ceremonies,[35] the
favourite sport of the men. A North American
Indian woman may mount a horse—but only
for transportation and usually seated behind or

in front of her husband, like our own colonial
dames or Spanish Americans of a later day.   No
Indian woman ever plays the great hoop and pole
game of all the North American tribes.[36]   The
Apache woman may not even see it played.   On
the other hand there is a game of double ball
played, outside of Northern California, exclusively
by women.[37]

Even if the same game is played by both sexes,
it is apt to be played with variations.   In playing
"lehal," a bone guessing-game, Thompson River
Indian men and women sing different songs.
Among the Wahpetou and Sissetou tribes the property of a dead person is gambled for at his or
her death feast, the guests—all men or all women—
playing against the man or woman representing
the ghost.   Formerly when the dice were figured
plum seeds, the men played with eight of them,
the women, with seven.   In the guessing or dice
games of many other Indian tribes, women are
apt to use a basket, men their hands.[38]   In the
card games of civilisation women usually play
for lower stakes than men, sometimes refusing
"to play for money" at all.

Nor in primitive culture do the sexes play any
game as a rule together.   In Leper's Island, a
game of guessing the identity of a person hiding

behind the door shutter of a house is played by both sexes, but never together.[39] There is a widespread hand-game among the American Indians, much like our "Jenkins up" or "hunt the button," which both men and women play, but usually apart. "Frequently there will be a party of twenty or thirty men gaming in one tipi," writes Mooney of this game among the Arapaho, "while from another tipi a few rods away comes a shrill chorus from a group of women engaged in another game of the same kind,"[40]—a game of "bridge" at the club and another at a ladies' lunch party.

When savage men and women do play together they are apt, like children everywhere, to line up against one another. The Crows play shinny, for example, and the Topinagugine, football,— men against women.[41]

On the whole more games are played, I surmise, and played more habitually, alike in savagery and in civilisation, by men than by women, particularly gambling and divination games. (Perhaps because of their sacerdotal origin.) In Vancouver tribes it is "indecent" for women even to look on at men gambling,[42] and from many of the gaming-hells of civilisation women are excluded.

It is undoubtedly because of its sacerdotal
origin that women are frequently excluded from
taking part in the drama or even from its circle
of spectators. A Japanese lady was told not to
"feed her eyes and ears" with ditties, ballads, or
theatrical performances.[43] It is a question whether
Greek ladies went or not to the comedies. At any
rate women took no part in the acting of Greek
plays. During the Renaissance a young prelate,
Tommaso Inghirami, was the "leading lady" at
the court of Leo X. We recall that even in
Shakspeare's day the women's parts had to be
acted by youths, that for a long period English
women did not go to the play at all and then
when they ventured that they went only with the
greatest circumspection. "There are few English
comedies a lady can see, without a shock to delicacy," wrote Dr. Gregory to his daughters. "You
will not readily suspect the comments gentlemen
make on your behaviour on such occasions. . . .
The only way to avoid these inconveniences, is
never to go to a play that is particularly offensive to delicacy."[44] In New York as late as 1830,
the pit was taboo to the ladies, and no man who
was careful about his womenfolk ever allowed them
to attend a *ballet*.[45] Until of late years in fact an
Anglo-Saxon often refused to take his wife to any
public show uncensored by himself.

Dancing, the elder relative of acting, and originally always a mimetic performance, has naturally varied a great deal with sex. In most communities one sex is apt to be precluded from the specialised dancing of the other sex, from war or harvest or court or temple dances. Even when men and women dance together their postures, steps, and positions are different. Recently I saw an Apache dance in which the men circled around the drum player in the centre, ring within ring, the women making the outermost ring. Felkin saw a similar figure danced by the Bari in the Soudan, the inner circle of men moving from left to right, the outer of women, from right to left. [46]   In the ball-game dance of the Cherokees the men danced in a circle around the fire and the women in line a few feet away, men and women singing separate songs. [47]   In a night dance of the Akikuyus the men stand in a circle with their backs to the fire in the centre. The girls face them, their hands on the men's shoulders. The men put their arms around their partners' waists, holding in both hands their long dancing-spear with its butt driven into the ground. Together men and girls sway from the waist backwards or forwards or from side to side. [48]   In our lancers the men stand or pirouette in one direction, the women, in another; the men bow, the women curtsey. In cotillion figures men and women play of course quite different parts. Even in the waltz, it is the gentleman who "holds" the lady and who starts to "reverse," mimicry which the defenders of the "old" against the "new" dances seem in their zeal to overlook.

In both play and work caste may break down some of the barriers raised by sex. Women, or rather some of them, have been let into men's play for the same reason some men have been let into women's work. The slave and the factory made possible a leisure class of women to become the vicarious consumers of men's wealth. For rich men, games and sports are one of the most prestige-ful means of consumption, so that it was natural for their unoccupied womankind to share in them— at least as soon as cloistering began to go out of fashion and the man too fastidious to see a woman take unbecoming exercise became rare.

On the other hand, the feminine chores that would have been degrading for a freeman, the slave, the feudal retainer, or the wage-earner have had to do. The original sex prejudice against particular jobs becomes a class prejudice. To be "in trade" or to spin cotton or weave wool in a factory disqualifies for the "best society."

Tailors are accounted one ninth of a man. Barbers fare somewhat better, but male house servants are so much disesteemed that they have to be recruited from the descendants of slaves or from countries where the feudal tradition is tenacious.

But caste may also raise up sex barriers in economy. Once housewives give up their places to slaves or wage-earners, their chief service, economically, is to be evidence of a man's wealth. The more idle they are, the more convincing. So it easily becomes discreditable to a man to have his womenfolk do any work at all. This theory, of course, can only be fully carried out in the highest ec·nomic classes; but where it prevails it more or less modifies the working habits of all classes of women. In early Victorian England, for example, there was a fiction in genteel middle-class families that the ladies of the house never did anything serviceable after the mid-day dinner, so that in the ceremonial of afternoon calling "no one was to be surprised in doing any kind of work."[49] Of this period too was the tradition that if a lady did work, it had to be without pay or merely for "pocket-money," a tradition still active in lowering women's wages. Even more persistent and far-reaching is the kindred theory that a girl works only because she has to, having none to work for her. It is primarily of course a middle-class theory, but even in organisations for the unemployed, insurance against worklessness is sometimes not open to women.[50]

When, in spite of these leisure-class traditions, women succeed in making their way into a new calling, it straightway tends to be disesteemed for men. I have known "men of affairs" who published their verses or their novels anonymously in order not to hurt their business or their professional standing. Painter and poet—in the United States at least—know that they are again and again discounted by practical men as effeminate. A Wisconsin Congressman of my acquaintance considers it expedient to keep his talent as a pianist a secret from his constituents. Nowhere has the male nurse as good a "social position" as the female. A man tutors or teaches school as a makeshift. There would be even more prejudice against a man kindergartner in the New York Department of Education than against a woman professor in Columbia University.

These anti-male taboos are the more striking because the callings from which art and teaching

10

and nursing were differentiated, priestcraft and medicine, are still a male monoply.

When the original medicine-man, the doctor-priest-chief, becomes even more disintegrated, will the split-offs in their turn be effeminised? Will the family doctor, already a disappearing type as a man, reappear as a woman*—thanks perhaps to the primitive sex prejudices which already serve the turn of the woman doctor in her struggle against the professional taboo? Long ago the Priest ceased to be poet, painter, musician, time-keeper, historian, naturalist. Since the Protestant Reformation, he has even lost prestige as a go-between for the gods. Now if Christianity becomes too metaphysical for practical life, and deity too remote for any communication at all, will ghost-worship be revived as spiritism and women, always more of a success as mediums than the men, come into their own again? Will the officials into whom the Chief is rapidly being differentiated also turn out to be women, men turning away from such routine jobs as public housekeeping, popular education, and international hospitality to the more exacting and interesting sciences back of them all?

Indeed, if ever medicine, religion, or politics

* Perhaps the visiting nurse is her forerunner.

become matters of routine, their practice or ad-
ministration may no doubt be safely entrusted
to women.   Is it not proper for women "to apply
the principles men discover,"* and have not
women always been depended upon in fact to keep
the social machinery running, "natural" conservatives as they are said to be?

Less well informed than our ancestors, apparently, about God's intentions for the sexes, we are
as yet not at all uncertain about Nature's, and
women we persistently classify as "naturally" imitative and conservative, and men as "naturally"
inventive and radical.   Who knows but in
society's re-alignments of sex to suit this classification, to be a conservative will become as
disreputable for a man as it was for a woman in
ancient Greece or feudal Japan to be a poet, or
to be "progressive"† will be as dangerous for
a woman in, let us say, the twenty-second century as it was in the seventeenth to be a natural
scientist.

And yet it is not danger, but derision, that
keeps men and women in their places.   Without
ridicule society would be topsy-turvy.   The

* Rousseau, *Emile*, Bk. V.
† We may remember that in a recent political campaign one
prominent woman at least was publicly scolded for affiliating
herself with the "progressives."

comic supplement is a social bulwark. Once it ceases to be "funny" for a man to thread a needle or shop or hold a baby, or for a woman to cast a ballot or sit on a jury or introduce a bill, domesticity and politics will become optional for both. Hitherto there has been nothing ridiculous in the man who imitates—providing his object is not a woman—or in the woman who invents—if she is modest about it—in a male reactionary or in a female radical; but as soon as our attention is focussed upon these types by the cartoonists and the "movy-man" we suspect that new fields for control will open up to all our grave Directors of Sex—and opportunely perhaps, a little *désœuvrés* just now as they seem.

XV

SEX DIALECTS

BARRIERS of nature, mountains, seas, deserts, are not, we well know, the only causes of dialect. The special interests which also split up a community acquire each a tongue of their own. Priestcraft always has more or less of an esoteric language, using foreign or archaic or quite forgotten forms of speech. Fishing and hunting, farming and industry, law, medicine, and science have all their technical vocabularies. Special words must be used or tabooed in addressing royalties, and Fifth Avenue excursionists have to learn the "expressions" of the East and West Sides.

Since different interests make for differentiated forms of speech, may we anywhere expect to find men and women speaking quite the same language?

Sacred words or dialects are generally kept secret from women. Kaitish tribesmen believe in a spirit they call Atnatu. Their women may not know his name or anything else about him; but they call what they believe to be his voice, the bull-roarer, Tumana.[1]   Shut out from the secret society of the men, its Papuan name, Asa, means merely something supernatural and fearful to Papuan women.[2]   In general the members of secret societies, Australian or Papuan, Melanesian or Bantu, speak a society slang never spoken of course before the uninitiated, *i.e.*, the children and the women.[3]

In self-protection, primitive fowlers and hunters, sailors and miners, use special terms to puzzle or placate the spirits of the animals or waters or soils they are upsetting or crossing or pursuing.   Of such sacrosanct lingo we may be sure the women are kept in ignorance, shut out as they are from the pursuit or calling itself.

A special taboo of this kind falls upon the Eskimo* women of Baffin Land.   As long as they are in mourning, they may not mention the name of any animal at all.[4]   Verbal taboos of mourning in general are apt to be heavier on women, like other mourning taboos, than on men.   There are tribes in Australia and in North America in which, speech being entirely taboo as we have elsewhere noted,

---

* Among other peoples the Eskimos believe that animals can hear and understand what is said of them at a distance.

widows use nothing but a gesture language. In many other communities in which a ghost is supposed to be attracted by his name or to object for some reason or other to its use, his kindred and particularly his widow become apt in periphrasis, avoiding not only his name but any common noun in which it or even any syllable of it occurs. Zulu women even taboo every sound at all like one in a tabooed name, and it is said that at the king's kraal it is sometimes difficult to understand the speech of the royal wives, tabooing as they do all the sounds in the names of all the king's deceased forebears, lineal and collateral.[5]

Ancestor worship and nature cults compromise with or cede to other forms of polytheism, but whatever course religion takes women continue to be excluded from its esoteric speech. Hindu women cannot read the Sanskrit of the Vedic texts.[6] Untaught in Hebrew, the Jewess has to pray in the vernacular.[*] During the Middle Ages comparatively few Christian women were able to read the Bible.

Nowadays men encourage rather than discourage women to read the Bible; but to one of their ancient religious privileges the men still cling.

[*] According to an Hebraic myth an ambitious Jewish maiden once reached Heaven by bribing one of the fallen angels to tell her the Ineffable Name.

Profanity, originally merely an appeal to the gods, belongs exclusively, they feel, to themselves, a prerogative they safeguard by not even availing themselves of it before a woman. And effectually, for "a woman does not know how to swear, even if she tries," the men say. Even where the company holds that swearing is "bad form" or "in poor taste" for men at any time, they find it far more offensive in women. A woman who swears "makes one shudder," and she is always criticised at least as "coarse." She has received even more drastic treatment. Moses à Vauts tells us that he had a wife who would not forbear swearing. So one day when after mild admonition she "let fly 2 or 3 bloudy horrid Oaths in my Face," he writes, "I bestowed so many Flaps with my bare hand alone on her Mouth, the Part Offending."*

We may notice, too, that the modified expletives dear to a boy, "Gee!", "By gosh!", "Golly!", are more or less taboo to little girls. Girls are expected in fact to use quite a different set of exclamations from their brothers—although "Oh my!", "Oh dear!", "Oh gracious!", "My good-

---

*The Husband's Authority Unvail'd; Wherein it is moderately discussed whether it be fit or lawfull for a good Man to beat his bad Wife, p. 84. London, 1650. This Englishman adds, to be sure, that for the same offence he would gladly receive the same treatment "from any Christian other than my Wife."

ness!", "Mercy!", may of course be only appeal to deity in the disguise of abbreviation.*

Excluded from statecraft as well as from theology, women have naturally been ignorant of the dialect of politics. Notwithstanding the very marked sex dialects of their daily life, the Caribs of the West Indies spoke a special jargon in their councils, a jargon quite unknown to the women and children.[7] In mediæval Europe, Latin was the language of statesmen as well as of churchmen, and only very enterprising women indeed learned Latin. It is "a rare unusual thing for a woman to understand Latin," said the German abbot who argued that that tongue was "not fit for a woman" because it contributed nothing towards the defence of her chastity.[8]

To-day it is only the conservative among our college girls who "elects" Latin; but even she finds outside of the classroom that the men who use it as a conversational garnish considerately undertake to translate it for her. As for our own political terms, woman suffrage has not yet been triumphant enough to deprive men of the pleasure

* The English-speaking Frank women of Smyrna are in the habit of prefacing their sentences with καλή as an equivalent of "I say." Lucy M. J. Garnett suggests (*The Women of Turkey: The Christian Women*, p. 371, n. 1) that the ejaculation may be a survival of the invocation of Artemis as 'Η καλή, Ephesus, the ancient centre of her cult, being only thirty miles or so distant.

of explaining them to women. Fortunately the meaning of primaries, of election districts, of moving the previous question, of scratching the ticket, etc., will undoubtedly survive for some time as helpful dinner-table topics.

Women are also unlearned in the dialects of business and trade, of war and its machines, and of sport. Few women understand the slang of Wall Street or are able to read stock quotations. How many women remain sufficiently unbewildered by new terms to go on listening when men begin to discuss the balance of trade or the theory of a central bank? Military expressions are rarely used by a woman and she is as uncertain in her reference to the parts of pistol or rifle as in her handling of them. Football, baseball, boats, horses, cards, drink, all have their technical vocabularies, and bits of them often come to be understood and adapted to other exigencies of description by the layman, seldom by the lay-woman. In critical circles, in fact, her use of race track, gambling, or tippling slang would be deplored, since it suggests a knowledge of the details of "sport" "distinctly unbecoming."[9]

Indeed our successive out-croppings of slang phrases—"It 's a cinch," "She 's a peach," " You 're easy," etc., etc., are both introduced and used

for the most part by men. That "slang is bad
enough in a young man, but in a young woman
it is disgusting," was once a widespread opinion.
Old standbys in fact like "hell" or "son of a
———" (various fanciful parents) no "gentleman"
will utter before a "lady" at all or at least without
begging her pardon.

Women too are apologetic about using certain
words to men. "Is that the right word?" or
"Is that the way you pronounce it?" is a kind of
self-deprecatory question they are apt to ask in
using unfamiliar or technical terms. It protects
them against an anticipated charge of pedantry,
recognising the fact of their trespass, but dis-
arming male criticism by its appeal.

On the other hand, women seem not to develop
to any extent special terms for their own interests.
Except in Nyasaland where women have a set of
special terms for food,[1] any man can understand the talk of any woman about household
detail—as far as words go. There are but few
peculiar terms for servants or babies, for shopping or marketing, for domestic hygiene or art.
Women use more colour terms than men—at least
in the United States—and the terminology of
women's dress men find puzzling—or pretend to.
But on the whole, do not men seem to run to

technical terms and women—away from them?—a differentiation the ethnologist may do well to notice when he considers the influence of sex on the origins of language.

In general the reason of this differentiation is not clear—to me, at least. One case in contemporaneous civilisation I may perhaps except. Men have what might almost be called a secret language of sex, whereas women have no words, secret or otherwise, to describe some of the simplest sex characters and expressions.* How does this happen? The making up of a sex vocabulary begins in the nursery. Given no names by their mothers for parts of their bodies, children very soon make up their own names. A child will always invent a name for the unnamed. Usually their "make up" calls forth mirth and soon goes the way of other "baby talk." But in this case a child is made to realise that its business of naming is objectionable. Now the little girl is readily shamed out of her newly coined words, but the little boy for some reason or other treasures them—in secret. And their secrecy gives them, of course, a new value.

* It is likely that savage women have a larger sex vocabulary than civilised women. Swahili women, for example, have one of their own made up of symbolical terms, archaic words, and words borrowed from other Bantu dialects. [Zache, H., " Sitten und Gebrauche der Suaheli," Zt. f. Ethnologie, xxxi (1899) 70.]

This nursery history explains, I think, *in part*, the obscenity of boys, and the state of mind in both sexes when adult that makes it necessary to duplicate college lectures treating of sex—even in a coeducational medical school.[11]

The sex taboos of the nursery become, of course, more and more exaggerated. The body is more and more hidden from sight and sex functions are carefully ignored. Boys escape from the nursery and learn, or mislearn, of sex; but for girls who commonly do not leave their nursery until they start to make another there is little opportunity to hear anything at all about sex. Husbands, as well as mothers, may be poor teachers, and we know that society at large habitually discountenances every explicit reference to sex. "We especially deplore," wrote a body of New England churchmen in 1837, "the intimate acquaintance and promiscuous conversation of females with regard to things which ought not to be named; by which that modesty and delicacy which is the charm of domestic life, and which constitutes the true influence of woman in society, is consumed, and the way opened, as we apprehend, for degeneracy and ruin."[12]

As, in accordance with this theory, no "decent" woman has been supposed to know anything about prostitution, much less to mention it, at least until very recently, its vocabulary, too, is necessarily unintelligible to her; many an "after-dinner story" it would be difficult for her to understand enough of to laugh at—if she wished.

But, as we know, there are also many general terms of sex which cannot be used in a "mixed" company.* An English lecturer on eugenics tells us that only with caution and anxiety does he ever venture to use the phrase "sexual selection" before a mixed audience, and that for many years he has found "racial" less disconcerting than "sexual," instinct. He advises the use of "parent-hood" instead of "reproduction," and he points out that Philaminte† is much less upset by "sex" (as an adjective) than by "sexual." He says that it is dangerous to use "pregnant" to her in any but its metaphorical sense, but that the para-

* Just as in Micronesia and Fiji there are many words which it is *tambu*, to use the Fijian term, to utter in female society. Before women, for example, Fijians must refer to a lad who has just been circumcised as *teve*, not *kula*, the proper term. (Williams, T., *Fiji and the Fijians*, I, 67, London, 1858. Cp. Brown, p. 383.)

† "Mais le plus beau projet de notre académie

C'est le retranchement de ces syllabes sales,
Que dans les plus beaux mots produisent des scandales;

Ces sources d'un amas d'équivoques infâmes,
Dont on vient faire insulte à la pudeur des femmes."
(Molière, *Les Femmes Savantes*, Act III, Sc. ii.)

phrase of "expectant mother" she hears with
equanimity.[13] The newspaper editor knows, however, that left to herself she prefers natural history
imagery.

Besides specific differences in sex interests,
differences in sex character and outlook in general
seem also to have made an impression on language.
It shows particularly in adjectives. For example,
are not "lovely," "darling," "sweet," "horrid,"
"mean" peculiarly girls' adjectives, and "bully,"
"fine," "jolly" "rum," "rotten," "bum," peculiarly boys'? Boys and girls may also use the
same adjective, "cunning" or "cute" for example,
in different senses.

Judging from their adjectives or descriptive
phrases, women tend to over- and men to under-
statement. Describing a fire, for example, a
woman would say that it was "perfectly frightful"
or "dreadful," a man, that it was "a pretty bad
blaze." On the other hand, in praise or de-
nunciation a man's terms are sometimes stronger
than a woman's. "Nice" "dear," "lovely" "just-
too-sweet," correspond to his "great," "fine,"
" capital," "stunning"; "poor thing" to his "dub"
or "slob"; "minx" and "cat" to his "skunk"
and "shark."

"Perfectly," as we have noted, is a woman's

word. So in hackneyed humour is "because."
The "bromidiom" or inevitable remark, as well
as slang and dictionary adjectives or adverbs, is
of course characteristic of the point of view, and
"bromidioms" have sex. I once classified Gelett
Burgess's original list of them to test his own sex
theory of the "bromide,"[14] and found one third
of them male, one third female, and one third
neuter. It was an amusing occupation, for one
was so certain of the classification and so uncertain
of its reasons. Could a man say, for example,
"I really ought n't to tell this, but I know you
understand," or "Why, I know you better than
you know yourself!" Or a woman, "I want to
see my own country before I go abroad," or "He's
told that lie so often that he believes it himself
now."

Men and women use different words in their
salutations. There is, for example, the difference
between "Hello" and "How do you do?"* We
may notice too that "Hello" is apt to be followed by "old sport," "old scut," "old goat,"
and "How do you do?" by "my dear," "you
sweet thing," "my love." Children are noticed

* A difference parallelled, we are told, in Fiji, and I venture
to say in many other primitive groups; but this sexual differentiation—like many others—has been unnoted as a rule by
ethnologists.

with two quite distinct sets of appellations—
"dearie," "sweetheart," "precious," etc., and
"captain," "snooks," "kid," etc.

Is sex also a factor in the written language?
Writing and reading in general were once hierarchi-
cal secrets. They were therefore likely to be
disclosed to men before women; but even when
they are fully secularised a reluctance to teach
them to women persists. "Some Stoicks indeed
there are," writes a seventeenth century Englishman, "who will not allow any Books to Womankind."[15] "What do girls want with τὰ γραμματικὰ?"
asked the Greek Christian of would-be school
teachers in the Turkish provinces. "We should
have to watch them more vigilantly than ever."[16]
"Teach a *girl* to read and write!" said a Moslem
mufti in Tripoli to Dr. Jessup. "Why, she will
write letters, sir,—yes, actually write letters! The
thing is not to be thought of for a moment."[17]
With a like point of view some of our mediæval
schoolmen also urged that women should not be
taught to write.[18]

Allowed to read and write, special books are
written for women, and sometimes even a special
script is required of them. The Japanese alphabet
has two sets of characters, *katakana* for the men,
hiragana for the women; and Japanese female

writing has its own syntax and many peculiar idioms. A woman versed in the learned script, a poetess, was admired, but, as in Greece, classified as a courtesan.¹⁹ Was not a "ladylike" handwriting an important part of the education of our great-grandmothers?

Nowadays there are signs of handwriting of any kind becoming a feminine specialty. We hear that letter writing, the last refuge of longhand, is becoming a lost art; but that women practise it more than men. Then, too, in sending a type-written letter to a woman most men apologise for it, and there are, in fact, women who resent receiving typewritten letters.

Started late in literature, it was natural that special books should be written for women, primers suited to their "natural" intelligence or to their un-trained minds. Otherwise, in reading men's books it was thought they ran the risk of discouragement—unless they "skipped." We may note, by the way, that for "skipping," we have as good an authority as Saint Teresa, since she begs her nuns when they read not to weary themselves with what they cannot understand, with "subtile discussions." "This is not fit for women. . . . Be always, then, on your guard against perplexing your mind. . . . Since women need no more than what suits their

.

capacity." And the Saint adds contentedly and
in a phrase many an anti-suffragist has since
paraphrased: "And in this respect God confers a
favour upon us."[20]

In writing books women could read without
skipping, authors had to appreciate, however, that
they might endanger their circulation. Francis
of Sales was told, for example, that because he
had dedicated his "Introduction to a *Devout Life*"
to Philothea he had kept many men from reading
it, men "who considered as quite beneath them
the counsels given to a woman." His next book
he accordingly dedicated to a man, opining that if
for that reason women did not read it, "the mistake
would be in them more excusable."[21]

Left to themselves, I doubt if women ever make
this mistake, however excusable. Teresa herself was quite subtle-minded enough to want to
read the arguments of the schoolmen. Even little
girls are as a rule glad to read boys' books. But as
they grow older they have not always been allowed
to read them. "It may here be questioned,"
writes the seventeenth century author of *Decency
in Conversation amongst Women*, "whether the
reading of Romances may be permitted to young
Ladies, of which divers men speak diversly according to the variety of their fancies." As for

"wanton" ballads and "loose pamphlets," "perilous books" which "learn young maids to sin
more wittily,"* "no Man can comprehend" how
they "may be justified."²²

A like opinion had been held by Vivès, the
Spanish pedagogue, and he implored mothers to be
more "strict" about the reading of their daughters, those emancipated "American" girls of the
Renaissance, as a conservative Frenchman calls
them. As a matter of fact, antique though their
criteria be, "careful" American parents do censor
the books their daughters read, and now and again
an American husband may be heard to say, "I
won't let my wife read that book."

Books to suit women's interests as well as their
mental or moral capacity have, of course, always
been written. In those calm days when the double
code of morals passed unchallenged, separate
moral tracts were written for women. The sexes
were not even scolded together, observes Mr.
Higginson.²³ The seventeenth century authors
of *The Whole Duty of Man* and of *Youths Behaviour*

* "In those vain Pamphlets, they do read how this Virgin
leaves her Countrey and her Parents to run after that Stranger;
another is in love in a moment, when she reads that she hath
received Letters from such and such a Gallant, and how they
have appointed private places where to meet together." (P. 168.)
—"Too much novel reading is very bad for girls."

published companion volumes called *The Ladies'
Calling,* and *Decency in Conversation amongst
Women.* A century or so later the Rev. Thomas
Gisborne wrote first his *Duties of Men* and then
his *Duties of Women.* Moral books for the young
were also sexed. *Letters* or *Talks* were addressed
specifically to Young Ladies or to Young Gentlemen. "Preceptors" and "instructors" were
compiled for each sex—like the "readers" of a
later day.

Children's books are still in general classified as
boys' books and girls' books, stories about boys
and their adventures for boys, stories about girls
and their virtues for girls. Female biography
was not so long ago addressed to adult females,
and collections of female poets dedicated to them.

Nowadays novels, having apparently lived down
their once suspicious character, are the nearest
approach to publications for women; the newspapers, for men. "I have no time to read novels,"
remarks in self-defence or self-satisfaction the
man who gives an hour a day to his newspapers.
"I am too busy to read the paper," says the
housewife who patronises the circulating library.

Half a century ago, when a lady did express any
desire to read the newspaper, the sheet containing
the advertisements, and the Births, Deaths and

Marriages was "considerately selected"[24] for her. To-day there is a "woman's page" for her in the daily newspapers, and entire weeklies or monthlies are published for her—even in China. So carefully adapted to her interests and mind are all of these publications that they undoubtedly reduce the danger of her defeminising herself by the reading of periodicals* to a minimum.

* Nietzsche, *Beyond Good and Evil*, § 239.

XVI

SEX IN DRESS

A CONTEMPORANEOUS Teufelsdroeck might be prompted to write the history of clothes, but not their philosophy. Shorn of their social significance, they are being lowered to a utilitarian basis, and even that is insecure. Thanks to railroads and steamships, illustrated newspapers, and picture postal cards, national costume has almost disappeared. Factory and democracy are making it impossible for any class to wear a distinctive dress. With the disappearance of age classes, dressing according to age of course disappears too. Except on babies or young women, long skirts or old ladies' caps are anachronisms.

And yet more stubborn than nationality, rank, or age, sex still exacts observance in dress. "She dresses like a man," is still a derogatory thing to say of a woman. If buff waistcoats, gilt buttons, and black beavers,* or linen collars, "tailor suits," and

* See Mrs. L. G. Abell, *Woman in Her Various Relations: Containing Practical Rules for American Females*, p. 307. New York, 1853.

sailor hats no longer subject her to this reproach,
short hair still does.   Long hair does even worse
for a man, classifying him as a "grind," a musician,
or a crank.   It was a costly mistake for an Abolitionist to let his hair grow.   At one time the
Massachusetts Puritan was ordered by the General
Court, true to its Roundhead traditions, not to
"wear long hair like women's hair"[1]; and China has
lately had to sacrifice her pigtails to get a position
in the world.   Dinka women wear an apron, and
the Dinkas call the neighbouring Nilotic tribes of
Bongo, "women," because their men wear one.
Schweinfurth, their dressy European visitor, they
called in irony the "Turkish lady."[2]   On the other
hand, their Bari neighbours consider it womanish to dress at all.   In dressing up they rely
entirely upon red paint.[3]   Until very recently in
the United States a man dressed up in a pleated
shirt or white socks at a considerable risk of it,
too, being "a shame unto him."   Even now a
bracelet watch may subject its wearer to a charge
of effeminacy.

More flagrant trespasses are penalised more
gravely.   Turkish trousers render their wearer
liable to jeers or even banishment.   In their
beginnings, bloomers and divided skirts entailed
difficulties almost as serious.   The New York

Herald of September 7, 1883, refers to bloomers as "eccentric habiliments, which hang loosely and inelegantly. . . making that which we have been educated to respect, to love, and to admire only an object of aversion and disgust."[4] After the berated garment had been limited to bicycle use, I remember on one occasion the indignation of a tourist "*en bicyclette*" who as I was going into a *château* in Touraine was being kept out—"*à cause de mes culottes*," she declared. And were not "all the kids in Bridgeport" after that enterprising bicyclist, Molly Donahue?[5] Nor are riding breeches even now "established" everywhere. Riding last year in Hayti "*salot*" was the "*injure*" cast upon me by the less polite, and the other day in New Mexico my hostess, a most independent woman, asked me to put on my coat as we neared the town near her ranch, otherwise the priest would be preaching against her. I doubt if there is a street in this country in which any woman as frankly betrousered as Dr. Mary Walker could not collect a crowd or induce her own arrest; and we have yet to hear of any board of aldermen repealing its customary ordinance against wearing attire improper to either sex, or of any judge refusing to fine or imprison such a disturber of the peace.

At other times or places the offence has been more than a crowd-gatherer or a misdemeanour. In ancient Mexico "the man who dressed himself like a woman, or the woman who dressed herself like a man," was hanged.[6] Gudruna's Icelandic lover Thord advises her to make her husband Thorwald a shirt with sleeves wide enough for it to be taken for a shift. She could then ask for a divorce on the ground that Thorwald wore female dress.[7] The Pelew Island goddess who put an apron of pandanus leaves upon her creature, First Woman, would certainly have punished her or her descendants if they took it off.[8] No doubt the leafy coverings of Adam and Eve differed. At any rate, after Hebraic dressing becomes more elaborate, it is decreed that "the woman shall not wear that which pertaineth unto a man, neither shall a man put on a woman's garment: for all that do are abomination unto the Lord."[9]

Do we wonder that the wife of the Brownist pastor of Amsterdam who persisted in lacing her bodice to her petticoat, "as men do their doublets and their hose,"[10] gave "an appearance of evil" to every Dutch Bible reader, or that their New York descendants, having relegated lacing entirely to women, scorn a corset-wearing male, or that the English swimming clubs of the Amateur Swimming Association have decided that the regulation swimming costume of the women must be about two inches longer than the men's?[11]

All these dress taboos are due, I suppose, to the distrust of primitive society about the natural differentiation of the sexes and to its never-failing confidence in its own ability to control it. Among its means of control, ornament and clothes are of course very important. They probably originated as a way of calling attention to and emphasising sex. And they still serve not to hide but to set off sex,—except in those callings in which sexlessness was once a means to supernatural power or position and in which sex is hidden under clothes worn by the opposite sex* or by neither sex.

We must also remember that conventional as dress may seem to us, to the more primitive it seems more than a mere form. Running through much of primitive thought is a theory of what has been called contagious magic. It is held that things which have been in contact become alike, get each other's traits, and are subject to each other's fortune. If, for example, you are by the

* From this point of view Pearson's theory that priests wear petticoats to assimilate themselves with the priestesses whose place they have usurped (*The Chances of Death*, IX; *Woman as Witch*, II, 19. London and New York, 1897) is questionable.

way of practising black magic, you can harm your victim by bedevilling (or, in one of the civilised forms of black magic, by ridiculing) his finger-nail parings, his spittle, his hair cuttings, or his ornaments or clothes.* They are all such an intimate part of him that what you do to them works also on him.   Furthermore, the mere wearing of the costume of a class or person or—sex may impart their traits.   The Khyoungthas of India tell of a king and his men who, persuaded to dress up as women, were attacked and overcome without a blow.[12]   And in order to subjugate the rebellious Lydians Crœsus advised Cyrus to order them to wear tunics under their cloaks and buskins about their legs,[13] a discipline which proved as effectual in changing their manners as that of Nurse when she makes her naughty little charge put on his sister's dress or hat.

Is not part of the severity of this punishment due to the dread in the boy's mind that he will not merely look like but become like a girl?   If an Australian Wiraijuri boy plays overmuch with girls, an old man takes him aside and pretends to ex-

*I suggest that this is the explanation of the popularity of the method of discrediting a woman by describing her dress.   This form of attack is used against men too, of course; but far less effectually, because a woman, social conservative as she is, is more identified with her clothes than a man.

tract from his legs strands of the woman's apron.[14]
Among the Yaunde, a Cameroon tribe, uninitiated
boys have to fasten banana leaves to their legs to
indicate their likeness to women,[15] humiliating
reminders which are torn off after initiation with as
much rejoicing as "putting on trousers" occasions
with us.

When the Galli devoted themselves to the cult
of the Mother Goddess they were presented with
a woman's outfit[16]; and wherever in savage tribes
men from religious or other motives temporarily
or permanently assimilate themselves with women,
they have perforce to don women's clothes,
whether for a day or a lifetime.

Agnodice, the enterprising Athenian girl who
studied medicine, cut off her hair and put on a man's
habit.[17] The first woman to study medicine at the
Sorbonne also dressed like a man, an example our
own Elizabeth Blackwell was advised to follow,
not as a disguise, but because, it was argued, it
made the University men free to help her.[18]
George Sand and many of the early Women's
Rights women in the United States took to wearing
modifications of men's dress. Their critics had
a habit of urging an absolute interchange of petticoats and breeches upon them all "to complete
the system."[19] For example, the editor of the

Rutland *Herald* advertised in his paper that after Clarina Nichols had appeared before a committee of the Vermont Legislature asking for the vote for women in district school meetings, he intended to come forward and present her with a suit of men's clothes.[20]   The Judiciary Committee of the New York Assembly, to whom, in 1856, petitions for "women's rights" had been referred, reported that in cases where both husband and wife had signed the petitions "they would recommend the parties to apply for a law authorising them to change dresses, so that the husband may wear petticoats, and the wife the breeches, and thus indicate to their neighbours and the public the true relation in which they stand to each other."[21]   For some such reasons husband and wife actually do interchange garments in many places. We remember how during child-birth a German peasant puts on some of her husband's clothes and how a sympathetic Erukala-Vandhu husband puts on his wife's. A bridegroom dressed as a girl, in the Greek island of Cos, when he received his bride; among the Masai he wore a girl's dress for a month after marriage. Argive brides wore false beards when they slept with their husbands.[22]

Where belief in the magical relation of clothes to personality persists, or where the suspicion is strong that sex left to itself may vanish at any moment and dread of this disappearance precludes toleration of any deviation from sex type, sex labels in dress will be made to stick. If, on the other hand, variation in personality ever comes to be considered more important than artificial distinctions of sex, or even an unvarying natural distinction, dress together with other sex labels or earmarks will soon wear off—and nobody will notice.

XVII

OTHER EARMARKS

"WHAT'S in a name?" Much, very much, and Juliet was indeed a very modern girl to even raise the question. In primitive culture it is often believed that the dead may be re-incarnated in the living through the appropriation of their name. Naming rites may determine a person's status and career. Then names are in themselves lucky or unlucky; a change of name will avert danger or bring one luck. An integral part of personality, a name may even affect character.

Sometimes names are kept secret, in the belief that knowledge of them gives power over their bearer. Ghosts may be lured back to their old homes by their names. Whatever the reasons, liberties may under no circumstances be taken with the names of the mighty, dead or living, chiefs or gods.

There are many name observances in family

life. Sometimes fathers-in-law or mothers-in-law, sometimes brothers or sisters may not be mentioned by name. Husband and wife quite commonly avoid using each other's name. A Zulu woman may not address her husband by name, particularly by his *i-gama* or real name. If she does, she is liable to a charge of witchcraft and killed.[1] In Nyasaland a woman will not even use a word synonymous with her husband's name, and were she to call him by name it would keep her from conceiving. Batchelor made his Ainu acquaintances blush by asking them the names of their husbands. In the course of ten years he found out that it was considered most disrespectful and extremely unlucky for an Ainu woman to mention her husband's name. In Southern India wives believe that to utter their husband's name even in a dream would bring him to an untimely end. Were a Nishinam husband to call his wife by name, she might divorce him.[2] Mrs. Grantley of England always called her ecclesiastical husband "archdeacon,"[*] and Mrs. Gaylord of New England thought of her husband and even dreamt of him as "Mr. Gaylord," and had never, in the most familiar moments, addressed him otherwise.[†] Squire and Mrs. Gaylord are of a past

* Trollope, Anthony, *The Warden*, ch. II.
† Howells, W. D., *A Modern Instance*, ch. IV.

12

generation, but throughout the United States, except in a few streets in Eastern cities, husbands and wives still speak of each other to their acquaintances as well as to their servants as "Mr." and "Mrs.," and, travelling *à deux*, a man registers as "So-and-so and wife." Husband and wife also refer to each other as "my husband" or "my wife," as "Father" or "Mother," "Poppa" or "Momma," as "my lord and master," "my better half," or in certain circles as "the old man" or "the old woman," or merely "He" or "She."

A Dyak couple also refer to each other as "He" or "She," if they are childless; otherwise as "father of So-and-so" or "mother of So-and-so."[3] A Hindu woman's periphrasis is "the master" or "the man of the house"; a Perak's, "house and house ladder"; an Ainu's, "my person" or "my man"; a Zulu woman's, "father of So-and-so;" a Zulu man's, "daughter of So-and-so."[4] So reluctant is the Moslem to refer to his wife at all that he may do so *via* male pronouns. "He has pain in his back, headache, and he will not eat," said the Mufti of Beirut in asking Dr. Van Dyck to visit his ill wife.[5] The Ainu speaks of his wife as "my person slow of foot" or "my person at the lower side of the hearth"; the Tuyang speaks of his, as "the mean one of the inner room," "my dull thorn," "the thorn in my ribs," to protect, it has been suggested, rather than to deride her.[6]—Luther also refers to his Kate as "my rib."[7]

In speaking of a married woman, either to her husband or another, there often seems to be some hesitation about using her name. Such reluctance is sometimes *de rigueur*. It is good manners in speaking to an Ainu of his wife to call her his *ketkimat*, "female doer of the heart." The polite term in New Britain for another man's wife is literally "a number of small children," and, if you are especially polite, you always refer to a man's wife in the plural, monogamist though he be. Zulus call a girl who is only betrothed "mother of So-and-so." In the New Hebrides, among the Todas, and in civilisation a married woman is referred to as the wife of So-and-so or by her husband's name.[8]

Pelew Islanders may not mention the names of married women at all or refer openly to them.[9] "A man can bear anything but the mention of his women," is an Arab saying. In speaking of any woman a Moslem adds *ajellak Allah*, "may God elevate you",[10] a disinfectant formula. A Solomon Islander rarely pronounces any woman's name and then only in a low voice.[11] In saluting women a Hindu was not to refer to himself by name." In China unrelated "male and female do not know each other's name; to find out a girl's name a man would have to ask her to marry him."

At primitive initiations youths are commonly given a new name, as our boys get a nickname at boarding-school. But an initiation name is generally less widely known than a nickname. It is kept secret from the non-initiates, *i. e.*, the women and children. The time comes with us too, however, when either nickname or "baptismal" name is more or less taboo to the other sex. I am told that in a well-known Boston dancing-school, the boys and girls of a certain age are formally told that the time has arrived when it is proper for them to address one another only by their surnames.

In love-making the great stress that is put on the use of the "Christian" name for the first time suggests how close an intimacy its use may, to be sure, involve. It appears to be also significant of a proprietary claim, and this may be the reason why men, particularly quite young men, are so shy about addressing a married woman by her "first" name. They probably feel, more or less unconsciously, that they are trespassing, misappropriating property. So they circumlocute or search for a nickname for the lady. One wonders if, where a husband takes his wife's name, as among the Andamanese,[14] the girls nickname him.

Sometimes a "tomboy" is given a boy's nickname, sometimes a "namby-pamby," a girl's; otherwise, sex is always very strictly observed in personal names. It, if nothing else, must appear in the name, and we never hear of even a feminist objecting.

Salutations or modes of address are very apt to vary with sex. The Fijian man, as we have noted, greets you in quite different words from the Fijian woman. In Chinese salutations "the upper place was given to the left hand," by men, "to the right hand," by women.[15] In addressing a man the Caffre woman always kneels.[16] In addressing a woman an American takes off his hat and in genteel circles keeps it off until she tells him to put it on. Meeting a woman on the road an American turns out for her, whereas a Yao or an Ainu expects her to turn out for him. An Ainu woman is also expected to take off her headdress to a man, whether she knows him or not. Saluting an acquaintance, she covers her mouth with her hand and fixes her eyes on the ground.[17] In the Russian pale only the unorthodox Jewess looks a man in the eyes or shakes hands with

him.[18]   An American "lady gives her hand to a
gentleman," writes the author of *Sensible Etiquette*,
"if she wishes to, but she does not shake his hand
in return." Nor should a gentleman grasp a
lady's hand "too cordially." Moreover, "*young*
ladies should not offer their hands to men who are
not relatives, unless under exceptional circumstances, such as after an absence of some weeks,
or to especial friends."[19]   Whatever the circumstances, handshaking is certainly less characteristic of American women than of American men.
In this country, too, the ceremonial kiss of greeting
is entirely confined to women. Girls are also
taught that "How do you do?" is the only "ladylike" verbal greeting, and that in saluting a man
it is their "privilege" to bow first.

Among savages, sex posture and gait and demeanour in general have been but little observed.
In civilisation they appear to be growing less
marked. And yet some of these habits are too
dependent upon dress, where sex differentiation,
we have observed, is peculiarly persistent, to vary
much of themselves. In bowing it would be
almost impossible for a woman to remove her hat—
even if she wished. Until recently she was loath
to take it off at the play, and she still willingly
acquiesces in the ecclesiastical requirement of

keeping it on in church. It would be hard, I suppose, for a girl to climb a tree in a hoop skirt. A "hobble" skirt or a Japanese *shigoki* precludes a "mannish" stride, many "shirt-waists," an overhand throw and, as Achilles once advertised the fact, any kind of a skirt will lead a woman to stop a ball in her own way.

Still, even when "hobble" skirts are not in fashion, a woman walks from the hips instead of from the knees at some risk. It makes her look so unfeminine. And, as Tertullian once pointed out,[10] a woman is expected to show modesty in her gait.

We ask only for short steps from women, but in many places in taking them a vibratory movement is considered pleasing. Little Papuan girls are made to practise this gait for hours at a time, and always walk in this way when men are about.[11] Had our own "Grecian bend" held its own, probably our daughters would also have had to be trained to it. To dance at the angle acceptable in their day, our great-grandmothers must have needed considerable training.

Dancing was the only form of gymnastic, I take it, they had. I suppose they never ran. An open-minded old lady said to me the other day that for her part she liked to see young women run.

"Nowadays, you know," she added ingenuously, "they teach girls how to run." Still "Marathon" races have not as yet been planned for girls, and a "grown woman" seen running for fun never fails to create amusement. But that in part may be because both sexes have begun to give up the use of their legs, too slow-going for modern requirements.

There is also a growing indifference about lady-like positions in sitting. Girls are no longer taught that lounging is "unladylike" as well as ungraceful, that only the other sex may sit cross-legged, "a gentleman, of course, being allowed more freedom than a lady,"* or that it is bad form to show their ankles or to cross their knees, a change in good taste for which bicycling and cross-saddle riding are probably in a degree responsible. Where these pastimes have not been introduced, for example in Bengal or in China, women are probably still expected to keep their legs parallel and to show the greatest possible modesty about their feet."

The demand for facility in fainting passed away with the eighteenth century, and other early requirements like taking a man's arm to "go out" or "in" to dinner or his hand to be ceremonially

* Sensible Etiquette, p. 395.

passed up or down, over or through, out or in,
are beginning to lose their vogue. Even the ceremonial positions in round dancing have lately
shown so many signs of passing that societies
have been organised in their defence.

Nowadays girls may whistle—or try to; but
our grandmothers, told us, with little attention to
rhyme, that

> Whistling girls and crowing hens,
> Never came to any good ends.

In Bohemia and Saxony a girl's whistling once
would have made the devil laugh, and in Austria,
Our Lady, cry.[23]

I am unaware of any present or past sex distinctions in sneezing or coughing except that
women are perhaps expected to sneeze or cough
less obtrusively than men, just as a strident voice
is peculiarly offensive in a woman. Hence American school girls were once required to recite in
accents "perfectly feminine,"[24] and in China a
boy is taught to "respond boldly and clearly"; a
girl, "submissively and low."[25]

But spitting in public was denied to women long
before it became a questionable habit in men or
prosecuted by boards of health. It is likely, too,
that the American spittoon will continue to be

a masculine property as long as tobacco chewing is a masculine specialty. Smoking is rapidly ceasing to be one. Among the Pueblo Indians only one woman in the pueblo, the *Pujo* or the "Woman," smokes[26] and among the Thompson River Indians only women "strong in medicine" smoke,[27] but in civilisation the habit is no longer confined to one type. In most parts of the United States it is still thought "fast" for a woman to smoke, but smoking no longer makes her "fast." She has still to smoke, however, with discretion. She is limited to cigarettes and she may not smoke in public places. As late as 1908 a resolution against smoking by women in restaurants was unanimously adopted by the New York Board of Aldermen. Mayor McClellan vetoed this ordinance, but in New York and in other cities whose mayor or aldermen have shirked their responsibilities in regulating women's habits, although there are restaurants where women may smoke, they have usually to depend upon the connivance of waiters instructed not to "see" them. Moreover in private houses many women smokers are always careful to ascertain if there is any man present who does not "like to see a woman smoke." Indeed I fancy that before long the formula "Do you object to my smoking?" at present quite pointless in a man's mouth will be appropriated by women and take on a new meaning.

The prejudice against their smoking in public together with the lack of smoking accommodations for them—men have not as yet resigned their smoking-cars or rooms to women nor are any other places provided for them to smoke in— makes smoking somewhat difficult for women who are much before the public. They have to resort to many curious devices, such as the pretext of chronic indigestion after eating, or cigarette cases in the shape of "housewives." I once knew a conspicuous damsel who in spite of all her consideration of the public was found out. "No, I have never seen a lady smoke and I hope I never shall," said my friend from the Middle West when she revealed to me this discovery. "But what can you expect of women," she continued, "when the daughter of our President smokes and— takes wine?"

This western lady herself drank whiskey toddies —her husband mixed excellent drinks and was always urging them upon her—but only when she had a twinge of rheumatism, and never in a mixed company. Rarely in the West, except in San Francisco, do men and women "take wine" together any more than they did in New York in

the days of Mrs. Pawkin's boarding-house, when
the women arose in a bunch from their places
side by side at the two o'clock dinner-table to go
to their bedrooms, leaving the men to first foregather with their tooth-picks about the spittoons
and then go on to the bar-room a block away.*
The natives of Australia are equally punctilious.
No man would drink out of a place where a woman
drank. So the drinking-holes are made circular
for the men and oval for the women. [28]

In the United States the public water fountains
are not differentiated for men and women, but
"bars" are invariably closed to women. Many
clergymen preach an annual sermon against
"growing intemperance among women," and a
drunken woman is universally held to be more
"disgusting" than a drunken man. Detestable
in all, the vice is "Prodigious in a Woman." †
Men were inclined to be prohibitionists for
women in fact long before women were for men.
The Japanese cautioned their women against much
drinking of wine or tea. [29] The wife of Manoah
is warned not to drink wine or strong drink. [30]
Rousseau's Sophie had never tasted them.‡ The

* *Martin Chuzzlewit*, ch. xvi.
† *The Whole Duty of a Woman*, p. 28.   London, 1712.
‡ *Émile*, Bk. v.

Hindus held that it was a "disgraceful fault" for a woman to "drink," and intimacy with her was a misdemeanour. After death she was reborn as a leech or a pearl-oyster.[31] The Babylonian priestess who opened a wine-shop or even entered one for a drink was burned alive.[32] (But her sacerdotal character may have had something to do with the rigour of this penalty, for the priesthood has always been formally restricted in its drinks.) Egnatius Mecennius was acquitted by Romulus for beating his wife to death after he caught her tapping a tun of wine. Another well-born Roman lady was starved to death by her family for misappropriating the keys of the wine-cellar. Cato states that men took to greeting their kinswomen with a kiss just to ascertain if they had been drinking[33]—the Romans were so practical!

Did Roman women, we wonder, have "soft drinks," drinking *syrop* or tea instead of absinthe or "cocktails"?

Eating as well as drinking is affected by sex. Were a Caroline Islander to eat blackbird, a favorite dish with the women, he believes he would lose his footing climbing cocoa trees.[34] The men of West Victoria may not eat the grey bandicoot.[35] All female animals and even hens and their eggs are taboo to Malekula

men. Once a Malekula died of anxiety after
eating sow.[36] Bangala men may not eat sweet
potatoes or frogs; or Dyaks, goat, fowl, or fern.[37]
If North Queensland women eat mullet or sting-
aree, fishing of every kind turns bad.[38] New
Guinea women may not eat pork or dog flesh, the
women of Unyamwezi, fowl; of Ankole, antelope
or buffalo; of the Sandwich Islands, cocoa or
banana, turtle or hog.[39] In some Naga and
Kabuis villages girls may not eat dog or goat or
the flesh of any male animal.[40] Nothing affronts
a Mandingo woman more than offering her an egg.
Egg eating would drive a Bayaka woman into the
bush, a lunatic.[41] In Fiji [42] and in several other
cannibalistic communities human flesh is an
exclusively masculine dish. With us no kind of
meat is taboo to women, but men are supposed
to care more than women for beef and to like it
less cooked. With the taste "characteristic of her
sex," Sophie ate very little meat. On the other
hand, Sophie, like other girls too, was fond of
"sweets," always of course in moderation.

How peculiar to women this taste may be, I
do not know, but, as a matter of fact, one never
sees a man with a box of candy on a railway car
or out driving or at the play, and when a man
helps himself from a girl's box he is apt to remark

—apologetically—that he has "a sweet tooth like a woman's."

Women usually eat less in general than men—sometimes because they have less to eat, sometimes from choice. A Lamotrek woman is forbidden to help herself to the first haul of fish. She knows that if she break this taboo her ankles will swell or elephantiasis will set in.[41] Eighteenth-century ladies had conventionally such light appetites that it was indelicate and unladylike to be hungry, and nowadays women are more apt than men to "bant."

"Banting" is, of course, a matter of sexual selection. Given our standards of feminine beauty, it is hard for a stout woman to be a "success"—wherever the women outnumber the men. This disproportion is undoubtedly the reason why a woman is so much more concerned over her own "figure" than over her husband's.* In fact we may expect to hear it said in course of time that God did not mean a woman to be fat, and moribund discussion over a "double code" may again wax lively.

* Harvey, p. 25.

XVIII

HER MARKET PRICE

WOMEN are an important item in primitive trade. Under the Australian betrothal system, a boy is expected to give his sister to one of the sons of his plighted mother-in-law. Later in life he gets another wife in exchange for a daughter.[1] Kinswomen are also exchanged in Sumatra.[2] In the Islands of Torres Straits, a match is readily made if the would-be bridegroom has a sister to marry to the girl's brother.[3] In Samoa, brides are bartered for canoes or pigs; among the Timor-laut, for elephants' tusks; among the Patagonians, for horses or silver trinkets; among the Indians of Oregon, for horses, blankets, or buffalo robes; among the Damaras, for cows; among the Samoyedes and Ostyaks, for reindeer; in Tartary, for horses, oxen, sheep or butter; in ancient Ireland and Wales, for vessels of gold or silver or bronze or for land.[4]

The bride-price is often more or less standardised. It is one goat among the Bondo, thirty among the Akikuyu plus five or six sheep. In Fiji it is a whale's tooth or a musket; in the Mangoni country, two buck skins; in Uganda, three or four bullocks, a box of percussion caps, or six sewing needles; among the Kisans, one rupee and two baskets of rice ‡; among the Kabuis, seven buffaloes, two *daos* and two hoes, two shears, two food vessels, two black cloths, two ear ornaments, two strings of conch shell beads and "meilon," i.e., some one thing of value [6]—in our terms a pearl necklace or a diamond tiara.

But a tiara or a real pearl necklace many a man cannot afford for his bride. Among the Mishmis the bride-price is twenty oxen for a rich man, one pig for a poor man [7]; and it ranges from four and a half *ackies* to two ounces of gold among the Tshis [8]; from three to thirty cows among the Caffres; from five to fifty roubles among the Chulims; from three thousand roubles to a cartload of wood or hay among the Bashkirs. Among the Californian Karok, a wife is seldom bought for less than half a string of dentalium shell, but if she belongs to an aristocratic family, if she is a skilful bread maker and basket weaver, and if she is pretty, she sometimes costs as high as two strings. [9] In the Venetian market the Italians of the Renaissance paid from six to eighty-seven ducats for their concubines.[10]

A maximum bride-price is sometimes fixed. A Shastika Indian or a Navaho will not pay more than ten or twelve ponies for a bride. The Cheurfa Kabyle who accepts a greater bride-price than thirty-five reals, four *sâa* of cheese, and four measures of oil, is fined one hundred reals. The bridegroom is fined the same amount and told to boot that he will die without sons. In the beginning of the nineteenth century the price of girls went up so high in Servia that Black George limited it to one ducat.[11]

It is likely that dowry and dower were originally forms of a bride-price, the theory having developed that it was improper for the bride's family to keep the purchase money for themselves. Hence they passed it on to her or her bridegroom settled it on her in the first place. Among the Bagobos of the Philippines the bride's father returns half the bride-price to the groom if the marriage turns out well. In Oregon, the relatives of the bride always raise as many horses or other things for her *dot* as her bridegroom has sent her parents, taking great care not to turn over the same horses or things.[12] Manu says: "When the relatives do not appropriate for their use the

gratuity given, it is not a sale; in that case the
the gift is only a token of respect and of kindness
towards the maidens[13];" and in modern India,
men of position lay out the "gratuity" in jewels
to give to their daughter on her wedding-day.[14]

In many other places too the bride-price masks
in wedding presents. In Florida, a Melanesian
island, the bride's parents give her family-in-law
from five to ten pigs in return for the *rongo* or
coils of native money they have received, saying
the money was for the pigs and not for the girl.[15]
The Yorubas also repudiate the idea of selling
their daughters; the wedding-gifts are merely
to offset the loss to them of her services.[16] In
Swahili opinion they are only to repay her mother
for the cost of bringing her up.[17] Among us they
are sometimes intended to give the bridal couple
"a start in life," but ordinarily they merely express
the "interest" of the "family connection," and
it is probably for this purpose rather than from
mere economic ostentatiousness that they are
ceremonially listed for the newspapers or displayed in the "spare room."

I have never heard of "placing down" or showing off the wedding-presents of a remarrying widow.
With us, in fact, she receives but few. What
are given, to be sure, she receives herself. Among

many peoples the family of her deceased husband
are the recipients. To them her second husband
has to pay the equivalent of her original bride-
price.

It is quite usual for the bride-price of a widow to
be lower than that of a virgin or even of a *divorcée*.
A widow is depreciated by her liability to the death
infection. She is damaged by corpse taboo.
It often happens therefore that a widow is the
only bride a poor man can afford. In primitive as well as in modern society, if for different
reasons, a second husband is apt to be poorer—
and younger—than a first.

This differentiation may not hold, of course,
when a man himself sells his wife to another. He
is apt to ask for her as much at least as he originally paid. He may be forbidden, as among
the Kabyles, to ask for more.[18]   Where he gets
another woman in exchange, as among the Eskimo,
the equivalence is necessarily uncertain. In two
of the recorded instances of wife-selling in England
in the nineteenth century, the price was half a
crown in the one case—the woman being sold in
open market with a halter round her neck—and
in the other, a two-gallon jar of gin—given by a
publican.[19]

In marriage, bride-price, dowry, and dower are

"settlements;" they are paid over once for all. Pecuniary transactions in other sex relations, on the other hand, although sometimes quite definitely regulated, are more or less continuous. The fact that their scale depends primarily upon the personal qualifications of the woman is another way of differentiating them from marriage transactions. A prostitute's income or social connections count for less than a wife's, although prices are probably much higher in the house of a competent than in that of an incompetent "madam."

Then too the exclusiveness of a prostitute enters largely into her price. As exclusive as a well-behaved wife, she may be even more expensive. In Borneo, a man who keeps a *bilian*, a dancing and singing girl, sometimes goes bankrupt through her demands.[20]

On the other hand, thoroughly commercialised, her price may be extremely low. It is fixed by law at a mere pittance in Dahomi, for example, part of it at that being paid over in the form of an annual tax to the king.[21] In Chicago, the brothel charges are fifty cents, one dollar, five dollars, half going to the prostitute and half to the keeper of the house.[22] Jane Addams tells the story of a Chicago factory girl earning six dollars a week who tried in vain for seven months to save enough for a pair of shoes. Twice during this time she had her old shoes resoled. When they became too worn out to stand a third soling, and she had but ninety cents towards a new pair, she gave in and, to use her own phrase, "sold out for a pair of shoes." For even less, for a ride on the merry-go-round, or an entrance ticket to a moving picture show, many a little girl has been entrapped by a city pander.[23]

Slave girls are distinguished from prostitutes by the multiplicity of their functions and by their dependence, or, if the modern white-slave traffic be under comparison, by the singleness of their dependence; from wives, by the subordination of themselves and their offspring in the household. Although their functions are more varied, their price is usually lower than that of male slaves.* The price-list of a <u>Richmond</u> <u>slave</u> <u>auctioneer</u> in 1853 was, for his young men, from $950 to $1300, for his young women, only from $800 to $1000. His boys ranged from $375 to $950; his girls from $350 to $850.[24] A few years later when the price of slaves had gone up, and an able man sold as high as $1800 or $2000, the lowest price quoted at a sale was $1140 for

* Definite information on this point about slaves, outside of modern civilisation, I have been unable to get.

one "Olivia."[25] But slave women who had marked sex qualifications sometimes went much higher. Harriet Martineau tells how a southern lady of her acquaintance sold one of her house slaves, a very pretty mulatto, to a guest who had fallen in love with her, for $1500. Asked the price of a beautiful young quadroon who was being held for sale at Alexandria, the slave dealers said: "We cannot afford to sell the girl Emily for less than $1800. . . We have two or three offers for Emily from gentlemen from the South. She is said to be the finest looking woman in this country." On the other hand, a woman of thirty who had borne five children was selling at this time for only $650.[26]

When the wage system takes the place of slavery the prices of women are lowered. Sex is no longer an economic asset.* Except on the variety stage or

---

* In a recent comparison of the earnings of Chicago working girls and prostitutes its commercialised value is plainly expressed. The average employee in a department store earns $7 a week; the average income of one hundred prostitutes, described in the Vice Commission's Report, ranged from $50 a week to, in exceptional cases, $100 (Addams, p. 68). Miss Addams has calculated that the average Chicago working girl may be capitalized at $6000; the average Chicago prostitute at $26,000 (*ib.*, p. 58).

I have no figures at hand on the weekly income of the London prostitute; but it is safe to assume that it is far more than 10s., the "customary" wage of the English factory woman (Hobhouse,

in an occasional store or factory, women employees
are sexually independent of their employer. On
he other hand the demands of husband or offspring
or in the case of the unmarried the expectation of
marriage are a handicap to the woman wage-
earner. Exclusion from a more or less large
number of occupations, thanks to the comparative
immobility of women workers, to popular prejudices against them, and to their own apathy and
notions of gentility, also depresses women's wages,
increasing the labor supply at certain points over
the demand.   Traditions in certain circles that a
woman is not entirely dependent on her wages, in
others, that no lady should work for her living, and
that "a gentleman's time is much more valuable
than a lady's," also militate against the theory of
equal pay for equal work.   Whatever the causes,
women's wages in all grades of work tend to be
lower than the wages of men, a disproportion
recently recognised by the English National Insurance Act in providing that the employer should
pay from six to twelve cents a day into the general
fund for a workman, from six to ten cents a day
for a workwoman. Among employees earning
more than sixty cents a day, the class in which

J. A.,   *The Evolution of Modern Capital*, p. 309.   London and
New York, 1902).

the employer pays six cents for both sexes, the men contribute eight cents, the women, six.

Blood-money as well as wages expresses the comparative economic value of women. Among the Moslems a woman's blood-money is half a man's. Among the Moslem Galla, for example, it is fifty oxen; a man's, one hundred.[28] For a pregnant Somali woman it is one hundred cows, if she is carrying a boy, if a girl, fifty cows.[29] According to Cambrian law a woman's blood-money was half a man's, her brother's; according to the laws of the Brets and Scots it was equal to her brother's if she was unmarried, but married, less than two thirds her husband's.[30] Among the Wanika, a man's blood-money is four slaves or twelve milch cows, a woman's, three slaves or nine milch cows.[31] Sick benefit in the English National Insurance Act is 10s. a week for men, 7s. 6d. for women.

Now and again the comparative estimates of the sexes are expressed quantitatively in terms still more naïve. In Sarae, the birth of a boy is heralded with seven ceremonial shouts of joy, that of a girl with five.[32] In Samoa, too, a birth is announced by shouting, five war-cries for a boy, two or three for a girl.[33] To the temple of Juno a Roman father had to pay a *quadrans* for a girl baby, a *sextans* for a boy.[34] In the old ecclesiasti-

cal law of England which forbade conjugal intimacy
after child-birth, the period was thirty days for a
son, fifty-six for a daughter. [35] In the Nága
village of Liyai twins of either sex are lucky, but
girl twins bring luck only to their parents, boy
twins to all the villagers. [36] Formerly in Switzerland, a father got one waggon-load of wood for a
girl, two for a boy. [37] In the scheme for the appor-
tionment of funds between the grammar and high
schools of Bedford, England, on the basis of
attendance three boys earned the same amount as
five girls [38]; and before the present salary bill was
passed the New York women teachers of boys'
classes were given a bonus of sixty dollars a year
—it being argued no doubt both in Bedford and
New York, not that boys were more worth while
teaching, but that they were more difficult to teach
than girls.—But for our habit of rationalising our
ancestral ways how difficult it would sometimes be
for us to "save our face."

XIX

"ONCE OUR SUPERIOR"

FROM blood-money or wages we get the comparative economic values of the sexes. Their comparative values in general are aften expressed in popular sayings or in literary flourish. "Better than a thousand women is one noble man," reasoned Iphigenia[1] as she went to her death. "The glamour of a man is a sevenfold glamour"—in Japan.[2] "One man is as good as five women," according to the Tarahuamaras of Mexico.[3] A wife is half the body of her husband, a woman half a man, held Hindu[4] and early Christian.[5] "The whole world was made for man, but the twelfth part of man for woman. Man is the whole world, and the breath of God; woman the rib and crooked piece of man," said the Christian of the seventeenth century.[*] "When nature divided the human race into two parts, she did not cut it exactly through the middle!" said a philosopher of the nineteenth.[†]

* Browne, Thomas. *Religio Medici*, Pt. II, Sect. ix.
† Schopenhauer, *On Women*.

Although the comparison is not always as frank as a numerical proportion, in any disparagement of woman the superiority of man is of course implicit. She is criticised for falling short of the masculine standard. About her shortcomings, whatever the reasons, men* have shown a striking unanimity of opinion. Against her they make perhaps five main counts. She is found to be unreliable or untrue, unreserved, unintelligent or unenlightened, unmagnanimous, uncourageous or unenterprising.

Double-tongued like a woman, is a slur often in the mouth of the American Indian. "Full of continual tricks, deceitful speeches and all other kinds of hypocrisy" are women, says the Essene Jew.[6]   Because of their apish or their snaky origin they are necessarily false, assert the Algerian Arab and the Bulgarian peasant.[7]   "They laugh with him who laughs, weep with him who weeps, with sweet words lay hold on him who dislikes them, all according to the requirements of the situation"; they "continually change their minds;" they are "fickle and wavering"; they "call falsehood truth, and truth falsehood," according to the Hindu, be he Brahman, Gaina, or Buddhist.[8]   "Souvent femme varie"; "la donna è mobile"; "a woman's 'no' by candlelight is not the same by day."

* And women, too, of course.

The penalties imposed upon prying women by primitive secret society men are so harsh that we can but infer that long before Eve or Pandora or Elsa von Brabant became a by-word, men thought of women as "curious." But women not only want to find out secrets, they cannot keep them. The Arunta youth has to wait a long time to be initiated into the tribal mysteries if he is *irkun oknirra*, "given to chattering like a woman."[9] In proof of his version of Eve's origin, the Hungarian peasant tells you a secret has as much chance tied to a dog's tail as on a woman's tongue.[10] The Buddhist is as thoroughly convinced as the Christian that if you tell a woman a secret it at once ceases to be one.[11]

" Women will talk"—of everything. "People strongly affirm that not a single silent woman has been found in any age up to this day," remarks a lady in one of the plays of Plautus.* "With the tongue seven men are not a match for one woman," is the Humanist statement† of a theme that has had many variations.

La plupart des femmes disent peu en beaucoup de paroles."[12] It goes without saying, however, that some women are more garrulous than others. Otherwise a Hindu would not be formally instructed

*Aulularia.   † Erasmus, *Colloquies*.

not to marry a chatterbox,[13] or a Chinaman or
Japanese, unluckily married to one, would not be
entitled, as he is, to divorce her.[14]

"A woman talks of everything as if she knew
all about it." And yet a woman has only the
knowledge of a Sudra, opines the Hindu. She is as
unable to master Sanskrit as a rope of lotus fibre
an elephant.[15] "Educate a girl! You might as
well attempt to educate a cat!" exclaimed a
Tripoli Moslem when Dr. Jessup asked him to send
his daughters to school.[16] "The fetichisms and
superstitions of this world are bolstered up mainly
by women," observed in 1872 the more optimistic
trustees of Cornell University in their report *in
favor* of a college for women.[17] "Ideas are like
beards—women and young men have none," said
Voltaire. "Tell that to women and children."
"You cannot reason with a woman." "A woman's
reason is 'because,'" and even "when they are
equal to primary reasoning, when hard pressed
they will take a swift leap past what they consider
a captious contradiction to a congenial conclusion"[18]—such is "woman's logic."

The lack of magnanimity in women is defined
and dealt with in a variety of ways. Victorian
boys may eat no female quadruped lest it make
them peevish and discontented.[19] To the Arab

a woman is one "who is always in contention without obvious cause."[20] Solomon fled from her to the house top; the less patient European ducked her or bridled her tongue with a pair of branks.[21] Discontent, jealousy, and slander are three of the five maladies the Japanese believe to infest seven or eight out of every ten women, and from which "arises the inferiority of women to men."[22] "Sweet is revenge—especially to women,"[23] writes the English poet, enough like them certainly to understand them. Malice was one of the unattractive traits Manu allotted to women when he created them.[24] Hence to the Brahman there was "no friendship with women"— "theirs are the hearts of hyenas."[25]—When Abby Kelly argued against slavery from the public platform, she too was called a hyena in ecclesiastical circles.[26]

"Frailty, thy name is woman!" The Thompson River Indians called men who shirked going on an avenging death-raid, "women."[27] If an Australian boy cries when his tooth is being knocked out during his initiation the women themselves taunt him with being a girl.[28] Among the Kuki-Lushai clans of Assam, the killer of a tiger performs a ceremony to enslave the feline ghost in the spirit world. He begins by disguis-

ing himself as a woman, for if the tiger believes
he has been shot by a woman he will be humble[29]
—like the modern boy who has been beaten by a
girl. In woman "energy or vital power is extinct,"
declared the Hindu, and prescribed that when she
was literally dead her burial mound was to be as
high as the hips, whereas a Kshatrya's reached as
high as a man with upstretched arms, and a
Brahman's up to the mouth—"for such like is
their vigor."[30]

Many another classification of woman is more
or less significant of her valuation or status in the
community. Arraigned with her by the Hindu
as undependable, were "a lustful, angry, timid
or bewildered man," he "who seeks for gain," a
drunkard, eunuch, and a child.[31] And not alone
in knowledge, but in many other attainments the
Hindu woman is rated with a Sudra, the lowest of
the castes. At one time the Athenians forbade
the study of medicine to women and slaves.[32]
Oberlin College, the first American college to be
so minded, opened its courses to negroes and
women at the same time. Not long ago an American President was hissed at a convention of
women for his reference in one breath to the en-
franchisement of women and of Filipinos—or was
it Hottentots? The Moslem rule forbids a fool, a

madman, or a woman to summon the faithful to prayer.

As a corollary to such classifications of woman, to be classified with her is belittling or derogatory. To make a refractory schoolboy sit with the girls is no trifling punishment. Public agitations or movements are sometimes discredited in the same way. One of the most biting taunts of the anti-abolitionists was a reminder to their opponents that they were associated with women. The Bull Moose party has been subject to sarcasm of the same kind. " To-morrow at noon there will open in the Coliseum a convention managed by women and has-beens," states the *Times* news-paper* of the first Bull Moose Convention. " Everybody who is not an ex is a woman . . . outside of the ex's the women are running things. It is to be a woman's convention." But although "its people are petticoated or backnumbered," don't "jeer" at them, counsels the paper, whether in irony or in discernment is somewhat uncertain.

Like all classifications or generalisations, the foregoing not only frame but breed ideas. Language is sometimes a very mirror of this mental process in relation to female character. Caroline Islanders very frequently use their word for woman,

* August 5, 1912.

14

li, in compound words for qualities or actions held in light esteem. *Li-kam* means a woman's fault, *i. e.*, a lie; *li-porok*, a woman's peering, *i. e.*, curiosity.[33] The Chinese affix their word for woman to many of their uncomplimentary adjectives,[34] a device we but clumsily approximate with our "like a woman," relying upon such adjectives as "womanish" or "effeminate" for greater emphasis.

Then too women try hard to live down to what is expected of them. In fact deviation from these expectations are not tolerated by either sex. Is not an "unwomanly" woman publicly more disesteemed and berated than a fickle or tricky or petty woman, than an ignoramus, a coward, or a chatterbox?

Of course "womanly" traits have to appear respectable. A change of name and a few ornaments do as much for them as for those they characterize. "It is a woman's privilege to change her mind," we say with an indulgent smile. That tact is indispensable to a woman may not be controverted, and the expedient deceit straightway finds a cloak. A woman ought to be "responsive" and vivacious, and so talk of any kind, providing it aims to please, "passes." That girls should be unsophisticated and innocent is a theory that makes any degree of ignorance supportable. Since a woman is "always a partisan," she may not be held to task for malice or intolerance. And then "nerves" preclude any searching analysis of disposition. Deficiencies in good taste, enterprise, or courage are due to "common-sense," "adaptability," or "refinement." Nor can much be asked of one who is "delicate" or whose "modesty" has to be safeguarded.

" Womanly" traits are protected by the social machinery as well as by euphemisms.

It is a truism that responsibility must be given to be taken. Themselves a form of property in communities where private property is at all well developed, women's rights to property either in tribal groups or in early civilisations are rarely equal with men's. Until 1882 an Englishman controlled his wife's earnings. In most of the United States a married woman is not permitted to enter into a business partnership exclusive of her husband's interests, and in general the courts do not favor a woman acquiring earnings for her separate use without her husband's consent. In Sweden, a husband still owns whatever his wife buys with her earnings.[35]

Since children, like women, are usually considered a form of property, a mother has seldom

the same rights as a father.*   Both the Babylonian and the Roman father could sell their children
—without maternal consent. (The Babylonian
could sell the mother of his children too.)³⁶ A
French mother has no legal authority at all over
her children during their father's lifetime and
after his death she has to share her control with
his kindred.³⁷ In our common law a mother is
not entitled, like a father, to the services and
earnings of minors, and in some States a father
can still will away the guardianship of his child
from its mother. In all the States a father has
the paramount right of custody.

Outside of her family, the law too gives a woman,
particularly a married woman, few responsibilities.
Among the Hindus no document was evidence
which had been executed by a woman. Nor might a
woman be a witness.³⁸ Among many African tribes
women are not allowed to testify.³⁹ English women
might not serve as witnesses until the eighteenth
century; nor Italian women, in civil suits, until
1877.⁴⁰   Caffre women are never proceeded
against for crime. Among the Bogos a woman
may not be punished even for murder.⁴¹ Hindu
women might not undergo ordeals by water or by

* Even under the matriarchate it is a woman's kinsmen who
control her offspring.

poison.[42] Among the Somali, women unlike men criminals are never sentenced to receive corporal punishment.[43] In English common law a woman might commit certain crimes before her husband and not be held responsible for them, the presumption being he had coerced her.

We allow women to serve as witnesses or to stand for trial like a man; although the courts still disincline to permit a personal judgment against a married woman, and for many years an American jury would not condemn a woman to death. Even now it is more difficult to get a conviction for crime against a woman than against a man. " They have n't th' right iv a fair thrile be a jury iv their peers; but they have th' priv'lege iv an unfair thrile be a jury iv their admirin infeeryors," says Mr. Dooley.[44]

When duelling was in fashion, it was only a very indirect means of holding women to accountability, and the opinion still prevails alike in the drawing-room and in the court-room* that you cannot hold a woman responsible for what she says. Schopenhauer questioned in fact whether they should ever be allowed to take an oath,[45] a doubt our Customs officials seem also to entertain.

* Consider how rarely libel suits are ever brought against women, and how seldom women are tried for perjury.

Nor is a man himself always responsible for
what he says to a woman. In English common
law, marriage voids all prematrimonial contracts,
nor can a man make a covenant of any kind with
his wife.[46] The Hindus formally allow a man to
"swear falsely" to the woman he desires and to
"speak an untruth at the time of marriage, during
dalliance."[47] With us too all is still fair in love
—if not in war—and most men consciously or
unconsciously feel that "a little exaggeration" is
a propriety of courtship—as well as of marriage
vows. To no woman must a warrior show his
whole mind, is the creed of the Ona tribesman of
Tierra del Fuego.[48]

Reserve is, in truth, a by-product of war; not
"to give oneself away," a habit engendered by
competition. As a rule women are shut out from
competition, except for men, and coyness is the
only kind of reticence of any use to them, and that
within limits. Reticence not based on the desire
to attract runs the risk in fact of passing for
"strongmindedness," a trait always deprecated
in a woman. Perhaps for fear lest they acquire
it, Chinese women are told that the "stillness"
with which they may overcome men is "a sort
of abasement."[49] Miri women are more frankly
forbidden to eat the flesh of tiger.[50]

One wonders if tiger would keep a woman from asking questions or succumbing in argument,—methods adopted by most occidental women to show they are *not* "strongminded." Australian women show it by expressing voluble surprise,—an Australian man is trained never to be taken by surprise,[51]—Chinese women, by "peeking"—"firm correctness" in a woman, but "a thing to be ashamed of in a superior man."[52]

In ancient China boys went to school at ten, but girls stayed at home to learn from their governesses "pleasing speech and manners," to handle hemp and silk, "to watch the sacrifices, to supply the liquors and sauces,—to fill the various stands and dishes with pickles and brine, and to assist in setting forth the appurtenances for the ceremonies."[53] Outside of China, too, girls have been educated at home, until comparatively lately, and their education as a rule limited to the "domestic sphere." Even when they have become learned in foreign subjects, they are often advised to conceal their knowledge, for in women there should be "a modesty about learning almost as delicate as that which inspires them with a horror of vice."*

" Je consens qu'une femme ait des clartés de tout;
Mais je ne lui veux point la passion choquante

---

* Fénelon, *De l'Education des Filles*, ch. vii.

De se rendre savante afin d'être savante;
Et j'aime que souvent, aux questions qu'on fait
Elle sache ignorer les choses qu'elle sait:
De son étude enfin je veux qu'elle se cache;
Et qu'elle ait du savoir sans vouloir qu'on le sache." *

Fénelon and Molière find support too in English-speaking countries. The author of *The Whole Duty of a Woman*, for example, commends the affectation of ignorance—on certain subjects—as a sure and invincible guard against that curiosity which "soil'd Humane Nature in Paradise."[54] And Dr. Gregory of Edinburgh advises his daughters, if they happen to have any learning, to "keep it a profound secret, especially from the men, who generally look with a jealous and malignant eye on a woman of great parts, and a cultivated understanding."[55]

Dr. Gregory seems to us a little severe and not very profound, but the Blue-Stocking, we must admit, is apt to be an object of derision. "A wise woman is twice a fool . . . as paniers don't become an ox, so neither does learning become a woman," declaims the sixteenth century German abbot. " The woman who thinks is like a man who rouges—ridiculous," is the way his modern countryman puts it. " How generous

* Molière, *Les Femmes Savantes.* Act I, sc. iii.

the conduct of Mrs. —," says Sidney Smith, of
some lady in favour. "As a literary woman, [she]
might be ugly if she chose, but is as decidedly
handsome as if she were profoundly ignorant. I
call such conduct honourable."

The theory of incompatibility between good
looks and a good education has always been a
bugbear. Even when it is admitted that education may not of itself destroy a girl's looks, somehow or other it is thought to handicap her in
the matrimonial market. "If all the men in the
world were sensible, every girl of letters would
remain unmarried all her life," is the last word
Rousseau has to say about the education of women.
"I shall not have Maria brought too forward.
If she knows too much, she will never find a husband; superior women hardly ever can," Margaret
Fuller represents an enlightened American father
saying in the fifties.[56] A half-century later the
same kind of father is saying: As a girl's "highest
development and greatest usefulness are likely
to come with marriage . . . pursuits that prejudice the chances of her marrying are on that
account the less desirable for her."* A college
education may keep her too busy or preoccupied
to meet or notice the right man,[57] Mr. Martin

* Martin.

continues, deviating, like a gallant American, from the earlier view* that it was the man who was inappreciative of his opportunities.

And yet attempts to reconcile educating girls with getting them properly married have not been lacking. There is none, I think, more valiant than Ruskin's: "A woman, in any rank of life, ought to know whatever her husband is likely to know, but to know it in a different way.† . . . Speaking broadly, a man ought to know any language or science he learns, thoroughly, while a woman ought to know the same language, or science, only as far as may enable her to sympathise in her husband's pleasures and in those of his best friends."[58]

Next to the matrimonial argument against

---

* And the English view. Mr. Higginson tells the story of how after having been shown over a girls' college by its head, a visiting Englishman said to her in an undertone: " All this is very interesting, very interesting, indeed, but what effect has this higher education upon—upon their chances?" "Upon their chances?" the dean naively asked, "chances of what?" " Why, of course," answered the Englishman, "their chances of getting a husband." (*Women and Men*, p. 65.)

† This idea had already been carried out, according to Margaret Fuller. " Women are now taught, at school, all that men are," she is quoted as saying, " but with this difference: men are called on, from a very early period, to reproduce all that they learn. . . . But women learn without any attempt to reproduce. Their only reproduction is for purposes of display."—*Memoirs of Margaret Fuller Ossoli*, i., 329.

educating girls, its first cousin, the modesty argument, has been perhaps the most reiterated and the most telling. Mary Wollstonecraft mentions a lady, for example, who vehemently asserted to her that instruction in "the modern system" of botany was "impossible" for modest girls.[59] And in the United States, in the 'thirties, people were still wondering how a well brought up girl could attend lectures on the subject.[60] In 1844 Paulina Wright gave public lectures here upon physiology. When she uncovered her manikin, ladies would drop their veils or run from the room; sometimes they "fainted."[61] Half a century later a New York physician confesses that for years he has been puzzled by the "practical" question of how to teach the functions of the body to growing girls, "and still leave them their modesty."[62] Having reached the limits set for the girls' class in arithmetic, an early nineteenth-century maiden once appealed to an older brother for help. "I am ashamed of a girl who wants to study interest," said he,[63] no doubt making her feel even more "ashamed," poor girl.

As late as 1884 it was argued that "to attend medical clinics in company with men, women must lay aside their modesty."[64] About this time the President of the British Medical Association, in

referring to medicine as a profession for women,
said publicly that he shuddered to hear of what
the ladies were attempting to do. "One can but
blush, and feel that modesty, once inherent in
the fairest of God's creation, is fast fading away."[65]
Of this same period must have been the lady who
had learned to swim—to the horror of her clergyman. "But," she said, "suppose I was drowning."
"In that case," he replied, "you ought to wait
until a man comes along and saves you."[66]

A narrow experience does not make for magnanimity, and life in close family quarters is not
good for one's temper. Native Australian girls
may never leave home unless accompanied by a
relative.[67]   At ten a Chinese girl "ceased to go
out."[68]   The Ewe term for mother is " She-who-
stays-in-the-house."[69]   A   well-bred   Japanese
woman was directed to "be constantly in the
midst of her household, and never go abroad but
of necessity." Without her husband's permission,
"she must go nowhere."[70]   In the great houses of
ancient Mexico, "if the women went one step
without the door [of their own apartments], they
were punished as were those that looked up, or
behind them."[71]   The Babylonian woman who
"gadded about" was thrown into the water.[72]
The Egyptian, like the Babylonian woman, had

unusual rights, but among them was not included
that of visiting without her husband's consent. [73]
"Teach the young women . . . to be keepers
at home," [74] advised Paul, and we remember he
did not spare the flighty widows who enjoyed
paying visits. To the Hindu, rambling abroad,
a "disgraceful fault," was one of the six causes of
the ruin of a woman, and it was a woman's duty
"not to stand near the doorway or by the windows
of her house." Against such evil inclinations
she had to be guarded. " By night and by day
she must be watched by her mother-in-law
and other wives belonging to the family." [75]
To Pontanus, the Renaissance poet, as to Hindu,
an unbolted casement was "the door to vice."
"Why should I admonish you to shun the seduction
of windows?" he queries in Latin verse. [76] With
much approval the German philosopher quotes
the English poet who writes that women "ought
to mind home—and be well fed and clothed—but
not mixed in society."* Once upon a time an
English woman or an American who went visiting
without the approval of her husband subjected
her host to a suit for damages and to imprisonment for two years. Even were she to miss her

* Schopenhauer, *On Women*. Quoting Lord Byron, *Letters
and Papers*, by Thomas Moore, II, 339.

way upon the roads, unless she were benighted
and in danger of being lost or drowned, hospitality
might not be lawfully proffered to her.⁷⁷   To-day
in Russia, a wife cannot get a passport without
marital consent.⁷⁸

Courage is in all communities one of the most
valued of traits—perhaps because the race started
as such arrant cowards.   But it is always considered far more important for the men than for
the women to be brave. Little if any ignominy
falls upon a timid woman and rarely is a girl
trained to be bold.   The youths of many a savage
tribe are forbiddden to eat the heart or other parts
of deer or of other timid creatures, a taboo not
laid upon their sisters.   Nor, as far as I know, are
women ever given the flesh of brave enemies to
eat, a favorite way with devotees of sympathetic
magic of growing brave.   On a recent visit to the
New Mexican pueblo of Santa Clara I was told
of still another way.   As little boys, the Santa
Clara Indians washed in running water, believing
that thus the free and gallant spirit of the water
became theirs.   "And the girls?" I asked.   " The
girls?   Oh, they were quite free to wash in stag-
nant water."   In it English girls might have been
made to wash a century or so ago—had the Santa
Clara theory of water prevailed in England.

" That bold, independent, enterprising spirit, which is so much admired in boys should not, when it happens to discover itself in the other sex, be encouraged, but suppressed," writes Hannah More,[79] pioneer though she was.

Important as water or food may be in developing courage, experience and independence are also factors—factors most women have to forego. Greek women and, before their latter-day emancipation, Roman women were, of course, ever under guardianship. Until the middle of the nineteenth century guardianship for unmarried women existed in most European countries. In the law of countries as "advanced" for women as the Netherlands, Finland, or Sweden, marital guardianship still exists. From English and American law it has disappeared, but "Why does n't her husband look after her better?" is still apt to be a query of the public about a woman it criticises.

The Frenchman and the Hindu, if not the Anglo-Saxon, know that a woman cannot be too carefully guarded. The apostle of the natural man advised French parents never to suffer their daughters for a single moment of their lives to know themselves free from restraint.* Nor was a Hindu woman "to act by herself in any matter."[80]

* Rousseau, *Émile*. Bk. v.

Without her husband's consent, a wife might not even pay a wedding visit or go on a girl's picnic.[81] "Day and night women must be kept in dependence by the males of their families," father, husband, sons. "Never is a woman fit for independence."[82] So stupid and silly is she in fact, remark the Japanese, that she ought "in every particular, to distrust herself and to obey her husband."[83] Self-distrust is also a Christian doctrine for women, and we have noted how well it may be inculcated in the Christian convent.

Closely related to the theory that the convent was to induce dependence was the theory that it was a retreat from temptations, a refuge from the "world," an asylum for women without "natural protectors." In these theories mediæval chivalry seconded the Church, for although it greatly increased the number of a woman's "protectors" —if she proved herself worthy of them—it greatly emphasised her need of a shield, alike physical and moral. Before the institution of knighthood had passed away, the idea that Dulcinda should never be exposed to the dangers or hardships of the world had become deeply rooted enough to live on and grow of itself. It flourished so well in fact that finally in the eighteenth century the feeling was general that there was nothing what-

soever a lady could not be guarded against or
"spared"—except child-bearing, that test of
courage and chance to meet reality face to face
men did not "protect" her from—until recently.

XX

√ ——→ POLICING HER SUPERNATURALLY*

IN primitive society bugaboos are not confined to
the nursery. Women, like children, are scared
into being "good." Again and again the men
invent spirits to aid them in their mastery of the
sex. The ceremonial bull-roarer or rattle of Australia, of New Guinea, of the West Coast of
Africa, is believed by the women to be the voice of
a terrifying spirit.¹ Among the Yorubans, women
are compelled on pain of death to act up to this.
belief by flying indoors when the bull-roarer or
the voice of Oro resounds in the streets.² On
Kiwai Island in the Fly Estuary and in the Elema
District of New Guinea, the women have even to
leave the village to escape the curse of hearing the
bull-roarer.³ Should Euahlayi women of child-
bearing age hear the spirit voice of Boorah, he
would first madden and then kill them.⁴

---

*Published, with minor changes, in *The Independent*, February
8, 1912.

The bull-roarer is evidently an effective curb
upon female curiosity. But prying women must
be restrained in other ways too. Were Kurnai
women to see or hear what goes on after a certain
point on the Jeraeil initiation ground, Tundun,
the Great Ancestor, would kill them.[5] Once in
an island of East Melanesia, Tepu, a ghost-god,
commanded that no woman should visit his shrine.
But the chief's wife did, and the god, having to
make an example of her, rendered her unconscious,
lay with her and then let her come to in a pool of
blood.[6] The Eskimo tell a story even more
alarming for Inquisitive Woman. Once upon a
time, against all warning, a woman entered the
Singing House when it was dark. For a long time
she had wished to see the Spirit of the House, and
so she summoned him. He came, and she felt him
all over until she touched his boneless and hairless
head. Then she dropped dead.[7] An Aleut Eskimo woman who trespasses on holy places always
runs the risk of illness, death, or insanity.[8] Fijian
women who spy about the *nanga* or cult house too
much go insane[9]—a somewhat severer penalty
than that visited on women indiscreet enough to
trespass in Catholic monasteries, or glance at club
windows on Piccadilly or Fifth Avenue.

A little religious knowledge, however acquired,

is a dangerous thing—for women. Should a Queensland woman touch or even look at a death bone, a bone for murder by magic, she would straightway fall sick.[10] So would a Mendi woman of Sierra Leone who found out the Poro secret society mysteries.[11] Any Jabim woman of Kaiser Wilhelm's land who saw the sacred flutes used in the initiation rites, would die.[12] All kinds of tribal misfortune come from an Aleut Eskimo woman finding out the least thing about the ritual.[13] Beguiled by the Serpent, Eve ate of the Tree of Knowledge, and only a few years ago a Protestant divine gravely declared that "she was at the beginning of all the trouble in the world."*

Serpents or bogies are useful to men not only in snubbing women who want to know too much; they help to keep women at home. In Australia there are the *iruntarina* and the *oruntja* to lie in wait for adventuresome women. An ever-present fear of these spirits cows the women into keeping close to their camp-fires,—"a wholesome check upon their wandering about alone too much,"[14] writes their English ethnographer, in full sympathy with their Blackfellow husbands. Fjort women are also timid about being alone at night,

* Dix, Morgan, *Lectures on the Calling of a Christian Woman*, p. 169. New York, 1886.

dreading the *bimbindi* or ghosts. And for good causes, for it is said that these *bimbindi* have made women live with them.[15] Tickolishe is another Bantu spirit who waylays women at night, coming out of the reeds to trick them.[16] In many an island of the Malay Archipelago women dare not venture alone in the forest at any time for fear of seductive spirits.[17]

In fact the ghosts or gods of many a tribe or race are given to seduction or rape, and women are taught to fear their devotion and avoid their haunts. Often to make their soliciting doubly fearful, illness or death is said to follow upon their attentions. Belief in such unpleasant wooers is undoubtedly more effective than any anti-feminist argument that woman's place is in the home.

Not content with merely threatening dangerous spirit encounters, the men of secret societies make their women believe that their own systematic spirit impersonations are actual spirit apparitions. During their funeral rites two or more of the Eastern Islanders of Torres Straits dress up as ghosts and bang and scrape on walls and doors, greatly frightening the women mourners within.[18] In the Elema district of New Guinea, men disguised as the spirit forerunners of Kovave, their

mountain god, terrify the women into staying at
home to cook food in great quantity for the
coming of the god.[19] If a woman neglect her
work during the initiation celebration in Kaiser
Wilhelm's land, the Asa descend upon the village
with a great hullabaloo, driving the frightened
women before them. The stick which the masks
then set up before the hut of the shirk is said to
be always effective.[20] Florida Island women also
cook for their "ghosts." During the day the
secret society men foregather undisguised among
the women, gossiping of what the "ghosts" have
done and are going to do.[21] In the Niger delta
the Ibo impersonation of the dead has a right to
any girl he can catch.[22] Yoruba women are
forbidden on pain of death to laugh at or even to
disparage the Egungun ghost impersonations,[23]—
a prohibition that suggests that even in Africa
woman may sometimes be flippant or sceptical.
According to a story of Mary Kingsley, they were
decidedly so once upon a time towards the Ikun
secret society—a society of the Bakele. The
heresy had spread so far that the women had to
be disciplined collectively. So what did the men
do but bury the Ikun impersonation under the
ringleader's floor, and when the ladies started to
say "what fools those men had been making of

themselves all the afternoon with their Ikun,"
appalling squeals and howls came from under their
feet. They stared at each other for one second
and then, feeling that something was tearing its
way up through the floor, they "left for the interior
of Africa with one accord." No arrests were
made—but Society was saved, adds Miss Kingsley,
clear as it is that it "cannot be kept together
without some superhuman aid to help to keep the
feminine portion of it within bounds."²⁴ And so,
to keep the women in order is one of the objects
of men's secret societies the world over—except
perhaps in New Haven.

Savage woman must neither pry nor roam. For
the comfort of the men in general she must be
unquestioning and unadventuresome. But furthermore, for the good of a particular man she
must be obedient and faithful. The Bangala of
the Upper Congo say that once a hunter called
Mokwete found that, thanks to his polygynous
habits, his allotment of meat was small. So going
into the bush he called out: "Wives of Mokwete,
wives of Mokwete!" They answered: "E!"
and heard: "When your husband comes with
meat you must not eat it, if you do, you will die."
Thereafter *all* the meat was brought to him—until
he was given away by his little son and deserted

by all the outraged women.[25] In California and
Australia, husbands manage better. A Pomo
Indian will terrify an unruly wife by himself
dressing up as an ogre. After such a scene she is
said to be unusually tractable for some days.[26]
To ensure wifely docility most of the men of
Central Australia carry a magic knout in their
wallets. The mere sight of it terrifies an offending woman; its stroke she believes to be fatal.
In spite of this implement or perhaps because of
it, wives sometimes run away in Central Australia.
Then the husband and his friends punish the runaway through black magic. They bewitch a
diagram of her which they have drawn on the
ground, and into a piece of green bark representing
her spirit they stick miniature spears. Sooner
or later her "fat dries up," she dies and her spirit
appears in the sky as a shooting star. In another
tribe a deserted husband catches a rabbit-bandi-
coot, renders it helpless by dislocating its hip
joints and leaves it to a slow death. As it dies,
the eloping wife wastes away.[27] In New Britain,
runaway wives are called *ia dapal*, after a woman
who once ran away from her angry and jealous
husband to a rock in the sea, only to be drowned
by the rising tide—a warning no doubt to other
refractory women.[28]

To test or ensure wifely fidelity, primitive
detective methods seem far fitter than modern.
Kayan and Kenyah husbands can tell from the
knots of camphor trees, while they are away
collecting, if their wives at home are unfaithful—
evidence enough to kill them on their return.[29]
Unsuccess in hunting is like evidence to both the
Wagogo and the Aleut husband.[30] On the Loango
Coast there is a special fetich to keep wives in
order and punish them for infidelity. A betrayed
husband finds the "medicines" in his fetich basket
wet.[31] An Ostyak husband has only to offer
his wife a handful of bear's hair. She believes
that if she takes it, being unfaithful, the bear
whose hair was pulled out would turn up in three
years to devour her.[32] Amara, a famous oriental
lady, refused to "wrong" her husband because
she could not keep it secret from spirits or from
"those of the gods who can read the hearts of
men."[33] "Men consider your religion as one of
their principal securities for that female virtue
in which they are most interested," wrote Dr.
Gregory to his daughters.[34]

Among several peoples a difficult labour, death
in child-birth, or the death of her child are promised
the unfaithful wife—sanctions that have also been
utilised from time to time by the modern novelist.

We have already noted that the modern novelist has made use too of the theory that conjugality may defy death, and that to more unsophisticated men a widow's mourning is no mere sentimentality. The primitive widow unquestionably believes that were she not to mourn with all propriety, her dead husband would harry her unmercifully. He is never too far away to observe her. Among the Unmatjera and Kaitish, he never leaves her side.[35] In Matamba he is even able to lodge himself in her breast—greatly to her discomfort.[36]

In developed tribal life and in early civilisations, supernatural reward or punishment is a more thoroughgoing affair than in savagery, and wifely subjection as well as the rest of the social order is thereby more systematically secured. A Japanese woman is taught "to look on her husband as if he were Heaven itself, and never weary of thinking how she may yield to him, and thus escape celestial castigation."[37] Even an unfaithful or worthless husband is to be constantly worshipped as a god by a Hindu wife. If undutiful, after death she enters the womb of a jackal, and is tormented by diseases. Hindus still believe that wifely disobedience or disloyalty or husband murder, in a former existence, are punished in the present birth by widowhood, that greatest of

Hindu curses. On the other hand, if a wife obeys her husband, she will for that reason alone be exalted in heaven, declares Manu, the sacred codemaker. A chaste widow is also promised a place in heaven beside her husband. As for that most devout of devout widows, the suttee, her term in heaven is immensely long. Moreover, she expiates her husband's crimes for him and sanctifies his and her ancestors.[38] Dr. Jessup once asked a Moslem fellow-traveller in the Damascus diligence if his wife would have any place in Paradise when he received his quota of seventy-two houris. "Yes," said the Meccca pilgrim, looking towards his closely veiled wife, "if she obeys me in all respects, and is a faithful wife, and goes to Mecca, she will be made more beautiful than all the Houris of Paradise."[39] Obedient to her husband the Parsee woman was accounted holy; disobedient, fiendish. Thrice a day a wife was to go before her husband, inquiring his wishes, and never, either by night or day, was she to avert her face from his command. Thus served she God.[40] "The well-ordered wife will justly consider the behaviour of her husband as a model of her own life, and a law to herself, invested with a divine sanction," writes Aristotle.[41] Simpler and even more forceful is the divine dictate of *Genesis* to the Hebrew wife: "Thy desire shall be to thy husband, and he shall rule over thee."[42]   Paul thoroughly agreed with this point of view and passed it on to Christendom. "Man is not of the woman; but the woman of the man. Neither was the man created for the woman; but the woman for the man."[43]   And until the _Origin of Species_, most men — and women too — undoubtedly held that the derivative nature of Eve was argument enough against rebellious wives.

Nowadays the deliberate anti-feminist must draw up a more critical kind of brief, but does not he or she depend at heart upon the religious sanction for the proper control of women?   Has not the proportion of women to men in the churches a bearing on this question?   Of the total number of confessions made every year in the Catholic Church, how many, we wonder, are made by men, how many by women?   Who at some time or other has not heard a Protestant non-church-going _pater familiæ_ declare: "But I don't interfere with the religious beliefs of my wife and daughters. I believe in their going to church."*   Why is Nietzsche so certain that a woman without piety would be "something perfectly obnoxious or

* Cp. Howells, W. D., _A Modern Instance_, ch. iv.

ludicrous to a profound and godless man?"*
"Without religion no ladies education can be com-
pleat," says the *American Lady's Preceptor*,** an
early nineteenth-century publication "designed to
direct the female mind," and only a generation or
so ago a girl was cautioned against going to college
because of its irreligious influence, a curious warning in view of collegiate origins.

Just to learn Hebrew and Greek one of the
devout girls of this period did nevertheless go to
college; she wanted to find out for herself whether
the Biblical passage *"and he shall rule over thee"*
had been correctly translated by the men.**
Why was Lucy Stone so concerned about this
translation? Why has a Khedivan princess written a commentary on the Koran to prove that it is
not unfavourable to women, and why have American feminists published a *Woman's Bible* in which
to scold Paul and the Patriarchs as they deserve?

Is a woman's fear of being out alone, particularly at night, always explicable upon rationalistic
grounds?

Why, in a society whose marriage and divorce

* *Beyond Good and Evil*, §239. A point of view held, too, of
course by women.
  "I am unwilling to believe, that there is in nature so mon-
strously incongruous a being, as a *female infidel*," wrote Hannah
More. (*Essays for Young Ladies*, pp. 164-5.)

laws are the same for men and women, is there more prejudice against a widow who remarries than against a widower, against a *divorcée* than a *divorcé?* And is not the widow who remarries within her year or two of mourning accused of heartlessness, and the remarrying *divorcée* of even worse?

In the thirteenth century, an erring nun was instructed to make a candid confession in these words: " Sir, I am a woman, and ought rightly to have been more modest than to speak as I have spoken, or to do as I have done; and therefore my sin is greater than if a man had done it, for it became me worse."[46]   We all know that nowadays also almost anyone talking about sex differences may be easily led up to saying: " A bad woman is worse than a bad man."   What have the mediæval penitent and the modern conversationalist in the back of their minds?

XXI

AS SHE CONCERNS HIERARCHIES

TO cast spells has always been a function of *das ewig weibliche*, and woman has always been reputed peculiarly versed in magic. Although when she practised it professionally she always had to compete with the male professional, it is only in the higher culture that he succeeds in relegating her to a poetical phrase or to a position of influence on the backstairs. In the lower culture, on the other hand, the female magician with her "intuition" and "charm" is an important figure. Like her male colleague, she cures, or kills, bedevils or exorcises, supplies charms for or against all kinds of disaster, controls the weather, guarantees professional success, ensures reproduction, interprets dreams, and, most important of all, serves the god as his mouthpiece or go-between.

Both medicine-man and woman practise their profession on the side, so to speak, living in every way like other people. They marry and rear offspring. They hunt or fish or fight, dig or forage or keep house, like lay men or women.

With social elaboration, this sameness ceases. It becomes unseemly for a priest to go to war—except as an army chaplain—or to go hunting, or to attend plays or dances, or take part in many of the games, pastimes, or interests of society. For a long time, however, his family life remains more or less normal. He may have more or fewer wives than his neighbours, in his excursions from home he may have to be more or less circumspect than others; but a family man he continues to be.

With women, on the other hand, maturing sacerdotalism very quickly precludes matrimony. The sacerdotal calling becomes too exacting for a husband to stand, particularly as, *pari passu* with its increasing demands, husbands themselves, as society develops, become more and more exigent and proprietary. Again and again the claims of husband and church are seen to conflict. While a Niger delta woman or an Ot Danom woman is harbouring a spirit, she has to withdraw from conjugal intercourse.[1] Tcham husbands lose all authority over wives who become spirit-possessed. Should they make the spirit jealous, they are also liable to be killed. As soon therefore as a woman "professes," her husband prudently divorces her.[2] An Ansayrii Arab knows that if he marries a saint-dedicated girl she will have to go on working on the property belonging to her saint's tomb.[3] In Fez, the husband of a newly "possessed" woman was called upon to give a banquet to her and her new friends, a demand that an independent man would sometimes frustrate by whipping the devil out of the baggage.[4]

On the Gold Coast, where husbands have ordinarily pretty much their own way, the husbands of sacerdotal wives have to approach them on their knees. Once a Gold Coast hyena god called Gbudu took possession of a married woman called Afiba. Whereupon he coolly ordered Afiba's husband to build him and Afiba a home. The husband complied and then eliminated himself.[5] But Ewe husbands are not always so obliging. We hear of one who pretends to sell his self-assertive wife to an European factor in order to break her spirit. His bluff is very successful. If he will only take her home, she promises to have only just as much religion "as my William likes." Another rebellious Ewe husband merely imprisons his wife at home, but in this case she succeeds with priestly aid in poisoning and paralysing him.[6] Such wayward wives are of course

unpopular, so that for the most part the priestesses
of the Gold Coast are unmarried.

In view of such incompatibility between sacerdotalism and domesticity, the one is often held,
as among the Tchams or the Ewes, to quite
preclude the other. The priestesses of Isis had
to separate from their husbands.[7] To get a
divorce, discontented African or Burman wives
have only to become serpent brides or Buddhist
nuns.[8]

Against such a contingency, husbands elsewhere
have provided more thoughtfully. "No sacrifice,
no penance, and no fasting is allowed to women
apart from their husbands, . . . a woman who
keeps a fast or performs a penance in the lifetime
of her lord, deprives her husband of his life, and
will go to hell," affirms the Hindu.[9] Neither her
"vow unto the Lord" nor her bond shall stand
if a Jewish woman's husband please to make
them void.[10] No conscientious Christian priest
consecrates a married woman without conjugal
consent. Told that it is a shame for women to
speak in church, and that "if they will learn anything," to "ask their husbands at home,"[11] it is
not so strange that many a Christian wife has felt
it her duty to join her husband's denomination or,
married to an unbeliever, has of her own accord

lapsed away from every church, acting perhaps upon the feeling that, "if he must be lost, then she did not care to be saved."[12] Parsee wives are formally forbidden to pray.[13] So are the Ainu women of Japan, lest they turn their prayers against the men and particularly against their husbands. Santal men take no chances whatsoever, keeping even the names of their household gods a secret from their wives.[14]

Unlike certain modern controversialists, priests realise, however, that all women are not married. There are the old or widowed, the young, the slave, and the unclaimed.

In ghost cults, widows are quite logically priestesses. They care for the needs of the marital ghost and they serve as mediums to mundane friends. We remember the oracular widows of Fiji and Urua. White Lady, the widow of the Kolor chief of Victoria, kept her tribe in constant fear of her supernatural power.[15] In India, the widows of saintly *gurus* have presided over their worshipful sects.[16]

The cult of a deified leader is apt to outlast the life of his widow. Hence ceremonial widows. When a royal Buganda widow dies, her place in the mausoleum is taken by a clanswoman.[17] The mummies of Incas and Pharaohs were cared

for by women, generation after generation.[18]
In 1349, Henry, Duke of Lancaster, founded an
endowment to support two anchoresses with their
two maid servants to live within the churchyard
of Whalley and pray there for the ducal soul. On
the ground that many of these anchoresses had
been unfaithful to the memory of the dead duke,
Henry VI dissolved their hermitage and appointed
instead two chaplains to say a daily mass.[19]

Whatever their conduct, widows, actual and ceremonial, always do run the risk of losing their job.
In Buganda, for example, where they were still
guardians of the royal grave, a high priest had
monopolised communication with the dead king,
setting up his claim by drinking beer out of the
royal skull.[20] In competition with overbearing
Buddhist, Christian, or Moslem hierarchy, widows
have even been ousted from their post at the grave.

Where the gods are without a ghostly character,
widows might seem to be as ineligible for religious
service as married women. But compromises
between the dead and deity are easier than between
deity and the living. Greek widows kept up the
perpetual fire in the pyrtaneum.[21] Anna, the
Jewish widow, served God day and night in his
temple.[22] "As my body cannot be buried with
you, I will have my head shaven and become a

nun," exclaimed an imperial Chinese concubine
at the death-bed of her lord.[23] We hear of a
Rajputani widow dissuaded from becoming *satī*
to care for the image of Krishna in the house of his
priest Ránávyás.[24] "They who have lost their
husbands are wedded to Christ in their stead,"
writes Chrysostom,[25] and we are told that as the
Reverend John Fletcher, a distinguished Metho-
dist, lay dying, he himself prayed aloud: "Husband of the Church, be husband to my wife."[26]
Mahâ-pagâpatî, the kinswoman who nagged
Gotama into admitting women to discipleship,
was a widow. In fact, widows have very largely
recruited the orders of all the churches.

During the first three centuries of Christianity,
widows even formed a distinct sacerdotal order.
The widow "professed" was the charity visitor
of the Church. She cared for the sick, the poor,
and the orphaned. She taught church doctrine
and she even officiated at baptism.

Like hierarchies elsewhere, however, the Christian Fathers took alarm over the ambitious widow.
They ordered her not to be so enterprising. She
was told that to baptise was very dangerous both
for her and the woman she baptised. Moreover,
had she been intended to baptise, Jesus would
have been baptised by his mother and not by John.

It was thought advisable for her, just as for the women members of a modern mixed hospital board, not to preside over meetings. She was to keep strictly within the limits of her woman's auxiliary society. As "God's altar," she was to remain steadfast in one place.[27] In fact, it was better for her to be cloistered. In the course of a century or two the widow "professed" seems to have submitted to this point of view and become a nun.

But the cloister furnished the Church with only a temporary solution for its old woman question. In later centuries, as we shall note, it was to become again acute.

The young, more amenable than the old, have often been dedicated to religious services. The gods are ever open to bribery, and children are acceptable *ex-voto* offerings. Ewe women who are barren or whose children die vow unborn children to their gods of fertility. While they are little these *klu* and *kosi* work for the priest of their god or goddess, and with their parents make him presents. The right of marrying off the girls belongs to him.[28] Shinto temples are served by little girls. They sing and dance for the gods and set out the food offerings on their altars.[29] Mexican mothers vowed their daughters to Quetzalcoatl or Tezcatlipoca. Tezcatlipoca's maidens went every day to his temple school to dance and sing in his honour. Quetzalcoatl's more aristocratic devotees lived in his cloister, took care of his temple, and catered for him and his priests. Every midnight in their devotions they bled themselves, piercing the top of their ears. When the girls were marriageable, their mothers brought presents to their sacerdotal superintendent and asked his permission to marry them off —a negotiation curiously like that narrated in the apocryphal histories of the Virgin Mary.[10]

According to Pseudo-Matthew, in fulfilment of a vow, Joachim and Anna had placed Mary, when she was two years old, in the community of the temple virgins who wove cloth and sang and danced in honour of Jahveh. When Mary was marriageable, "Abiathar, the priest, offered gifts without end to the high priest in order that he might obtain her as wife to his son." For, ever since the days of Solomon, said the priest, the temple virgins, daughters of kings and prophets and priests, having arrived at the proper age, had been given in marriage.[11]

Like these apocryphal Jewish maidens, the *kosi* of the Gold Coast, the *miko* of Japan, as well as the Mexican Maids of Penance, as the Spaniards

called them, all leave their sacerdotal tasks for
the world. Elsewhere, as we have noted, girl
devotees remain cloistered. Married to the god
himself, they are called upon to spend their lives
in his service and, what seems to amount to the
same thing, in that of his priests, apt to act as his
proxies in every particular. In the cloisters of
Christendom and of the Peruvian Sun-god, such
a complete identification of god and priest was
more or less irregular and surreptitious, but in
India the Brahmans are as a matter of course the
lovers of the *deva dasi*.

Many of the *deva dasi* are slave girls. As slave
girls are commonly immolated at the funerals of
the mighty, and in bloody sacrifice to deity, they
are naturally appropriated to gods in need of live
servants or of being placated with very special
gifts. Once when Lake Victoria Nyanza was in
flood, King Mutesa sent one hundred women to the
shrine of its god.[32] In classical antiquity, hun-
dreds of women were vowed annually to deity to
bring men "comfort and hope in danger."[33]

The votaries of India, of Corinth, and of Western Asia are religious prostitutes, prostitution
being an essential rite in the cult of their deity.
But even the lay prostitutes of India and Corinth,
as of other places, have a *quasi* religious character.

Moreover, the unclaimed or "loose woman" is free to give herself to religious service if it appeals to her, and again and again it seems to. Too worn out when she joins the church or perhaps too masochistic to be enterprising, we find her conventionally recruiting existing orders of nuns—in India, in Japan, in Christendom.

Thanks to their age or birth or mode of life, all these devotees are evidently amenable to their church,—slave women and prostitutes, humble alike from birth and life's vicissitudes, young girls disinclined to take their passing profession seriously or brought through their theogamy into a meek relation to the god and his proxies, widows cut off from communication with deified husbands or from society by segregation in tomb or cloister.

In the cloister the subordination of nun to monk or priest is as a rule carefully planned. "A Bhikkunî, even if of a hundred years' standing, shall make salutation to, shall rise up in the presence of, shall bow down before, and shall perform all proper duties towards a Bhikku, if only just initiated." This is the first of the Eight Chief Rules the Buddha lay down for the women whom, against his better judgment, he had taken into his order. His kinswoman, Mahâ-pagâtî, a wo-

man of character, suggests that this etiquette
of personal relationship should be based on senior-
ity, not on sex. But the Blessed One refuses
to consider her suggestion. It is "impossible," he
says. Even teachers of "ill doctrine" do not allow
"such conduct towards women." To be doubly
safe, he thereupon makes it an offence in a
bhikkhu to treat a bhikkhuni as a superior. Nor
is a bhikkhuni on any pretext to revile or abuse
a bhikkhu. "Official admonition" of bhikkhu by
bhikkhuni is forbidden, but not of bhikkhuni by
bhikkhu. Bhikkhus also heard confessions and
administered penance for the bhikkhunis, until
the provision gave rise to scandal and the bhikkhus
were limited to merely initiating proceedings
against an offending bhikkhuni.[34]

" Confession" of nuns by their "directors"
has given rise to scandal in Christendom too;
but the priesthood has never on that account
shirked its task or delegated it to others. As recently as 1890 the Pope forbade a mother superior,
whatever her rank or eminence, endeavouring,
"directly or indirectly, by command, counsel,
fear, threats, or blandishments" to induce her
subjects to make her any "manifestation of
conscience."[35]

In all other important matters, a Catholic

sisterhood is also under the orders of bishop, cardinal, or pope. Their prayer-books must be passed upon by their bishop, and even their private devotions must have his approbation. "The very nature of religious life demands from the Sisters submission to the ecclesiastical hierarchy."[36]

In spite of all this regulation of women by the churches, the primitive medicine-woman fights for her own. Generally old and familyless, she is comparatively unfettered, and she lives in more or less secret rebellion against ecclesiastical domination. But the position of such refractory old women is always extremely dangerous. Maligned to society as witches, they are accused of practising only black magic, of wrongfully recalling the dead, and of being in league only with malevolent or outcast spirits. As any misfortune can be put to their credit, they are often, to be sure, a convenient scapegrace. Still, their direct relation with their "familiars" never fails to alarm the hierarchy. The independence of the witch threatens their own monopoly. A witch is a poacher.

And she is generally made to feel it. We recall the suspiciousness of the Witch of Endor when she was called upon by the orthodox to display her power, and undoubtedly her timidity was justified. Snubbed as she was by the Jewish hierarchy, at the hands of the neighbouring hierarchy of Babylonia she would have fared even worse. Like the Europeans and the colonial New Englanders, the Babylonians burned their witches.[37]   The Chinese still execute theirs.[38]   In the reign of Constantine, the sacerdotal sisters of a Christian bishop, a "vowed virgin" and a "widow professed," were killed by the Persian hierarchy for causing their queen to fall ill through enchantments.[39]

But the priesthood must be well organised and self-confident for such thorough persecutions. Paul merely cast out the devil from the slave woman of Thymira and depreciated her market value.   Bishop Ageric could not even effect this much against the Frankish sorceress who appeared one day on the streets of Verdun in the gorgeous raiment she had earned by "smelling out" thieves. Failing to exorcise her "familiar," the Bishop had to let her depart to the court of Queen Fredegonde.[40] In the old ecclesiastical law of England the woman who "practised divination or diabolical incantation" had only to do penance for one year.[41] In Merida, Yucatan, a *mestiza* called Belinda started recently to found a cult for a patron saint. The Bishop kept her from completing her half-built

chapel, but Belinda herself is still at large. Our own Mother Ann, Mother Tingley, and Mother Eddy have been ignored by the churchmen altogether.

Unable to persecute the intrusive prophetess, hierarchies have usually realised, however, that the only safe alternative was to bring her into close relationship with themselves. We recall the theogamic wives of the priests of the Pelew Islands. Cavazzi tells of a Congoese priest called Ngosei who had to share a wife with each of his eleven gods. The gods answered his questions only through the women. [42] We hear of another African priest, a Caffre called Umhlakaza, "managing" a girl who received messengers from the ancestral spirits. [43] Among the Dravidian Tuluvas, the priest's wife is possessed by his *Bhûta* and sings the *Bhûta* stories for him. [44] The Delphic Pythoness was celibate, but her oracles were published by the priesthood. They were, moreover, careful to select for the important office a woman of humble birth, very ignorant and inexperienced. [45]

Both orthodox Buddhism and orthodox Christianity determined to do without prophecy—a decision very unfavourable to women. But Buddhist and Christian sectaries alike proved unable to forego such a prestigeful religious asset.

Consequently women had a prominent position among them.   In *Málaté and Mádhava*, a classical Hindu play of the eighth century, a Buddhist priestess is a leading figure, thwarting as she does the machinations of the priest and priestess of Kali.   She lives in her own house surrounded by her female disciples and, judging from the boasts she makes of her powerful knowledge of mystic rites and prayers,[46] she was far from orthodox. In the Japanese Nichiren sect, the Buddhist sect most influenced by Shinto and most characterised by "possession," the possessed are always women. In the other sects affecting possession, the men have been ousting the women from the rôle.[47]   It was a prophetess who contaminated Dean Nicholas, the first of Christian heresiarchs.   Priscilla and Maximilla of Phrygia were the inspirers of Montanus, and Philumene, of Apelles, a Marcionite. Marcellina, together with Carpokrates, led a sect that associated with "familiar spirits and dream-sending demons."[48]   Marcus, a prominent Gnostic, was bitterly arraigned by the orthodox for his devotion to women.   Too clever a fellow by far, he seduces them, according to his detractors, with a promise of the gift of prophecy.   The timid woman who urges that she has never prophesied and does not know how, he reassures, saying,

"Open thy mouth, speak whatsoever occurs to thee, and thou shalt prophesy." Greatly "puffed up" and overcome with gratitude to Marcus, the new prophetess gives him herself and her fortune, "that she may become altogether one with him."⁴⁹

Justified by Paul's tongue-tying ordinance and his notorious prejudice against women teachers, the Fathers gravely disapproved of the "wanton" women of the heretics. The scandal of them was one of their strongest arguments for the cloister. And yet from time to time even in the cloister a "mystic" asserted herself. Hildegard of Bingen, "filled by the Holy Ghost and acquainted with things which are hidden from mankind generally," was able to "uncover the past and foresee the future."⁵⁰ The nun Mechthild of Hackeborn and the Beguine Mechthild of Magdeburg see visions. Bridget of Sweden writes down "revelations." Monks beg Elizabeth Barton, the prophetic nun of Kent, to pray for them, and bishops "believe in" her.⁵¹ Teresa of Spain, the most famous prophetess of them all, even appeared to her own nuns after death. One of them, Catherine of Jesus, writes to Father Gracian, the Provincial, that Teresa has just appeared to her, bidding her tell him not to allow any of his " Religious to write about revelations, nor to make any account

of them; for though some of them may be really
authentic, yet it is quite certain that many are
false; and it is very difficult to discover the truth
amidst a hundred lies."[52]   Whether this subtle
mandate was inspired by Teresa or by Father
Gracian himself, it probably kept the itch to
prophesy from spreading in the nunnery.

The actual or potential competition of mystic
or witch is not the only form of the woman question which has been troublesome to the Church.
The effect of the female upon the male worship-
pers is a far graver matter.   It probably begins
to cause concern to the theologians just as soon
as they modify their policy of strictly excluding
women from their cults.   The admission or even
the partial admission of women into secret societies
is ever a sign of their decadence.   The Yale
senior society men who decided that the wives of
graduates should not be admitted into their society
building were wiser than the Masons who organised
the Society of the Eastern Stars.   Just as when
mildew falls upon a fine field of rice, or blight upon
a good field of sugar cane, that field of rice or
sugar will not last long, just so "under whatever
doctrine and discipline women are allowed to go
out from the household life into the homeless state,
that religion will not last long," resignedly observed

Gotama, [53] after he had succumbed to Mahâ-pagâtî.

At some time or other Roman priests must have been as weak as the Buddha, for in Strabo's day Roman women seem to have monopolised the cults—much as Christian women monopolise them nowadays. "All agree in regarding women as the authors of devotion to the gods," he says, "and it is they who induce the men by their example to a more attentive worship of the gods, and to the observance of feast-days and supplications; for scarcely is there found a man living by himself who pays any regard to such matters." [54]

Indifferent students of social psychology though they are, churchmen do realise that it is a perilous time for a religion when men have to be attracted to it through women. Even in antiquity women were not admitted into all the cults. That their husbands may not turn away from the household gods of Christianity "in grieved contempt," Ruskin urges women to keep away from the *dangers* of theology. [55] Realising perhaps that but for the crusades men would have lost interest much sooner than they did in Christianity, within the last year or two evangelists have been organising a great revival for men *and for men only* in the United States. It is an intelligent if somewhat belated endeavour.

XXII

IN 1850 Harvard refused to admit Harriet Hunt into its medical school after its students had pleaded "that whenever a woman should prove herself capable of an intellectual achievement, this latter would cease to constitute an honour for the men who had previously prized it,"—a theory of female—and male—intellect the Harvard Medical School appears to still entertain. Wesleyan undergraduates have been like-minded. About twenty years ago they expressed their disapproval of the admission of women into the college by excluding them from class-day exercises, tactics which they have kept to ever since and through which they have at last succeeded in forcing the university to drop its coeducational rôle.

But Harvard and Wesleyan students have had support outside of their faculties. In fact some time ago so loud was the outcry against feminisation of the colleges that a witty essayist felt called upon to make a persuasive plea against the further

258

chaperoning of his sex. He argued that you could not make a man by hiding him from women, that Woman was not contagious, and that at any rate she had at some time or other to be encountered.* That he had himself encountered her I happen to know, having once been a member of a college class which he taught (I trust I am not giving him away), but in making these statements did he nevertheless fully appreciate his own boldness and the fact that the majority of mankind disagreed with him?

He certainly seemed a little surprised that the idea prevailed that "as soon as women broke into a college" the men would all take "to piling up fruits and flowers and birds on their hat brims," and that any university professor could bleat "over the danger to his manhood from the fact that there were so many women near him."

But one has to ignore academic history not to expect the university to tremble for its "imperilled manhood" at the approach of Woman. This terror was put into its heart originally of course by the Church. The Church itself has always been very much afraid of Woman. Its manifest dislike of her has been primarily an expression of its fear.

* Colby, Frank Moore. *Imaginary Obligations: The Co-Education Scare*, pp. 178–81. New York, 1905.

But whence in turn this particular ecclesiastical timidity? Conservative as it is in general, the Church naturally holds conservative ideas about Woman. Now in primitive thought Woman, as we have repeatedly noted, is not only dangerous— even Mr. Colby admits she may be "damaging" —she *is* contagious. We remember for what good reasons the youths of Australian tribes had to be shy with women. Malagasy porters believe that if a woman strides over their poles the skin will peel off the shoulders of those next using them.[2] If a South African woman steps over her husband's stick or *assegai* he will never be able to hit any one with it. Were a man ever to touch his wife with his right hand, he would grow weak and certainly be killed in war. Barea couples do not sleep together, for "the breath of the wife weakens her husband."[3]

Exposure to Woman being so rash, it should indeed be avoided or undergone only with the utmost precaution. Should a woman of South-East Australia step over anything belonging to a man, he would throw it away. In the Solomon Islands a man will never go under a fallen tree for fear a woman may have gone over it.[4] A New Britain man dare not look at a woman, and still less would he risk laughing with his eyes upon her.[5]

One of Hesiod's maxims is a prohibition against
washing in water used by a woman.[6] The wise
Hindu was "never unguarded in the company of
females," and after touching one he "purified"
himself by bathing in or touching or sipping water.[7]
Woman "desires most of all to set off the blandishments of her beauty, and thus to rob men of their
steadfast heart!" declaims Gotama. "How then
ought you to guard yourselves?" he asks his followers as they are approached by the Lady Âmra,
a good and generous—but beautiful—woman.
And the Buddha answers himself: "By regarding
her tears and smiles as enemies, her stooping form,
her hanging arms, and all her disentangled hair
as toils designed to entrap man's heart."[8] On
another occasion a disciple asks Gotama: "How
are we to conduct ourselves, Lord, with regard to
womankind?" "Don't see them, Ânanda." "But if
we should see them, what are we to do?" "Abstain
from speech, Ânanda." "But if they should speak
to us, Lord, what are we to do?" "Keep wide awake,
Ânanda."[9] Equally prudent were the early Christians. A holy man would neither eat nor drink
with nor sleep anywhere near women. He would
not let them wash his feet, or anoint him, or
make his bed, or wait on him in any way at all.
When the Christian salutation was called for, it

was to be exchanged with hands wrapped in garments and eyes cast upward.[10]

.Christian and Buddhist ascetics are of course
celibate; but there are other anti-feminists less
logical. After a week of "trial marriage," Man
went to Twashtri, his creator, and said: "Lord,
this creature that you have given me makes my
life miserable. She chatters incessantly, and
teases me beyond endurance, never leaving me
alone: and she requires incessant attention, and
takes all my time up, and cries about nothing, and
is always idle; and so I have come to give her
back again, as I cannot live with her. So Twashtri
said: Very well: and he took her back. Then
after another week, Man came again to him and
said: Lord, I find that my life is very lonely since
I gave you back that creature. I remember how
she used to dance and sing to me, and look at me
out of the corner of her eye, and play with me, and
cling to me; and her laughter was music, and she
was beautiful to look at, and soft to touch: so
give her back to me again. So Twashtri said:
Very well: and gave her back again. Then after
only three days, Man came back to him again,
and said: Lord, I know not how it is; but after
all, I have come to the conclusion that she is more
of a trouble than a pleasure to me: so please take

her back again. But Twashtri said: Out on you! Be off! I will have no more of this. You must manage how you can. Then Man said: But I cannot live with her. And Twashtri replied: Neither could you live without her. And he turned his back on Man, and went on with his work."[11]

Much the same view of marriage was taken from time to time by the ancients. "If, Romans, we could do without a wife, we should all be without that source of vexation," opined the Roman Censor, Metallus Numidius. "To marry is an evil, and not to marry is an evil," wrote Simonides, the poet.[12] Better marry than burn, counselled the embittered and disastrous Tarsian. "It is a hazard either way," added Robert Burton[13] sixteen centuries later, and his view is still popular.

Nevertheless matrimonial dangers may be reduced. Such appears to be the aim of many marriage rites. In Celebes as the bridegroom's soul is apt to fly away at the wedding, rice is scattered to induce it to stay. A Matabele bride "purifies" the groom by dousing him with water as soon as she arrives in his house. At a Malay wedding bride and groom are first fumigated with incense and then smeared with the "neutralising paste" which averts ill luck.[14]

A bridal veil is a very common means of mutual protection.   The Zulu bride wears a veil of beads; among the Yezedee and the Armenians the veil covers the bride from head to foot.   The Roman veil was bright yellow; among the Druses it is red; ours is white.   The Corean bride veils her face with her long sleeves.   In Melanesia palm leaves are held before the bride's face; among the Abipone, a carpet[15]; among the Australians of Victoria, an opossum skin—for two moons after marriage.[16]   The Armenian bride wears her short veil of crimson wool (a substitute for her all-enveloping wedding veil of silk) still longer—until her first child is born or, if she impresses the household head unfavourably, even longer, perhaps for years.[17]

Friends also help to lessen the perils of a wedding. From six to twelve groomsmen attend the Abyssinian bridegroom.   The South Celebes bridegroom is accompanied by a "double," a favorite device in primitive society for diverting danger.   The Egyptian bridegroom has two such "best men," and several bridesmaids stand with the bride under her canopy.[18]

Wedded, the right kind of conjugal traditions must go far to make marriage tolerable for men. In the Islands of Torres Straits to be called a "good wife" a woman had to be proud of her husband's success with the girls." A Japanese wife is bidden never to "even dream" of jealousy." At their nubility ceremony the Awemba women chant

" The husband is powerful within the hut,
We the women are merely as the chaff which hangs
    from the roof."

In passing out from the great gate of her father's house, a Chinese bride follows her bridegroom, and "with this the right relation between husband and wife commences." As soon as the Russian groom and bride enter their bedroom, he bids her take off his boots. Obeying, she finds in one of them a whip, symbol of authority over her person. That "the husband is the head of the wife" and that " the wife hath not power of her own body, but the husband," are Christian beliefs the Anglo-Saxon finds thoroughly embedded in his common law* and adequately expressed in his marriage service and wedding symbols.† Saint Teresa tells us she has many Spanish friends who never com-

---

* Allowing, as it does, a husband to whip or lock up a misbehaving wife (Blackstone, Bk. i, ch. xv).

† Originally the English bridegroom symbolised his power by treading ceremonially upon his bride's foot (Howard, i, 273). Nowadays only an old shoe or slipper is thrown after her.

plain of their maladies for fear of displeasing their husbands.[25]   Manu teaches that however "destitute of good qualities" a man may be, he must be deified by his unquestioning wife.[26]   During the speechifying at a recent woman's lunch party in Washington, the wife of a noted Democrat is reported to have perorated with: "My husband, may he ever be right, but right or wrong my husband!"   To "truly love her husband a woman must regard his affection and his *honor* as her dearest earthly treasures.   For the preservation of these she will endure privation, bear any reverse, encounter any labor."*   This American sentiment is dated 1840, but it finds many a latter day echo. I know one young wife who, taller than her husband, has worn since her wedding day heelless slippers.

Wives who are self-sacrificing, uncritical and confiding, uncomplaining, submissive, humble, not jealous, can surely give their husbands little trouble.

Liability to involve a man in awkward relations with other men is an unquestionable disadvantage in a wife; but there are many ways in which she may minimise this danger too for him.   After her

---

*From an editorial on *A Husband's Duty* in the Philadelphia *Saturday Courier*, quoted by the *Newport Mercury*, Saturday, Jan. 25, 1840.

wedding Arabella Trefoil felt that "she need never again seem to be gay in order that men might be attracted."[*] To make themselves unalluring, Polynesian and Greek and Anglo-Saxon brides always had their hair cut.[27] Orthodox Jewish brides put on a wig. New Guinea and Borneo wives have to forego all ornaments.[28] "The ornament of a matron does not consist in fine clothes or other deckings of the body," says the dutiful German wife, "but in chaste and modest behaviour, and the ornaments of the mind. . . . Whores are tricked up to take the eyes of males but we are well enough drest, if we do but please our own husbands."[29] "Submit your head to your husbands, and you will be enough adorned,"[30] taught the early Fathers. "Let none of you think that, if she abstain from the care of her person, she will incur the hatred and aversion of her husband." Beauty in fact truly Christian husbands do not require. "You will please them in proportion as you take no care to please *others*."[31]

It is perhaps with such aims that for years after marriage Gilbert Island women wrap themselves up in a mat with only a small hole to peep through and that young Wataveta wives wear from the temples a veil of iron chain which hangs in close

[*] Trollope, *The American Senator*, iii, ch. xxii.

lengths to below the lips.[32] Greek and Roman matrons also wore a veil. Writing how satisfactory he finds his wife, Pliny describes her standing nearby when he speaks in public, "listening with delight" to his hearers' praises of him, "*under the cover of her veil*,"[33]—"eternally, necessarily feminine."[*]

Gratifying as a veiled wife must be to a proprietary husband, a veil may be an impediment to conjugal companionship. Nofel Effendi, a distinguished Moslem, once told Dr. Jessup he was unwilling to walk with his wife in the street lest, closely veiled as she was, she might be taken for another man's wife. "You cannot expect a respectable man to put himself into such an embarrassing position!" he exclaimed.[34]

For no other reason than to preclude conjugal intimacy pregnant Masai women have to forego every adornment, for they are given explicitly to understand they have no business to make it difficult for their husbands to keep the rule of continence.[35] Among the Nootka Indians and in Vancouver pregnant women also discard their necklaces, bracelets, and anklets[36]—perhaps to make themselves unenticing, perhaps more directly for the good of the unborn child.† Women in

* Nietzsche, *Beyond Good and Evil*, § 239.   † See p. 78.

civilisation are also apt to utterly neglect their "looks" at this time—also for uncertain reasons.

A woman considerate of her husband's "honour" will be particularly careful not to imperil it in his absence. Not only was the Hindu wife not to decorate herself while her husband was away, she was not to dance or sing, not to eat meat or drink intoxicants, not to attend public shows or festivals; and, truly devoted, she was to keep herself "squalid and languid" until his return.[37]   In East Central Africa the wife of an absent husband could not anoint her head or cut her hair or wash her face.[38]   The wife of a Galla pilgrim had to barricade herself indoors with the branches of trees, besides, as we have noted elsewhere, dieting herself.[39]   In Alaska a Koniag woman fasts and lies wrapped in a bearskin in a corner of her hut when her husband goes whaling.[40]   Such self-sacrifice insures him a good kill, just as we have seen that in many another community "sympathy" in wives is a guarantee of success to husbands "away on business."   Incidentally, however, this faithful or "dignified" conduct at home must always conduce to marital monopoly.

"Grass widows" are in fact quite modern. There were seventeenth-century Englishmen who held that a wife "ought not to speak many words

but in her Husbands presence," and he being
absent "she ought to be Invisible," not appearing
"in her full splendour but when she comes near
the Sun."⁴¹ Even in the United States I have
heard of wives who will not have a solitary man
guest stay overnight in their house or even dine
with them if their husband is not there.

It is the duty of all women, not merely of the
young wife, to be as little dangerous to men as
possible. The colour and pattern of a Japanese
woman's garments "should be unobtrusive,"
for "it is wrong of her, by an excess of care,
to obtrude herself on other people's notice."⁴²
Let women "adorn themselves in modest apparel, with shamefacedness and sobriety," wrote
the Jew who ever protected himself against the
allurement os sex. Nor were women to tempt
him, or others who wished to remain even as he,
with "braided hair, or gold, or pearls, or costly
array."⁴³

Do you not know that you are each an Eve?"
asks Tertullian, and do you "who persuaded him
whom the devil was not valiant enough to attack,"
who "destroyed so easily God's image, man,"
on whose account "the Son of God had to die,"
do you dare think of adorning yourselves "over
and above your tunics of skins?" "Are you to dye

your hair or paint yourselves that your neighbours may perish?"[44]

Tertullian argued that virgins as well as matrons should go veiled. Were not the virgin daughters of men the cause of the angels' sinning? "So perilous a face, then, ought to be shaded, which has cast stumbling-stones even so far as heaven."[45] Clement of Alexandria was like-minded, urging women away from home, even in church, to go veiled. By not uncovering their face they would invite none to fall into sin or fall themselves.[46] Indeed so fearful a thing is comeliness and grace, so imperilled are all ages in your persons, declares Tertullian to both maids and matrons, that you must hide and neglect them. "Put on the panoply of modesty; . . . rear a rampart for your sex, across which none may even glance."[47]

Ever since the days of Clement and Tertullian men have been very urgent upon women to "dress modestly" for their sake. "For a woman to make her appearance in the society of young men with such displays of person as are made in what is so mistakenly called 'full dress,' is a shame to her," writes Timothy Titcomb, "for I know not one young man in one hundred who comes out of 'a full dress party' as pure and worthy a man as he went in."[48] As for the young man exposed on the streets to an acquaintance "with rouged cheeks, blackened eyelids, and enamelled complexion," although as a gentleman he may not "cut" her, he "may surely be excused for persisting in not meeting her eyes."* Some protection he must have.

To objectify psychological peril seems to be a natural human tendency. Danger from without is so much easier to understand and meet—or dodge—than danger from within. For an Arab or a Carthaginian or Alexandrian Christian to call women "the whips of Satan"[49] or "the devil's gateway,"[50] for a Hindu to believe that it is "the nature of women to seduce men" into slavery to desire or anger,[51] for a Gaina to teach that women are "female demons" leading men "to pain, to delusion, to death, to hell, to birth as hell-beings or brute beasts,"[52] for a Frenchman to "chercher la femme," for an Anglo-Saxon to use the term "women" as a synonym for dissipation, is obviously the line of least resistance. Moreover, it fosters that demeanour in women which most men, together with Clement and Tertullian, have called modesty and which they all have greatly valued,

*Sensible Etiquette, pp. 282–3. Similarly the Brahman householder desirous of energy was warned not to look at a woman who applied collyrium to her eyes or anointed or uncovered herself. (Manu, iv, 44.)

Clement and Tertullian because it secured their path to heaven, others, somewhat less foresighted, because, as a property safeguard, it protected them from theft, by themselves or others, and its consequences.

Nevertheless, devised for self-protection or for self-delusion though it be, this objectifying of temptation cannot fail by a process of natural selection to develop at least one type of male courage. A dangerous woman makes a brave man, and it is after all the men most willing to take chances with women who father the race.

For the sake of humanity can Woman therefore afford to forego her danger signals and appear less hazardous? The query is well worth the consideration of all our most esteemed Regulators of Sex, of Mrs. Grundy, of the Churchmen, of a Weininger or a Nietzsche.

18

XXIII

WHETHER in direct or indirect self-protection, the professional man at large, not alone the schoolman, has always wanted to shut women out of his calling, out of theology and politics, learning and pedagogy, law and medicine.

The methods of the theologian are usually drastic and thorough. In South-Eastern Australia no woman trespasses on the initiation ground for fear of being killed by the magic scattered in it by the medicine-man.[1] If a Brazilian woman sees the Juruparí trumpets, a sacred kind of pipes, she is killed by poison.[2] Should a Torres Straits woman see the men preparing the food for the "ghosts," she too would be killed.[3] By merely touching a holy image, a Hindu woman—together with a dog or a Sudra—destroys its godship.[4] Similarly, if a West African chief wishes to destroy his *ju-ju*, he has merely to show it to a woman.[5] Bini women are forbidden to look the leopard, a sacred animal, in the face.[6] In early Christendom

274

women were enjoined not to approach the altar during mass[7] and in Greek churches to-day the *gynaikonitis* is curtained off from the altar.[8] Among the Pima, cosmological narrators will not talk with women around[9]—a reserve customary in many other ecclesiastical circles. We remember too the hard life of the witch, the snubs given to worshipful widows by the churches, the reluctance of Gotama to consecrate women, and Paul's uncompromising order to them to "shut up," an order so scrupulously followed by Christians that until recently only the very heretical among them have ever called it into question. It has just been re-endorsed by the Presbyterian General Assembly.

Women are quite generally excluded from a share in public affairs. The Nāgas have a war stone no woman may look upon and live.[10] In anti-suffrage argument a voting booth seems to be nearly as dangerous a spot for women. When you ask an East Central African mother whether the child in her arms is a boy or a girl, she answers, if it is a girl, "it belongs to the sex that does not speak" (in the village council).[11] Seldom, indeed, among savages have women a voice in the tribal council or among the governing Elders. So unquestioned until recently has been their disfranchisement in civilisation that in many cases it did not even occur to lawmakers that in designating citizens or taxpayers or heads of families as entitled to vote they might also be including women. New York did not formally restrict the franchise to males until 1777; Massachusetts until 1780; England until the thirties; the Netherlands until 1883. And it was not until 1906 that any European state fully enfranchised women. Even where women vote in the United States the women members of the State legislature are seldom invited to the party caucuses[12] or appointed to important committees.

Nor until the last half-century were women ever expected to join publicly* in social reform movements. In 1837 the General Association of Massachusetts sent out a pastoral letter to its churches deploring "the mistaken conduct of those who encourage females to bear an obtrusive and ostentatious part in measures of reform, and countenance any of that sex who so far forget themselves as to itinerate in the character of public lecturers and teachers."[13] The women referred to who had forgotten themselves were probably abolitionists. The women abolitionists had begun at this time

---

* Or sometimes privately. "Éloignez avec un soin extrême toutes les pensées de critique présomptueuse et de réformation indiscrète," Fénelon counsels the educators of girls. (De l'Éducation des Filles, ch. vii).

to give men, abolitionists and anti-abolitionists, much trouble. In 1840 at the annual meeting of the Anti-Slavery Association the right of a woman* to serve on its business committee was challenged. The meeting voted in her favor, but on her appointment the men on the committee, two of them clergymen, asked to be excused from serving. In this same year women delegates were sent by several American abolitionist societies to the convention of the British and Foreign Anti-Slavery Society in London. The women came as a great surprise, for the Society had expected them so little that it had not even thought of limiting its invitation to men. So vigorous was the opposition of the clerical delegates, British and American, to the women, that they were denied seats in the convention—in accordance with "the plain teaching of the word of God."[14] To the unseated women delegates the teaching seems not however to have been so plain; for on their return to the United States they organised their famous Woman's Rights Convention at Seneca Falls, the first of that series of gatherings which accustomed the public to women on the platform.

So thorough were these pioneers that it is hard for us to realise to-day that in a coeducational col-

* Abby Kelly.

lege* courses in elocution were not open to the girls,[15] that the mere appearance on the public platform of a woman provoked hisses, and that on many an occasion a vote was called for on her right to speak.   Miss Anthony tells us that after complimenting her on a report on coeducation she had just made to a teachers' convention at Troy, the president of the Association added: "And yet I would rather follow a daughter of mine to the grave, than to have her deliver such an address before such an assembly."[16]   At a public meeting in Columbus, Ohio, a lady in the audience said to the Rev. Antoinette Brown after her address: "How could you do it? My blood ran cold when I saw you up there among those men!" "Why, are they bad men?" asked the preacher. "Oh, no! my own husband is one of them; but to see a woman mixing among men in promiscuous meetings, it was horrible!"[17]

As the universities were originally but a school for church and state, they were naturally not open to women. Their exclusion of women continued however long after the purpose of an academic education had become generalised. Margaret Fuller went with a man friend to the Sorbonne to hear Leverrier, the astronomer, lecture. "*Mon-*

* Oberlin.

sieur may enter if he pleases," said the *concièrge* with a disdainful air, "but *Madame* must remain here in the courtyard"[18]; and it was not until 1862 that the Sorbonne gave its degree to a woman. The Universities of Cambridge and Oxford did not open their Local Examinations to women until 1863 and 1870. Until 1878 the University of London refused degrees to women and several universities still refuse them,—Cambridge and Oxford in England; Trinity in Ireland; Princeton and Harvard in the United States; the University of Tokio in Japan.

The exclusion of girls from the schools which prepared for the universities was also a matter of course, and here, too, exclusive habits persisted after the schools were no longer merely "preparatory." In Massachusetts, for example, Boston girls were admitted to the "free schools" only during the summer term. Arithmetic was not in the summer curriculum, for of it, it was said,[19] "all a girl needs to know is enough to reckon how much she will have to spin to buy a peck of potatoes in case she becomes a widow."[*] In its early days the town of Newburyport was even

[*] At any rate, it was thought unnecessary for her to "understand it so perfectly as a man." "As her sphere of action is more confined," adds the *New Pleasing Instructor* (p. 12), "so her knowledge, in this respect, should be more confined likewise."

more cautious than Boston about schooling its girls. Admitted as in Boston in the summer "when the boys in the school had diminished," the master was directed to teach them grammar and reading for only an hour and a half "after the dismission of the boys." Even this innovation was not established at once, for the master was at one time ordered "not to teach females again."[20]

Aversion to coeducation has lingered on in New England. Not so long ago a President of Dartmouth College declares that "almost every department of study, including classical studies, inevitably touches upon certain regions of discussion and allusion . . . which cannot be treated as they ought to be in the presence of both boys and girls."[21] Whether because of this taboo of speech or for other reasons, girls are still excluded from many New England schools. It has never even been suggested, I think, to open St. Paul's or St. Mark's or Groton to them.

In England likewise girls are still excluded from Eton and the other public schools which are the prototype of the American boarding-school. Nor are girls admitted to the boys' *lycées* or state high schools of France.[22]

There are to-day independent schools for girls

in France; but in the sixteenth century when Françoise de Saintoges wished to found a girls school she was hooted in the streets, and her father called together four doctors of law "*pour s'assurer qu'instruire des femmes n'était pas un œuvre du démon.*"[23]

The first college for girls, Queen's College, an outgrowth of the Governesses' Benevolent Institution and the forerunner of Girton, was founded in London in 1848. In an inaugural lecture one of its professors deplored its name—to English ears, he said, the word "college" in connection with the education of females has "a novel and ambitious sound." And he added: "I wish we could have found a simpler one which would have described our object as well."[24] If the boundary line of the "higher education" had indeed not been so blatantly proclaimed, it might have been easier to cross. Unprotected by phrases, parents might by this time have stopped asking you if you "believe in sending a girl to college." Still naïve enough to argue against "the *higher* education," they would hardly risk a stand against merely completing their daughter's schooling. Nor does "she may have an education if she wants it," sound quite as liberal or advanced as "she may go to college if she wants," the last stand of the parent who has always tried to turn a girl away from every thought of going there.

The intellectual damsels of the Renaissance were taught by tutors. The Humanists were down on governesses. "I allow women to learn; to teach, never," said Bruno.[25] Nevertheless once systematic schooling for girls did set in, women school-teachers were bound to follow— largely for the same reasons which in the most conservative of countries, like India or the United States, have made possible the practice of law and medicine by women for women. Established in girls' schools, women teachers slipped into "mixed" and then into boys' schools, becoming so entrenched in them all—being far cheaper and, it is sometimes said, better teachers than men—that the periodic agitations against the feminisation of the schools prove fruitless.

Against feminisation by women teachers, if not by women students, the universities still for the most part protect themselves. More than half a century ago Emerson wrote that "prescription almost invincible the female lecturer or professor of any science must encounter,"[26] a prescription in this country little modified. In continental Europe a few university chairs are held by women.

Outside of the schools, the picking up of learning or the practice of "letters" has also been dis-
couraged in women.   The Ká-to and Kai Pomo
of California forbid their women to study any of
the Pomo dialects in which they are themselves
fluent.[27]   The German abbot we have found so
quotable was a little more liberal than the Cali-
fornians.   French he did not object to his trying
interlocutor learning and reading, although at Latin
books, as we have noted, he did draw the line.
And he was not alone.   "From a braying mule and
a girl who speaks Latin, good Lord, deliver us,"
was a popular jest.[28]   Now to Latin, a later and
more famous ecclesiastic, Archbishop Fénelon, did
not object—providing a girl was not overcurious.
But no amount of discretion, the Archbishop
seemed to think, could justify girls learning Italian
or Spanish, languages of no use to them and only
leading them to read books dangerous to their
sex.[29]   For like reasons Vivès, the celebrated
Spanish tutor of the Renaissance, cut out French
and Italian from his pupils' curriculum.[30]

And yet during the Renaissance in Spain and
elsewhere, women seemed comparatively free to
learn languages and to read whatever books they
liked.   Lady Jane Grey read Greek, Mary Stuart
orated in Latin, and Queen Elizabeth translated

The Mirror of the Sinful Soul from the French of
Margaret of France.

Margaret was quite as independent a lady as
Elizabeth herself. In those days a woman was
as severely chided for finding a second husband
as for not finding a first.[31]   And Margaret married
twice.   She also wrote books, a far more questionable habit even in the Renaissance than reading
them.   "Some find it strange," says Jean Bouchet
of one of the learned ladies of his day, that this
lady employs her mind in composing books, saying
that "this is not the business of her sex," a super-
ficial judgment the gallant Frenchman at once
controverts, opining, like some of our contem-
poraries in trying to conciliate a suffragist,
that women of position might well be learned
—or have a vote—but the women without any
should of course not be educated—or enfranchised; they "must needs busy themselves
with familiar and domestic matters," whereas
"queens, princesses, and other ladies who have
men-servants and maids to relieve them of vul-
gar tasks will do much better to use their minds
and time in good and honorable study than in
dancing and feasting."[32]

With this opinion of the Frenchman one often
hears Americans—usually middle-aged gentlemen

—concurring. It is much better, they say, for a girl to have "serious interests" than to stay up all night dancing or spend all her time "calling." Let her be as "literary"* as she likes. We shall fail to fully appreciate the liberality of this concession—in the East at any rate—until we recall the fact that Hannah Adams shocked Boston when she took to reading in the Boston Athenæum,[33] or that Governor Winthrop believed that one of his guests, the young wife of the Governor of Connecticut, had gone insane "by occasion of giving herself wholly to reading and writing." (Had she "not gone out of her way and calling," Governor Winthrop assures us, "to meddle in such things as are proper for men, whose minds are stronger, etc., she had kept her wits,† and might have improved them usefully and honourably in the place God had set her.")[34]

From law as an offshoot of statecraft women have been logically excluded. Valerius Maximus tells us to be sure of a Roman woman, Afrania, wife

* Brought up in a circle of society opposed to college-going for girls, the rather curious formula most commonly used to put me in my place during my college years was "I hear you are so *literary*, Miss Clews."

† In the controversy over the University of London opening its examinations to women, it was argued that half the young ladies in the country would be in a brain fever or a lunatic asylum if they tried for them (Davies, p. 55).

of Licinius Bucco, a Senator, impudent enough
to plead her own causes before the prætor. But
her death occurred 48 B.C., the one event in the
life of such a monster deserving record, adds
the historian; and her name became a byword
at Rome for unexampled feminine forwardness
and immorality. After her day it was considered
so inconsistent with modesty for women to mix
themselves up in other people's affairs and to assume functions appropriate to men, according to
a quotation from Ulpian in the Digests of Justinian,
that no woman was allowed to practise law.[35]
American lawyers held the same point of view as
Roman. The Supreme Courts of Illinois, Wisconsin, Massachusetts, and of the United States refused to admit women to their bars until directed
to by acts of the state legislatures and of the
federal congress. In the opinion of the Supreme
Court of Illinois a married woman would not be
bound by contracts proper between attorney and
client.[36] In the opinions of the United States
Supreme Court and the Supreme Court of Wisconsin, it was bad public policy "to tempt women
from the proper duties of their sex," "the domestic
sphere," by opening to them a profession quite
unfit for them. "It would be revolting to all
female sense of the innocence and sanctity of their

sex, shocking to man's reverence for womanhood
and faith in woman, on which hinge all the better
affections and humanities of life, that woman
should be permitted to mix professionally in all
the nastiness of the world which finds its way into
courts of justice, . . . incest, rape, seduction,
fornication, adultery, pregnancy, bastardy, legiti-
macy, prostitution, lascivious cohabitation, abor-
tion, infanticide, divorce,"[37] an enumeration which
suggests that the Court of Wisconsin was thinking of protecting but one group of women only
from itself. The English bar still protects women
in this way, not admitting them on the ground,
some say, that they would have to dine periodically
with the men lawyers.

On what given grounds French women were
excluded until 1899 from the French bar, I do
not know, nor why Russian women, like English
women, have been disqualified. In Russia, however, a bill has been pending* in the Douma qualifying women to practise law.[38]

There is still in many court rooms a tendency to
question the presence of women at cases "not fit
for a lady to hear." At a recent trial for rape in
Chicago, for example, counsel for the defence
asked to have the two women present—a truant

* Whether or not it has been passed I have not heard.

officer and an agent of the Vice Commission—
leave the court room. The Judge, however, allowed them to remain. To one of them the little
girl who occupied the witness chair for a day and
a half said later: "The men [there were about
seventy-five of them in the court room] looked at
each other and smiled at what I said; that was
what made me get nervous and jerk so."*

In medicine female encroachment is no novelty.
In very few primitive societies can women be kept
altogether from doctoring, and in their competition with medicine-women, medicine-men are
sometimes worsted. The Kirghiz call in their
"old women" before they resort to their medicine-
men.[39]   More important than the *papa* in Greek
and Bulgarian villages is the old woman who drives
away the demon of fever and diagnoses illness by
the position taken by the knot in her scarf as she
measures it along her patient's arm.[40]   In the
Congo, husband and wife sometimes practised
medicine together, and with equal privileges,
but we hear of one case in which the woman, a
stomach and lung specialist, must have got the
better of her original doctor mate, having come to
run a polyandrous establishment.[41]   After many

* *The Social Evil in Chicago*, p. 274. The Vice Commission
suggested excluding men from the court room in such cases.

adventures Thecla, Paul's convert from Iconium, settled down in a mountain cave in Seleucia to practise medicine. So successful were her cures that the Seleucian doctors lost their *clientèle*[42]— and, like the Athenian doctors down on Agnodice, their tempers.* Sozomen, an early Christian historian, relates that Nicarete, a "vowed virgin" of Bithynia, worked cures beyond the skill of the lay doctor.[43] At Esslingen there once lived too "a great virgin" who outwitted even the most famous physicians with her magic[44]—a lady whom Pearson identifies with one of the ancient healing goddesses of that Mother Age so greatly rejoiced in by him and other encouragers of womankind.

Mediæval lay doctors must have been at a disadvantage too in competition with the nuns of Walton, who had the healing waters of their holy well to draw upon,[45] or with such noted eye-specialists as Saint Lucia and Saint Ottilia, or with Sœur Jeanne des Anges whose cures were famous enough to bring Cardinal Richelieu to her feet.[46]

Lucia and Ottilia were canonised by the Church; and the tomb of Sœur Jeanne it suffered to become a shrine for pilgrims; but outside of the cloister women healers ran great risk from ecclesiastical

* They claimed that Thecla's power was due to her chastity, and they resorted to one of the expedients often used by men to show a woman her place (*Acts of Paul and Thecla*).

suspicions. Ann Hutchinson was exiled from Massachusetts to a colony whose standards were lower—and pleasanter. Margaret Jones was hung for a witch—so simple were her medicines and yet so wonderful her cures.[47] The Brahman tells women that it is their duty "not to practise incantations with roots or other kinds of witchcraft," and "decent" women are warned not to have anything to do with women who practise "magic with herbs."[48] Even Madame Guyon was accused of sorcery by the "envious"[49] and eventually thrown into prison.

Backed up by an organised church, the doctor attempts to fully down the doctress, forcing her to practise on the sly and at great risk. Nevertheless not until the last witch was burned or hung was even the doctor of our civilisation freed from at least potential female competition. And then his monopoly was short-lived. It was but little more than a century from the hanging of Margaret Jones to the entrance of Elizabeth Blackwell into the Blockley almshouse in Philadelphia as an *interne*.

But the men doctors have fought hard against the women. The men *internes* at Blockley stepped out of the wards as Dr. Blackwell stepped in. They stopped posting the patient's history above his bed, thus handicapping their obnoxious

colleague in diagnosis,[50] a device a distinguished
woman doctor* in Washington tells me was tried
against her when she was an *interne* in the hospitals
of Germany.   Until 1859 the Philadelphia County
Medical Society threatened to expel any physician
teaching in the Woman's Medical College or con-
sulting with its teachers.[51]   When in 1872 the
London University declared women eligible to its
degrees, physicians throughout England protested
against the innovation, declaring, like the Harvard
medical students,† that it lessened the value of
their own degrees.   In 1887, the New York College
of Physicians and Surgeons refused to accept
endowed scholarships for women, and it still ex-
cludes women students.

Medical exclusiveness has not gone unsupported
by the lay public.   When Dr. Longshore set up
her sign in Philadelphia, it attracted a mocking
crowd.[52]   While Elizabeth Blackwell was in the
medical school at Geneva, a doctor's wife at the
table of her boarding-house would not speak to
her, the townspeople stared at her in the streets
and in general gave her to understand they thought
she was either "a bad woman"‡ or insane.   In

* Dr. Nordhoff-Jung.   † See p. 258.
‡ The usual sneer against the pioneer woman.   Agnodice was
charged with corrupting her patients, Sappho, her disciples.   I
venture to say that to-day any American woman advocating any

later years, forced to found her own hospital in
New York City, she received insolent letters[53]
telling her that her hospital would be under enough
suspicion for the police to interfere.*

Exclusive as men have been in their professions,
they are even more so in daily life. "A lady never
calls upon a gentleman unless professionally or
officially,"† instructs a much read American book
on *Manners*.‡ To close his house to every woman,
whether on business or otherwise, a Bavili of
Loango has only to put a few leaves of manioc,
banana, or palm tree about the latch of his
door.[54] An Anglo-Saxon says "you can't reason
with a woman" to close the argument. Belief
in "woman's sphere," or, in more modern terms,
"disbelief in identity of function between the

---

radical social change would be pilloried as "immoral." The
author of a fairly conservative text-book on the family tells me
that after it had been given some newspaper notoriety she received letters from all over the country telling her what a "bad"
woman she must be, and, in more than one case, asking if she had
not been so professionally.

* An empty taunt, for in this case even the New York Police
Department declined to interfere.

† Part of the selling success of *The Fruit of the Tree* was due, I
think, to the discussion provoked by it in polite circles whether or
not the heroine should have "called" upon the hero or *quasi* hero.

‡ Hale, Sarah J., *Manners*, p. 223. Boston and New York,
1889. Its sub-title is *Happy Homes and Good Society All the
Year Round*, and it is dedicated to "all who seek for happiness
in this life, or for the hope of happiness in the life to come."

sexes," justifies most men in locking women out of any place they call their own. Only with women confined to "*Kirche, Küche, und Kinder*" do William III and many other bellicose men seem to feel quite safe from invasion. "Not that we believe in identity of function," qualifies Mr. Roosevelt to reassure his less progressive followers, suspicious of the vote as an open sesame for their womankind. Equally devoted to this disbelief, the Todas keep whole villages shut to women,[55] South Africans forbid women to enter their villages by the paths taken by the men,[56] and no well brought up girl in Cambridge, Massachusetts, would think of taking a short-cut across the campus.

Women are excluded from other regions besides walks and arguments. Of the causes of divorce in Connecticut in 1704 we are informed by a well trained lady that they are not "proper to be related by a Female Pen."[57] "It has been inculcated in women, for centuries, that men have not only stronger passions than they, but of a sort that it would be shameful for them to share or even understand," remarks Margaret Fuller. Hence to the "good" woman a "bad" man may readily seem only "bold and adventurous, acquainted with regions which women are forbidden to explore—."[58] A strange advantage, when you come to think of it, for his rivals to have left so long undisputed to the "bold, bad man."

Less strange, perhaps, is the exclusion of women from the privilege, such as it is, of enjoying their own company. There is a very strong tradition in all classes that away from home a woman must never be alone—except when it cannot be helped. It is one of those facts about which to be at all convincing you must give personal experiences. I give my latest. On a walking trip this autumn in New Hampshire I dropped in one mid-day at a gubernatorial campaign meeting. Unconcealed was the candidate's surprise to find that I was "alone," not only in the town hall, but in his State. Early that evening in the village street, in front of the post-office, to which every one was going for the incoming mail, a village yokel asked me, with an unmistakable emphasis, if I was alone. A day or so later I was home in New York and had occasion to go to a trial in the Criminal Courts building. "I kept two seats for you," said the well-mannered young clerk of the District Attorney's office, "for I thought you would certainly not come down here *alone*." In the place in the court room to which I was shown sat an acquaintance. "What, are you *alone?* What a brave woman," he remarked, and considerately took the seat next to mine to keep me, I suppose, from feeling embarrassed in the court room.—Still more recently returning from Yucatan, I fell into talk on the train with the wife of an American engineer whose perspicacious New York office had just ordered all the women and children in its camps out of Mexico. My exiled acquaintance had been telling me of the success of coeducation in her college, the University of Texas. "And throughout Texas," she continued, "it is just the same; except that women have n't a vote, they are treated just like the men." "Do you go out alone at night?" I asked. "Would you in San Antonio go to the play alone, if you happened to want to?" "No," and a little perplexed, she added: "I never thought of that before." Then with a look of relief at being after all able to make her point, she said: "But two women could go together and no one would say anything"— *vamos siempre dos* as the wife of a fisherman at Campeche had said a few days before after asking me the question which opened all conversation in Mexico, "*'stá sola¿*" So courteous are Mexican manners that I never knew what chance my answer, "*si, sola*," had of being believed. Back in New York when I was again called upon to reiterate it incidentally to the curious about Mexico, it was easy to realize it had no chance whatsoever.

THE LADIES' GALLERY AND AMAZONS

ODDLY enough in the clamours of sex controversy men's chief claim to superiority is
rarely emphasised. To have kept half the world
their interested spectators for innumerable centuries is surely no meagre achievement. Not
once have they had to step off the stage. Recently
to be sure their audiences in some parts of the
globe, notably in the United States, have been
showing signs of becoming a little bored—they are
growing restless. Perhaps the stage management
has been getting slack.

No matter how uncritical your onlookers, it
is rash to grow careless. Secret society men, who
are of all actors the most dependent on their
audience, always realise the imprudence of not
playing up; they always take a great deal of
trouble with their womenfolk. Kurnai initiates
walk around the hidden parts of the encampment
swinging the bull-roarer to frighten the women by
making them believe it is the voice of Tundun, the

Great Spirit. Should a Chepara man give the show away by letting a woman see the bull-roarer, both he and she would be killed by the tribal medicine-man.[1] The Torres Straits Islanders insist on the women believing in their disguised ghost dancers. Were a woman to find them out, "she died that night."[2] In the Banks' Islands the *Tamate* men chase the women through the village and beat those they catch.[3] During the periodic secret society shows of the Tatu Indians, the chief actor, a devil of a fellow, charges among the squaws. The Gualala Californian woman is made to believe that were she merely to touch the stick of the devil dancer, her children would die.[4] When civilised American girls ask impertinent questions of a Greek letter society man, he has to turn on his heel and leave her—whatever his inclinations.

Rôles of mystery and exclusiveness are by far the easiest ways of holding popular interest; but such powerful appeals to the imagination have, in course of time, to be given up. Everywhere esotericism tends to go out of fashion and democracy to come in. Egugun of Yorubaland has become a joke to the men and, as we have seen, even the women have to be forbidden to laugh at him. I doubt if Masons can any longer get their wives to take them seriously. Since the secret societies of American colleges have been written up* and boys have been known to decline election to them, American girls are sure to become frivolous about them.

Handicapped by a general demand for publicity and democracy, men have had one other reliable device to depend upon in dealing with women— giving them minor parts. We have already noted how even the Church has had from time to time to resort to this plan, how women have been allowed to keep house for the gods, to earn an income for them through mendicancy, prostitution, or handicraft, to sing and dance for them, and even to be their mouthpieces. How to give women enough to do along these lines to secure their devotion and interest without making them independent has ever been, we observed, a nice question for the priesthood, one they have often met by bringing their devotees into an intimate personal relationship with themselves. We recall the digamic prophetesses of the Pelew Islands and the nautch girls of India. "The nun is the wife of the monk," is a saying of the Chinese layman.[5] The intimacies between the Brethren and Sisters of the early centuries and the relations between the "double

* Johnson, Owen, *Stover at Yale*. New York, 1911.

monasteries" in a later period made an analogous impression upon lay Christendom.

From time to time the Christian mystic is herself a witness to her equivocal position. Of her relation to Father La Combe, her director, Madame Guyon writes: "My heart had in it as it were a counterpart, or an echo, which told it all the dispositions which he was in. . . . Our hearts spoke to each other, communicating a grace which no words can express. It was like a new country, both for him and for me, but so divine, that I cannot describe it."[6] Even more direct than the French prophetess is the Spanish. "I saw our Lord in the form under which He is wont to appear to me," writes Teresa of Spain of one of the visions of her "heavenly bridegroom." "On His right side was Father Gracian and I myself was on His left. He took both our right hands, and joining them in His own, said to me: This is he whom I will have stand to thee in my place as long as thou shalt live."[7]

We have noted too that kings and statesmen have been wont to secure feminine devotion in the same way as priests, that the Ccoya of Peru represented the Moon, that the Queen of Egypt served in the temples with the Pharaoh, and that many an Asiatic queen bore the name of the goddess consort of her husband's god. European princesses have to receive visits, lay corner-stones, attend bazaars, and be present ceremonially at festivities. The wives of American statesmen perform a card ceremony supposed in some way to affect their husband's career, and outside of Washington they are said to "help" their husband in Washington. Lately political wives have even been encouraged to form women's auxiliaries in their husband's political districts.

But lately too in many places politicians have been giving minor political functions to women quite irrespective of husbands. In Colorado, the office of State Superintendent of Public Instruction is regularly held by a woman; only once from 1894 to 1909 was a man nominated for it by either of the two leading parties. In some Colorado counties it is the custom to appoint a woman the deputy county clerk, treasurer, or assessor. In some of the smaller towns the offices of city treasurer or city clerk are always given to a woman*—often to needy widows.[8] Throughout

* And yet since the early years of equal suffrage in Colorado, women have lost ground, except in the school system, in the distribution of elective offices. Party leaders have discovered that to keep women under the party whip they do not have to yield them as many offices as they first thought necessary. (Sumner, pp. 147-8.)

the United States and in many European countries
there are women factory and sanitary and school
inspectors, police matrons, poor law administra-
tors, women employees in the postal and telegraph
services, and women clerks in other government
departments. The Provincial Government of
Moscow has appointed women as fire insurance
agents. In France there is a woman member of
the state boards of education, of labour, and of
charity. In Austria a woman is chief of the Sanitary Bureau of the Labour Department.[9] President Taft appointed a woman head of the
Children's Bureau, the new bureau in the Department of the Interior. During the last national
campaign the Republican National Committee
organised a "Woman's Department." Its Advis-
ory Board established headquarters in New York
on the fifteenth floor of the Waldorf Hotel, where
they distributed "literature" and to which they
invited "representative women" to come—to
meet each other.

Outside of Church and State, many new opportunities have been given to women during the last
half-century to work for men—opportunities in
teaching, in medicine, in business. It is a striking
fact that some of these opportunities are embraced
more contentedly by women than others. School-

teachers are comparatively restless and ambitious,
whereas the trained nurse never dreams of promotion in her profession and has an even greater
contempt than her chief for the woman doctor.
"Woman was designed to be the helpmeet for
man . . . it is appropriate that man be the
physician and woman the *nurse*," a Quaker
physician once declared to Dr. Blackwell,[10] laying
with these words one of the corner-stones of the
profession of nursing.

"Business women" are also as a rule satisfied
with their position. Shop girls resist trade union-
ism. Stenographers make no demands for "equal
pay for equal work." As for women clerks and
secretaries, they are said to do office work so well,
not merely because they do not clamour to be made
partners, but because "they develop a sort of
wolfish wifehood on behalf of the invisible head of
the firm."[11] Can it be that in applying the helpmeet theory physicians and business men have
established a more satisfactory relationship with
the women who work under them than school
superintendents?

In comparison with housewives, too, trained
nurses and "business women" seem, at least in
the United States, particularly content with their
lot. The women who are classified in the Amer-

ican census as *N. G.*—"not gainful"—are in fact
of a peculiarly dissatisfied type. One of their
observers declares that the corners of their mouths
habitually turn down. Moreover the very women
who made cheerful and devoted stenographers and
professional housekeepers and nurses may make
peevish and incompetent wives. For a man to
marry "beneath him" is much more a matter of
faulty reasoning than of questionable taste.

And yet American husbands have such a good
reputation, none better. Where else can husbands
be found so hardworking for their families, so
generous about bills, so uninterfering in the household arrangement, so unobtrusive in the bringing up of the children, so tolerant of a wife's
friends of either sex, or so blind to feminine
idiosyncrasies?

How comes it then that the American housewife
is so discontented? Why has she deserved the
reproach of being the most unquiet and the most
disquieting part of man's audience?

Can it be that American husbands, thanks to
their notorious indifference to feminine psychology,
have misinterpreted their wives? It has long
been a joke with most men that a woman would
rather work for a man than for another woman;
but outside of the criminal classes and a stray

writer or painter who keeps his wife happy reading
his proof or posing for him, it has occurred to
comparatively few men in this country that a
woman would rather work for a man than have him
work for her. When Mr. Donohue staid in bed
in the morning to teach Mrs. Donohue a lesson,"
it was a good joke, but was it quite as good as
Mr. Donohue—or Mr. Dunne—thought? Or was
the judge who granted a woman a divorce the other
day because her husband habitually took his
breakfast in bed quite justified—at least on the
aforesaid point? Is it possible that as soon as
women keep house for themselves as well as for
one another they get tired of housekeeping—
mistress as well as maid? And can this be the
explanation in part of the apartment house vogue
as well as of the vexatious servant girl question?
Why does public housekeeping seem more alluring
to women at present than private? May not
even race suicide be due to the prevailing theory
that in the number of her children a woman has
only herself to satisfy? Wherever a woman has to
give proof of her fertility in order to marry well
and wherever a wife's prestige grows with every
son, barrenness is her greatest curse.

Then too in foregoing actual wife-beating were
Americans a little precipitate in undervaluing the

psychological whip as well? May they have been too quick to conclude that because a woman as a rule does not like the one, she dislikes the other? Or that because primitive man bullies woman only as a sex, no other line of browbeating is open to civilised man?

Have American men been even a little selfish in their unselfishness? It is possible they may never have noticed that women liked to be bullied or to wait on men, but is it certain that their reluctance to issue orders to "pay, pack, and follow," to many women besides Lady Burton a formula of happiness, is not also due to a desire to protect their own "sense of chivalry"?

For "the chivalry of American manhood" to be properly protected, American women have also to be "protected." And so American men punctiliously go on taking the outside of the walk—a habit which seems to have held over from the days when there were no sidewalks and to give a person the wall was indeed a courtesy. In certain circles men also support a woman's elbow across the curbs. They insist on paying her carfare or other expenses even when she prefers to pay them herself. They never sit while she stands, forcing her, like royalty, to sit down when she would rather stand. In cars, playhouses, or churches they always take the end seat on the theory that although it is the pleasantest it is also the most exposed. They will have a woman go first—through a door or into a lifeboat—whatever inconvenience or tragedy such precedence may cause her. They even "help" her over a fence when obviously they should but turn their back on her—or take her into their arms.

Of course I do not wish to be understood as denying that American chivalry needs *no* protection. It *does* appear to be frail. One hears of women kept as a sex out of men's clubs—in the case of one country club I know of, to the applicants' real inconvenience—merely because the members are fearful they might sometime have to blackball a woman or be "rude" to her. Then chivalry is so easily hurt by contact with an "unwomanly woman." In the days, for example, when it was generally considered very unladylike to study medicine, women medical students met with curious experiences. Once Dr. Elizabeth Blackwell presented a sealed letter of introduction from a Boston physician to a distinguished Frenchman.[13] The letter proved to be nothing but an insult to her.* In the clinic of the Philadelphia hospital where

* Later in their acquaintance its recipient gave her the letter to read, pointing out that for future self-defence she should know

Dr. Blackwell had been ostracised by her male colleagues, the male students one day introduced a male patient entirely nude in order to "shock" the girls studying with them.[14] Among lawyers and lawmakers the unwomanly woman may also work havoc. Judges themselves have recognised the danger. In denying in 1869 Mrs. Bradwell's application for admission to the bar, the Supreme Court of Illinois cautioned woman as follows: "Whether . . . to engage in the hot strifes of the bar, in the presence of the public and with momentous verdicts the prizes of the struggle, would not tend to destroy the deference and delicacy with which it is the pride of our ruder sex to treat her, is a matter certainly worthy of her consideration."[15] She certainly has to admit at times the truth of this observation. It was once proved, for example, by a group of New York women engaged in petitioning the legislature for equal suffrage and for equal rights to the inheritance of matrimonial property. Reporting adversely upon their petitions, the chairman of the Judiciary Committee pointed out to his hilarious

---

its contents. And yet her American doctor friends had urged her not to study in Paris. "You, a young unmarried lady . . . go to Paris, that city of fearful immorality! . . . Impossible, you are lost if you go!" (*Pioneer Work in Opening the Medical Profession to Women*, p. 63.)

colleagues the unreasonableness of the female
lobbyists, for "the ladies always have the best
place and choicest titbit at the table," said he.
"They have the best seat in the cars, carriages,
and sleighs; the warmest place in winter, and the
coolest place in the summer. They have their
choice on which side of the bed they will lie, front
or back. A lady's dress costs three times as
much as that of a gentleman; and at the present
time, with the prevailing fashion, one lady oc-
cupies three times as much space in the world as a
gentleman."[16]

A disorderly house is of course no fitter place
for a lady than was once a clinic or a court-room
or a legislative chamber, and so perhaps it is not
so amazing to find that girls imprisoned in them
are very rarely helped to escape by their patrons.
Last year New Yorkers heard* of how the daughter
of a well-known family who had been kidnapped
and held a prisoner was for *three weeks* unsuccess-
ful in finding a knight able to see a dragon in the
keeper of the house and in herself a pitiful victim.

Untested protective theories have long been
popular in America—applied to chivalry or women,
to cotton goods or steel rails. A few years ago,
however, an expert commission on the tariff was

* Not through the newspapers.

secured. Now that this commission has reported on the most urgent economic schedules and been told by a self-sufficient Congress there is nothing more for it to do for American trade, might it not be directed to draw up a revised schedule for American chivalry, determining how much "protection" is necessary to a successful appeal to the feminine imagination. Surely in the United States as elsewhere

> "Every Jack must study the knack
> If he wants to make sure of his Jill."

Certain industrial trusts have reported of late that over-protection is actually harmful, and unless men do something about it before long, is it not possible that, outside of comparatively small professional or business circles, they may look up some day to find their ladies' gallery quite empty? The ability of Americans to play to empty galleries is notorious, but our countrymen may find this particular dispersal discouraging.

And yet, incurable sentimentalists as they are, they may not mind the vacancy at all, for does not their inattention to details in relation to this gallery justify a suspicion that they have been thinking more of their own attitudes than of its occupants? For example, should they not have

raised a grille in front of it? The enclosed ladies'
gallery in the House of Commons is certainly more
stimulating to the feminine imagination than the
open balcony in the House of Representatives.
And when it comes to leaving, would not women
prefer to be forcibly ejected, padlocks, railings,
and all, than to have their exit excite no notice
whatsoever?

Again, would it not be much more satisfactory
to American women for their men to say with
the Englishmen, "*We* shall give you the vote,"
or even "*We* shall not give it to you" than for
them not to vote at all on the question when it
is submitted to them at the polls or to close the
subject in the drawing-room with, "You women
shall have the vote as soon as *you* want it"? It
may be good strategy, the feminine habit of want-
ing things through men only being so ingrained,
but is such masculine indifference magnanimous?

When William Lloyd Garrison was a delegate to
the London anti-slavery congress he sat with the
disfranchised women delegates in the spectators'
gallery. Following his example, were men nowadays to refuse to vote themselves until women did,
would women be altogether pleased? Would it
be fair to so utterly deprive them of the salt of
male arrogance?

Whatever the reasons, Europeans certainly give themselves a good deal more trouble than Americans to find out what women like. And they refuse to believe that normal women can be more interested in each other than in men. I doubt if a European who had never visited the United States could be persuaded that women ever dressed for women or organised clubs or wrote stories or "entertained" for them. An American women's lunch party would have to be seen—or heard—to be believed.

The European doubts too that women ever surmise that second-hand interests like second-hand clothes may not fit. An Englishman will remind you that the most conspicuous feminist movement of the eighteenth century was named after a man's pair of stockings, that contemporaneous militant suffrage was inspired by a *pater familiæ*, and that the heroine whom equal suffragists have taken for a symbolic figure in their parades lost her life for the sake of a man. To English or to any other European eyes the most self-assertive woman never seems to be stepping out of her gallery; she seems merely to be doing it over to look like an office or a workshop or a laboratory.

To the ancients, too, oriental or occidental, it

was inconceivable that women living with men could fail to be supremely interested in them. And so when they had to find a habitat for the Amazons they segregated them at the ends of the Chinese Sea or among the outer barbarians, in regions remote from culture and almost as unknown in those days as the New World. It was left for that world alone to have the originality to seat *its* Amazons at the breakfast table.

XXV

SEX AFTER DEATH

L IKE other primitive habits, "mourning" has been rationalised, but it is not difficult to follow its history back to the time when ghosts were important members of society. Prone as they were to interfere in the affairs of the living, it was necessary either to keep them at a distance, or, if that was not possible, in a good humour. Strict attention to their wants, at their funeral and afterwards, was, therefore, for the timid, expedient—particularly if they were ghosts of position.

We have been speaking, of course, primarily of male ghosts. As rank in death is largely determined by that in life, female ghosts are usually of little account. At Saa, for example, a village in Melanesia,—all Melanesia is notable for its ghostly snobbishness,—it is quite settled that no woman's soul can be a ghost of power, a *lio'a*, but only an *akalo*, a departed spirit.[1] A like insig-

nificance must attach to women's ghosts in the
Islands of Torres Straits. The Islanders drink
the juices of mummifying corpses in order to
become impregnated with the qualities of the
deceased. The juices of dead women are never
drunk.[2] Nor, in fact, in the many places where
this kind of magical cannibalism does exist, does
one ever hear of female titbits. Sometimes a
dead first wife, spiteful against a living second,
or a woman dead in childbirth against a successful mother, may have to be exorcised or placated,
but as a rule female ghosts rarely walk and are
too insignificant to require much care from their
kinsmen. Their valuation is patent at their
funerals, far less elaborate and costly affairs than
those of men. "Mourning" for women is also
more economical, being less characterised by
bodily mutilations, by village or house movings,
or by destruction of property.

Compare widower with widow rites. An Australian widow burns her body with a fire stick
or becomes a mute or carries her husband's bones
around with her for months[1]—attentions never rendered a deceased wife by her widower. Whereas
African widows fast and sequester themselves,
and go unwashed or mud bedaubed or nude, African
widowers only shave their heads—as unexacting

in comparison as wearing a black hatband instead
of a crape veil. For three years a Tolkotin widow
must carry her husband's ashes on her back, weed
out his grave, and be tyrannised over by his village. A Tolkotin widower is expected to pass
through a like ordeal but—he runs away. [4]

And we hear of no evil consequences. On the
other hand widows, anywhere, who shirk their
obligations run, as we have noted, a great risk—
especially if they remarry too soon, the jealous
marital ghost being sure to punish them or their
second husbands. Although remarriage is generally taboo to widowers too during a set time,
the period is much shorter and the only penalty
one ever hears of for its non-observance is the
covert reproach that John Smith, the widower,
could not have been really very fond of his late
lamented Mary Jane.

Nor, unlike widows, are widowers suicidal.
A widower is never bullied or, like the Hindu
widow, cajoled into following the deceased. He
is comparatively free to escape from a reproachful
or tormenting family; nor would promotion in a
ghostly harem or perhaps even a long conjugal
life in heaven appeal to him.

In spite of threats or bribes the immolated is
far commoner than the suicidal widow, the suttee.

A real chief should always be accompanied in
death by one or more women. They are necessary
to his ghostly position and comfort. So undoubted
is this view of the posthumous requirements of
rank in early culture, that the slaves, sometimes
even the male slaves, of women of high rank are
immolated at their funerals also, considerations
of rank overcoming those of sex. Brynhild of
Germany orders to be burned with her and Sigurd
her own thralls, five women and eight men; and
Austrechilde makes her husband, King Goutran,
promise to kill her two physicians when she dies—
for company.[5] In 1633 a queen of Bali died and
twenty-two of her slave women were first stabbed
and then burned in her honour. In accordance
with custom her own corpse was conducted with
great pomp to the funeral pyre and for five or
six weeks afterwards her water vessels, betel-box,
clothes, and toilet articles were set out daily before
her calcined bones; then a band played and her
bones were devoutly washed.[6] In some minds
at least, if not in Melanesian, women may have
prestige in ghost land.

Funeral immolations ceased to be the fashion
among Aryans, but entrance into heaven has
ever been made agreeable for titled ladies. At
the New England funeral of Lady Andros volleys

were fired over her grave, her hearse was drawn by six horses, and six "mourning" women sat in front of the draped pulpit⁷—an advance upon immolating them. When the Grand Duchess Paul died, the Prelate of the Russian Church is said to have written to his "master and friend, St. Peter, the gate-keeper of the Lord Almighty: We announce to you that the servant of the Lord, Her Imperial Highness, the Grand Duchess Paul, has finished her life on earth, and we order you to admit her into the Kingdom of Heaven without delay, for we have absolved all her sins and granted her salvation. You will obey our order on sight of this document which we put into her hand."⁸

Such a passport to heaven would be greatly prized by the tribeswomen of Assam. The ghost of their First Man guards the approach to Mi-thi-Khua, the village of the dead. Infants and men who have been often in love he may not molest, but at women he always shoots.⁹

There are peoples among whom even a Russian passport would be unhonoured, since they hold that no woman, whatever her rank, has a soul. The For of Central Africa eat liver, the seat, they say, of the soul, to increase their own.¹⁰ But, instead of encouraging their women, whom they account soulless, to ensure themselves a future

life, by eating a great deal of liver, they forbid
them to touch it.*　In view of their objectionable
origin, Nusairiyeh Arab women are also naturally
without a future—"like animals," adds an Arab
writer.[11]

Wherever "salvation" depends upon an "initiation" or upon a knowledge of sacred texts, the future
life of women is uncertain.　In New South Wales,
for example, it was well known that the uninitiated,
women (and boys), did not go to the men's heaven,
but ideas about theirs were vague.[12]　So concerned was the Hindu author of the *Ramayana*
and *Mahabharata* over the linguistic inability of
women,—not understanding Sanskrit, how can
they be saved, he queried,—that he wrote his
great poems in the vernacular.[13]

In the Islands of Torres Straits, women had
souls, but in the funeral ghost dances men always
represented the female ghosts.[14]　The Egyptians
also seemed to think of women in the next
world as males, for they called them, as they did
dead men, "Osiris," and attributed to them
male soul-birds.[15]　Christians also refer to their
winged souls or angels as males.　Not long ago
the sculptured angels of a New York cathedral

* One is reminded of persons who believing in "the educational
influence of the ballot" are against woman suffrage.

had to come down from their niches to have their
sex changed: the ecclesiastical committee evidently disagreeing with the poet who wrote:

"O woman! lovely woman!
Angels are painted fair, to look like you.[16]"

Although usually very insistent upon sex distinctions, the Fathers too were quite positive
that on the Day of Resurrection there would be
none. "For you too (women as you are),"
writes Tertullian, "have the selfsame angelic
nature promised as your reward, the selfsame
sex as men."[17]

One wonders about the point of view of these
churchmen, ancient and modern. Knowing that
heaven is not dependent on women for its popula-
tion, are they merely of the same mind as Euripides
and Sir Thomas Browne who both longed for a
world independent of women? Do they think that
heaven cannot be heaven with women in it?
Or, firm believers in the reward and punishment
theory of a future life, do they think, perhaps, that
heaven cannot be heaven to women as women?

Once the reward and punishment theory has
begun to encroach upon the continuance theory
of life after death, reincarnation theories become
prominent. In them a change of sex is quite a

common form of reward or punishment. According to the Ansairey Arabs a bad man dying becomes a woman, a good woman, a man.[18] In a "fervent moment" an admirer once said to Margaret Fuller, "You deserve in some star to be a man."[19] When they are "free from birth" Buddhist devotees are expected to despise their female nature so that if they *are* born again they will be born male.[20] A deceased Brahmanic perjurer was loaded down with chains for a hundred years, then he was reborn a woman.[21] Plato too suggests[22] that the man who misuses his opportunities becomes a woman, and, failing even in this character, a bird.

In order to avoid a double penalty *Manu* carefully provides in some cases against a change of sex. Stealing grain, a man becomes a rat; honey, a stinging insect; milk, a crow; meat, a vulture; fat, a cormorant; salt, a cricket; silk, a partridge; linen, a frog; molasses, a flying-fox; perfume, a muskrat; fire, a heron; fruit or roots, a monkey; cooked food, a porcupine; raw food, a hedgehog, etc. Thieving women are to become "the females of those same creatures."[23]

In China it is not the desert of the dead, but funeral ritual which may cause a change of sex in reincarnation. The Hakka, a Mongolian tribe,

will often put a girl to a cruel death to bully her
soul into reappearing in the shape of a boy.[24]   If
a dead man is wrapped up in *Yin* ciphers, even
numbers identified with the cold, dark, and evil
part of nature, the female part, he loses all his
luck in the grave.   He is reborn a woman and
a woman, too, apt to give birth to girls.[25]

21

LOCATIONS OF LESS WELL-KNOWN PEOPLES
CITED

Abipones: Paraguay
Acaxée: Durango, Mexico
Admiralty Islanders: North-western Melanesia
Ainu: Northern Japan
Akikuyus: British East Africa
Amboina Islanders: Moluccas, Malay Archipelago
Andamanese: Bay of Bengal
Angoy, Natives of: West Coast of Africa
Apache: New Mexico and Arizona
Arapaho: Plains, North America
Aru Islanders: South of New Guinea
Arunta: Central Australia
Ashanti: Gold Coast, West Africa
Atjehs: Northern Sumatra
Awemba: Rhodesia, East Africa

Babar Islanders: Moluccas, Malay Archipelago
Baganda: Uganda, East Africa
Bageshu: East Africa
Bagobos: Mindanao, Philippine Islands
Bahima: Ankole, East Africa
Bakele: West Central Africa
Bakongo: Central Africa, Congo
Bali Islanders: Indian Archipelago
Bangala: Upper Congo
Banks' Islanders: Melanesia

Barea: East Africa
Bari: Soudan
Bashkirs: Slopes of Ural Mts.
Basuto: South Africa
Batta: Interior of Sumatra
Bayaka: French Congo
Bechuana: South Africa
Bedui: North-east Africa
Beni-Harith: Arabia
Beni-Mzab: Algerian Sahara
Bhuiyâr: India
Bini: Benim, Gulf of Guinea
Bogos: East Africa
Bondo, Negroes of: Soudan
Bongos: East Africa
Bornu: Soudan
Buru Islanders: Moluccas
Bushmen: South Africa

Caffres: South Africa
Ceram Islanders: Moluccas
Cherokees: Southern Alleghanies
Chepara: South-east Australia
Cheyennes: Plains, North America
Chippeway: Lakes Huron and Superior
Chiquito: Brazil
Chiriguana: Brazil
Chulims: Russia
Creeks: Alabama and Georgia
Crows: Rocky Mts.

Dahomi: Hinterland, Slave Coast, West Africa
Damaras: South-western Africa
Dinkas: Soudan

Dorah, Papuans of: New Guinea
Druses: Syria
Duke of York Island: North-east of New Britain,
   Melanesia
Dyaks: Sarawak, Borneo

Euahlayi: New South Wales
Ewes: Slave Coast, West Africa

Fjorts: West Coast of Africa, Congo
Florida Islanders: Banks' Islands

Galela Islanders: Indian Archipelago
Galla: East Africa
Gilbert Islanders: South-east Micronesia

Hopi: Pueblo Indians, Arizona
Hottentots: South Africa

Ibibio: West Coast of Africa, Nigeria
Isleta, Pueblo Indians of: New Mexico

Jabim: New Guinea, Kaiser Wilhelm's Land
Jekri: Nigeria

Kabuis: Manipur, India
Kabyles: Algeria
Kaffa, Natives of: East Africa
Kaitish: Central Australia
Kamchadales: Siberia
Karoks: California
Kayans: Sarawak, Borneo
Kaya-Kaya: Dutch New Guinea

Kei Islands: Malay Archipelago
Kenyah: Sarawak, Borneo
Kharwars: North-west India
Kirghiz: Central Asia
Kisans: Bengal
Koloshes or Thlinkets: North-west Coast, North
America
Kumaun: Northern India
Kurnai: South-east Australia

Lakor Islanders: Moluccas
Lamotrek Islanders: Caroline Islands
Laos: Indo-China
Leper's Islanders: New Hebrides, Melanesia
Leti Islanders: Moluccas
Lillooets: British Columbia
Luang Sermata: Malay Archipelago

Mabuiag Islanders: Torres Straits
Maidu: California
Makalolo: Branch of the Basutos
Malekula Islanders: New Hebrides
Mălers: Rajmahal, India
Mandingo: Senegambia, West Africa
Mangoni, Natives of: East Africa
Maoris: New Zealand
Marquesas Islanders: Eastern Polynesia
Măsai: East Africa
Matabele: South Africa
Menang-Kabaws: Interior of Sumatra
Mendi: West Coast of Africa, Sierra Leone
Menomini: Wisconsin
Minahassers: Celebes
Miris: Bengal

Mishmis: Assam, North-east India
Mosquito Indians: Central America
Musquakie: Kansas

Nāgas: Manipur, Assam
Nandi: British East Africa
Narrinyeri: South-east Australia
Navaho: Arizona
New Britain Islanders: Melanesia
New Caledonia Islanders: Melanesia
New Hebrides Islanders: Melanesia
New Ireland Islanders: Melanesia
Nias Islanders: West of Sumatra, Malay Archipelago
Nīshinam: California
Nootkas: Vancouver Island
Nusairiyeh: Syria
Nyasaland, Natives of: East Africa

Omaha: Nebraska
Ona: Tierra del Fuego
Ostyaks: Siberia

Pelew Islanders: Caroline Islands
Pentecost Islanders: New Hebrides
Pima: Arizona
Prince of Wales Islanders: Torres Straits
Pshaves: Caucasus

Quakeolth: Oregon
Quayquirie Indians: Orinoco

Samoyedes: Siberia
Santa Cruz Islanders: Melanesia
Santals: Bengal
Saraē, Natives of: East Africa

Sarts: Turkestan
Sennar, Negroes of: Soudan
Serua Islanders: Malay Archipelago
Shastika: California
Sioux: Plains, North America
Sissetou; Sioux: Plains
Solomon Islanders: Melanesia
Somali: East Africa
Surinam, Aborigines of: Dutch Guiana
Swahili: British East Africa

Taculli: North-west Coast, America
Tatus: California
Tcham: Cambodia
Thlinkets: Coast of British Columbia
Thompson River Indians: Interior British Columbia
Tjingilli: Central Australia
Timor-Laut: Malay Archipelago
Todas: Nilgiri Mountains, Central India
Tolkotins: North-west Coast, America
Tonga Islanders: Polynesia
Torres Straits Islanders: Between Australia and
    New Guinea
Tshi: Gold Coast, Gulf of Guinea
Tsimshian: British Columbia
Tuluvas: Southern India
Tuyang: China

Uliase Islanders: Malay Archipelago
Unmatjera: Central Australia
Unyamwezi: South of Victc ia Nyanza, East Africa
Upsala, People of: Sweden
Uripiv Islanders: New Hebrides

Veddah: Travancore, Madras Presidency

Wabemba: East Africa
Wagogo: East Africa
Wahpetou; Sioux: Plains
Wanderobbo: British East Africa
Wanika: East Africa
Warramunga: Central Australia
Warrau: British Guiana
Warua: Congo Free State
Wataveta: East Africa
Watubella Islanders: Malay Archipelago
Wetar Islanders: Moluccas
Wichita: Kansas to Texas

Yahgan: Tierra del Fuego
Yakuts: Siberia
Yao: North of the Zambesi River, East Africa
Yaraikanna: North-east Australia
Yaunde: Cameroon, West Africa
Yezedee: Kurdistan
Yokaia: California
Yoruba: Slave Coast, West Africa
Yuki: California

Zulus: South Africa
Zuñi: Pueblo Indians, Arizona

REFERENCES

I

1 *Brihadâranyaka-Upanishad. Sacred Books of the East*, xv
2 DORSEY, GEORGE A. *The Mythology of the Wichita*, p. 1. Washington, 1904
3 BAIN, F. W. *A Digit of the Moon*, pp. 32-3. New York and London, 1906
4 CURTISS, S. I. *Primitive Semitic Religion To-day*, p. 74 n. 3. Chicago, New York, Toronto, 1902
5 *Anthropophyteia*, i (1904), 10-11

II

1 *Reports of the Cambridge Anthropological Expedition to Torres Straits*, vi, 109. Cambridge, 1908
2 *Sacred Books of the East*, v, 344
3 KIDD, DUDLEY. *Savage Childhood*, p. 26. London, 1906
4 PLOSS, H. *Das Kind*, i, 70. Leipzig, 1884
5 *Ib.*, i, 68, 70
6 *Ib.*, i, 70
7 *Ib.*
8 *Qur'Ân*, xvi, 60-1. *Sacred Books of the East*, vi
9 PLOSS, H. H., and BARTELS, M. *Das Weib*, i, 390. Stuttgart, 1876
10 *Letter* cvii, 3. *Nicene and Post-Nicene Fathers*, vi (Sec. Ser.)
11 PLOSS and BARTELS, i, 391
12 JESSUP, HENRY HARRIS. *The Women of the Arabs*, p. 2. New York
13 *Reports of the Cambridge Anthropological Expedition to Torres Straits*, v, 196
14 PLOSS and BARTELS, i, 809
15 GARNETT, LUCY M. A. *The Women of Turkey, The Christian Woman*, p. 239. London, 1890

16 PLOSS and BARTELS, i, 809
17 PLINY, *Natural History*, Bk. xxx, ch. xiv
18 *Reports of the Cambridge Anthropological Expedition to Torres Straits*, vi, 105
19 PLOSS and BARTELS, i, 396
20 CHAMBERLAIN, BASIL H. *Things Japanese*, p. 375. London, Tokyo, 1890
21 *Vishnu, The Institutes of*, xxvii, 4–13. *Sacred Books of the East*, vii
22 CRAWLEY, ERNEST. *The Mystic Rose*, pp. 208–9. London and New York, 1902
23 *Ib.*, p. 210

III

1 BARNES-GRUNDY, MABEL. *Hilary on Her Own*, p. 10. New York, 1908
2 *De l'Éducation des Filles*, ch. v
3 PLOSS, ii, 437
4 CHAMBERLAIN, p. 368
5 HALL, G. STANLEY. *Adolescence*, ii, 233. New York, 1905
6 *Lî Kî*, Bk. x, Sect. ii, 36. *Sacred Books of the East*, xxvii, xxviii
7 HALL, ii, 233
8 CRAWLEY, p. 220
9 FRAZER, JAMES G. *Golden Bough*, i, 208. London, 1900
10 *Ib.*
11 BROWN, GEORGE. *Melanesians and Polynesians*, pp. 105–7. London, 1910
12 FRAZER, *Golden Bough*, i, 210
13 PUTNAM, EMILY JAMES. *The Lady*, p. 5. New York, 1910
14 *Why the Oracles Cease to Give Answers*, 46
15 *Decency in Conversation amongst Women*, p. 2. London, 1664
16 HIGGINSON, THOMAS WENTWORTH. *Common Sense about Women*, p. 106. Boston and New York, 1881
17 *Letter* cvii, 13. *Nicene and Post-Nicene Fathers*, vi(Sec. Ser.)
18 MARCHAIS, R. *Voyage en Guinée*, ii, 144–5. Amsterdam, 1731; Ellis, A. B. *The Ewe-Speaking Peoples of the*

Slave Coast of West Africa, pp. 57–8. London, 1890;
BOSMAN, WM. *Coast of Guinea*, p. 372. London, 1705

19 ALLDRIDGE, T. J. *The Sherbro and its Hinterland*, xiv.
London, 1901; LEONARD, A. G. *The Lower Niger and
its Tribes*, pp. 408–9. London and New York, 1906;
HEARN, LAFCADIO. *Japan*, pp. 158–9. New York and
London, 1904; SAHAGUN, BERNARDINO DE. *Histoire
générale des choses de la Nouvelle-Espagne*, pp. 14, 15,
459. Paris, 1880

20 CLAVIGERO, D. F. S. *The History of Mexico*, ii, 48. Philadelphia, 1817

21 ACOSTA, JOSEPH DE. *The Natural and Moral History of
the Indies*, Bk. v, ch. xv

22 JEROME, *Letter* cvii, 5; *Letter* cxxvii, 5, 8

23 *Didaskalia*, ch. xiv. *Texte und Untersuchungen zur
Geschichte der alt-christlichen Literatur*. N. S. x, 1904

24 HEFELE, C. J. von. *A History of the Christian Councils*,
v, 213. Edinburgh, 1871–96

25 DE GROOT, J. J. M. *The Religious System of China*, ii,
756. Leyden, 1892–1910

26 *Ib.*, ii, 406, 409

27 CUNNINGHAM, J. F. *Uganda and its Peoples*, pp. 230–2.
London, 1905

28 *Qur'ân*, xxxiii, 54

29 GARNETT, LUCY M. J. *The Women of Turkey and their
Folk-Lore*, pp. 591, 593. London, 1893

30 FRAZER, J. G. *Totemism and Exogamy*, ii, 284. London,
1910

31 CRAWLEY, p. 37

IV

1 *Lî Kî*, Bk. x, Sect. ii, 37

2 *Vanity Fair*, ch. iii.

3 PLOSS, ii, 437

4 *Ib.*, ii, 425 ff

5 *Ib.*, ii, 437: ELLIS, *The Tshi-Speaking Peoples of the Gold
Coast of West Africa*, pp. 235–6. London, 1887

6 HALL, ii, 234

7 *Ib.*, ii, 235

8 OWEN, MARY ALICIA. *Folk-Lore of the Musquakie Indians
of North America*, p. 70. London, 1904

9   ELLIS, *The Tshi-Speaking Peoples*, pp. 234-5.
10   PLOSS, ii, 429, 443
11   *Ib.*, ii, 425, 437
12   *Ib.*, ii, 439; CRAWLEY, p. 272
13   *Ib.*, p. 270; PLOSS, ii, 439
14   ELLIS, *The Ewe-Speaking Peoples*, p. 155
15   PLOSS, ii, 438, 440, 441

V

1   WESTERMARCK, EDWARD. *The History of Human Marriage*, p. 213. London and New York, 1901
2   CODRINGTON, R. H. *The Melanesians*, p. 237. Oxford, 1891
3   SPENCER, B., and GILLEN, F. J. *The Native Tribes of Central Australia*, pp. 558-9. London and New York, 1899
4   FRAZER, *Totemism and Exogamy*, iv, 235-6
5   DAWSON, JAMES. *Australian Aborigines*, pp. 30-1. Melbourne, Sydney, and Adelaide, 1881
6   CRAWLEY, p. 315
7   OWEN, pp. 74-5
8   *Lt Kt*, Bk. 1, sect. i, pt. iii, 36
9   CRAWLEY, p. 316
10   *Ib.*
11   *Ib.*, pp. 328, 329
12   CODRINGTON, p. 240
13   TEIT, JAMES. "The Thompson River Indians," *Memoirs*. American Museum of Natural History, vol. ii, p. 324
14   WESTERMARCK, *Marriage*, p. 71
15   *Ib.*
16   BROWN, p. 113; ZACHE, H. "Sitten und Gebräuche der Suaheli," *Zt. f. Ethnologie*, xxxi (1899), 79
17   CRAWLEY, pp. 315, 316
18   *Lt Kt*, Bk. 1, sect. i, pt. iii, 34
19   P. 337
20   HOWARD, GEORGE ELLIOTT. *A History of Matrimonial Institutions*, i, 267. Chicago, London, 1904
21   KOVALEVSKY, MAXIME. *Modern Customs and Ancient Laws of Russia*, pp. 40-1. London, 1891

22 *Nârada*, xii, 32, 35. *Sacred Books of the East*, xxxiii
23 CRAWLEY, pp. 238–9
24 WOOD, EDWARD J. *The Wedding Day in all Ages and Communities*, p. 167. New York, 1869
25 WESTERMARCK, *Marriage*, p. 401
26 ELLIS, A. B. *The Yoruba-Speaking Peoples of the Slave Coast of West Africa*, pp. 153–4, 185. London, 1894
27 *Nârada*, xii, 38–44
28 WESTERMARCK, *Marriage*, p. 402
29 *Manu*, v, 153. *Sacred Books of the East*, xxv
30 *Li Ki*, Bk. x, sect. ii, 37
31 *The Code of Hammurabi*, § 128. Ed. HARPER, R. F. Chicago and London.
32 WESTERMARCK, *Marriage*, p. 415
33 *Ib.*, p. 444
34 CRAWLEY, p. 333
35 GARNETT, *The Women of Turkey; The Christian Woman*, p. 324
36 CRAWLEY, p. 333
37 *Deuteronomy*, xxiv, 5
38 FRAZER, *Totemism and Exogamy*, iv, 234; GARNETT, *The Women of Turkey; The Christian Woman*, pp. 203, 205
39 CRAWLEY, pp. 333–4
40 NIEBOER, H. J. *Slavery*, p. 11. The Hague, 1910

VI

1 *Pahlavi Texts: Shâyast Lâ-Shâyast*, x, 19. *Sacred Books of the East*, v
2 *Manu*, ix, 4, 90, 93
3 ANTIN, MARY. *The Promised Land*, p. 35. Boston and New York, 1912
4 *The Whole Duty of a Woman*, p. 38. London, 1702
5 ERASMUS, DESIDERIUS. *Colloquies. A Lover and Maiden*
6 §§ 178–81
7 PLUTARCH. *Numa*, x
8 GARCILASSO DE LA VEGA. *Royal Commentaries of the Incas*, i, 293. Pub. Hakluyt Society
9 *Ib.*, i, 296–8; ii, 163
10 PUTNAM, pp. 90 ff

336

VII

1. *Epistle to the Ephesians*, v. 28
2. BLACKSTONE, WILLIAM. *Commentaries on the Laws of England*, Bk. III, ch. iv
3. *Manu*, ix, 22
4. *Brihaspati*, xxiv, ii. *Books of the East*, xxxiii
5. *Vishnu*, xxii, 19
6. *Âpastamba*, i, 4, 14, 21. *Sacred Books of the East*, ii
7. CHAMBERLAIN, pp. 370-2
8. KOVALEVSKY, p. 45
9. FRAZER, *Totemism and Exogamy*, i, 72
10. *Decency in Conversation amongst Women*, p. 71
11. SCHOULER, *A Treatise on the Law of the Domestic Relations*, §§ 37, 39. Boston, 1895
12. MOONEY, JAMES. VII (*1885-6*) *Annual Report American Bureau of Ethnology*, pp. 338-9
13. FEATHERMAN, A. *Social History of the Races of Mankind*, Second Division, p. 178. London, 1881-91
14. SPENCER, B., and GILLEN, F. J. *The Northern Tribes of Central Australia*, p. 474. London and New York, 1904
15. PLINY, Bk. XXVIII, ch. vii
16. DOBRIZHOFFER, M. *An Account of the Abipones*, ii, 264. London, 1822
17. PLOSS and BARTELS, i, 929
18. *Ib.*, i, 931
19. *Ib.*, i, 890, 930-1
20. SPENCER and GILLEN, *Native Tribes*, etc., p. 471
21. BEARDMORE, EDWARD. *Journal Anthropological Institute*, xix (1889-90), 462
22. CALLAWAY, *The Religious System of the Amazulu*, p. 443. Natal, Capetown, London, 1870
23. DE GROOT, v, 538-9
24. ROSCOE, J. "Notes on the Bageshu," *Journal Anthropological Institute*, xxxix (1909), p. 184
25. PLOSS and BARTELS, i, 929-32
26. BOWRING, JOHN. *The Philippine Islands*, p. 120. London, 1859
27. SPENCER and GILLEN, *Native Tribes*, etc., pp. 466-7
28. *Reports Cambridge Anthropological Expedition to Torres Straits*, vi, 106

29 KUBARY, I. S. *Aus dem samoanischen Familienleben.*
 Globus, xlvii (1885), 70
30 TEIT, p. 305
31 PLOSS, i, 36.
32 CRAWLEY, p. 426
33 *Anthropophyteia,* iii (1906), 35
34 CRAWLEY, p. 424
35 PLOSS, i, 35–6
36 CRAWLEY, p. 392
37 COLQUHOUN, A. R. *Across Chrysê,* i, 335. London, 1883
38 *The Indian Antiquary,* iii (1874), 151; CRAWLEY, p. 425
39 *History of Woman Suffrage,* i, 322. Ed. ELIZABETH
 CADY STANTON, SUSAN B. ANTHONY, MATILDA JOSLYN
 GAGE. New York, 1881
40 HOWITT, A. W., *The Native Tribes of South-East Australia,*
 p. 397. London and New York, 1904; SPENCER and
 GILLEN, *Northern Tribes,* etc., p. 293
41 *Reports Cambridge Anthropological Expedition to Torres
 Straits,* v, 439
42 *Journal Anthropological Institute,* xix (1889–90), 467
43 KOHLER, J. "Das Recht der Marshall-insulaner," *Zt. f.
 Vergleichende Rechtswissenschaft,* xii (1897), 453; CHAL-
 MERS, J. "Toaripi," *Journal Anthropological Institute,*
 xxvii (1897–8), 332–3; CHRISTIAN, F. W. *The Caroline
 Islands,* p. 239. London, 1899; FRAZER, J. G. *The
 Golden Bough: Taboo,* p. 191. London, 1911; *Narrative
 of the Adventures and Sufferings of John R. Jewitt,* pp. 108,
 111. Ithaca, N. Y., 1849; WEEKS, J. H. "Anthropo-
 logical Notes on the Bangala of the Upper Congo River,"
 Journal Anthropological Institute, xxxix (1909), 458, 459;
 BRASSEUR DE BOURBOURG, E. C. *Histoire des Nations
 Civilisées de Mexique et de l'Amérique-Centrale,* ii, 565.
 Paris, 1857–9; HERRERA, ANTONIO DE. *History of
 America,* iii, 1, 4
44 ROCHAS, VICTOR DE. *La Nouvelle Calédonia,* p. 286.
 Paris, 1862; BARBOT, JOHN. "North and South Guinea,"
 Churchill's Collections, v, 121; TOUT, C. HILL. "Report
 on the Ethnology of the Statlumᴴ of British Columbia,"
 Journal Anthropological Institute, xxxv (1905), 139;
 RIVERO, M. E., and TSCHUDI, J. J. VON. *Peruvian Anti-*

quities, pp. 157, 158. New York, 1855; DIODORUS SICULUS, i, ch. vi; KAEMPFER, E. *The History of Japan*, ii, 69. Glasgow and New York, 1906; DE GROOT, ii, 613; MARCHAIS, ii, 168; ROSCOE, J. "Further Notes on the Manners and Customs of the Baganda," *Journal Anthropological Institute*, xxxii (1902), 47; DALTON, E. T. *Descriptive Ethnology of Bengal*, p. 274. Calcutta, 1872; CROOKE, W. *Natives of Northern India*, p. 218. London, 1907

45 FEATHERMAN, Second Division, p. 93; TATE, H. R. "Further Notes on the Kikuyu Tribe of British East Africa," *Journal Anthropological Institute*, xxxiv (1904), 263, 264; HOLLIS, A. C. *The Nandi*, p. 52. Oxford, 1909; LUMHOLZ, CARL. *Unknown Mexico*, ii, 170. New York, 1902; FEATHERMAN, Second Division, p. 259; SPIETH, JAKOB. *Die Ewe-Stämme*, p. 642. Berlin, 1906; FEATHERMAN, First Division, p. 446; MELDON, J. A. "Notes on the Bahima of Ankole," *Journal African Society*, vi (1906-7), 144; FEATHERMAN, Third Division, p. 269; BOAS, F. "First General Report on the Indians of British Columbia," *Report of the British Association for the Advancement of Science*, 1899, p. 846; STEVENSON, M. C. "The Zuñi Indians," XXIII (*1904*) *Annual Report Bureau American Ethnology*, p. 15; DORSEY, G. A., and VOTH, H. R. *The Oraibi Soyal Ceremony*. Pub. Field Columbian Museum. Anthropological Ser. iii (1901-3), p. 59 n.; CLAVIGERO, D. F. S. *The History of Mexico*, ii, 46, 62-3, 64. Philadelphia, 1817; OVIEDO Y VALDÉS, G. F. DE. *Histoire du Nicaragua*. TERNAUX-COMPANS. *Voyages*, xiv, 43; HERRERA, iii, vi, 1; iv, 139; GARCILASSO, i, 278; SHAW, TH. "On the Inhabitants of the Hills near Rájamahall." *Asiatick Researches*, iv (1795), 59; *Madras Government Museum Bulletin*, No. 4, pp. 193, 198; FRAZER, *The Golden Bough: Taboo*, p. 11; PORPHYRY, iv, 7; PAUSANIAS, ii, 14; viii, 13; OVID, *Fasti*, ii, 328-30; *Âpastambâ*, ii, 2, 3, v. 13; *Âkârânga Sutra*, Bk. ii, Lect. 15, iv. "Gaina Sûtras," *Sacred Books of the East*, xxii; *Pâtimokkha Pârâgikâ Dhammâ*, i. "Vinaya Texts," *Sacred Books of the East*, xiii; SMITH, R. ROBERTSON. *Lectures on the Religion of the Semites*, p. 435. Edinburgh, 1889;

Luke, i, 8–9; 1 *Corinthians,* vii, 5; *Nicene and Post-Nicene Fathers,* xiv, 613

46 CRAWLEY, p. 394

47 COLE, H. "Notes on the Wagogo of German East Africa," *Journal Anthropological Institute,* xxxii (1902), 318

48 FRAZER, *The Golden Bough,* i, 28

49 FURNESS, WILLIAM HENRY. *The Home-Life of Borneo Head Hunters,* p. 169. Philadelphia, 1902

50 FRAZER, *The Golden Bough,* i, 28

51 *Ib.,* i, 30

52 ELLIS, *The Tshi-Speaking Peoples,* p. 226

53 CRAWLEY, p. 395

54 *Ib.,* p. 396

55 PAULITSCHKE, PHILLIP. *Ethnographie Nordost-Afrikas,* ii, 67. Berlin, 1893–6

56 BOAS, FRANZ. "First General Report on the Indians of British Columbia," pp. 846–7

57 KUBARY, J. *Die Religion der Pelauer.* BASTIAN, A. *Allerlei aus Volks- und Menschenkunde,* i, 34. Berlin, 1888

58 BASTIAN, A. *Loango-Küste,* ii, 169, 170. Jena, 1874; CAVAZZI, *Relation Historique de l'Ethiopie Occidentale,* i, 270. Paris, 1732; DENNETT, R. E. *At the Back of the Black Man's Mind,* p. 89. London and New York, 1906

59 CAPART, J. "Sur le prêtre In-mwtf.," *Zt. f. Ägyptische Sprache u. Alterthumskunde,* lxi (1904), 88–9

60 DEMOSTHENES, *Against Neæra,* §§ 73–6

61 AULUS GELLIUS, x, 15; PLUTARCH, *Roman Questions,* 50, 86

62 TERTULLIAN, *Against Heretics,* ch. xxx; SULPETIUS SEVERUS, *Sacred History,* ch. xlviii; LEA, H. C. *Sacerdotal Celibacy in the Christian Church,* pp. 41–2. Boston and New York, 1884

63 *Leviticus,* xxi, 13

64 *Ib.,* xxi, 14; *Apostolical Constitutions,* vi, xvii; *Ante-Nicene Christian Library,* xvii; *Nicene and Post-Nicene Fathers,* 363

65 HEFELE, i, 227

66 1 *Timothy,* iii, 11

67 GARCILASSO, i, 274

68 MORET, A. *Du Caractère Religieux de la Royauté Pharaonique*, pp. 49–52. Paris, 1902
69 CRAWLEY, p. 9
70 *Ib.*, p. 168
71 *Ib.*, pp. 394–5. (Not found in Bancroft as cited. i, 581)
72 SAXO GRAMMATICUS. *History*, i, 25–6. London, 1894
73 *Vašishtha*, xxi, 15. *Sacred Books of the East*, xix

VIII

1   SPENCER and GILLEN, *Native Tribes*, etc., pp. 124–5
2   HARTLAND, E. S. *Primitive Paternity*, i, 22, 149–50.
      London, 1909
3   MARCHAIS, ii, 149–50
4   CASALIS, E. *Les Bassoutos*, p. 283. Paris, 1859
5   MARRIOTT, H. P. F. "The Secret Societies of West Africa,"
      Journal Anthropological Institute, xxix (1899), 22
6   JUSTIN, xi, ch. xi
7   LIVY, xxvi, 18
8   FISON, LORIMER. *Tales from Old Fiji*, p. 33. London,
      1904
9   *Ib.*, p. 200
10 CUSHING, F. H. *Zuñi Folk Tales: The Maiden the Sun
      Made Love to, and Her Boys*. New York and London,
      1901
11 MORET, pp. 49–52
12 HARTLAND, i, 25
13 MONIER-WILLIAMS, M. *Brāhmanism and Hindūism*, pp.
      354, 355. London, 1887
14 CURTISS, p. 117
15 PURCHAS, S. *His Pilgrimage*, iii, ch. ii, § 4. London,
      1813
16 *Untrodden Fields of Anthropology*, i, 67–9. Paris, 1898
17 HOPKINS, E. W. "Position of the Ruling Caste in Ancient
      India," *Journal American Oriental Society*, xiii (1889),
      64–5
18 2 *Kings*, iv, 8–17
19 ROTH, W. E. *North Queensland Ethnography*, Bull. No.
      5, p. 22. Brisbane, 1903
20 *Sûtrakritânga*, Bk. ii, Lect. 2, 25–7. *Sacred Books of the*

East, xlv; *Kulavagga,* v, 33, 2.   *Sacred Books of the East,* xx
21 *Manu,* ix, 49, 51–2, 54
22 *The Social Evil in Chicago,* pp. 273, 283.   Chicago, 1911
23 PLOSS and BARTELS, i, 389

IX

1 Bull. No. 5., pp. 25–6
2 *Reports Cambridge Anthropological Expedition to Torres Straits,* vi, 105
3 PLOSS and BARTELS, i, 910
4 KIDD, *Savage Childhood,* p. 8
5 TEIT, pp. 303–4
6 PLOSS and BARTELS, i, 910
7 *Ib.*
8 *Ib.,* i, 925, 926
9 PACHINGER, A. M.   "Die Schwangere und das Neugeborne in Glauben und Brauch der Völker. *Anthropophyteia,* iii (1906), 34, 39
10 PLOSS and BARTELS, i, 890
11 CRAWLEY, pp. 8–9, 226
12 PLOSS and BARTELS, i, 890, 893
13 CRAWLEY, p. 54
14 *Li Kî,* Bk. x, sect. ii, 16
15 PLOSS and BARTELS, i, 906
16 CRAWLEY, p. 167
17 PLOSS and BARTELS, i, 905
18 PACHINGER, iii, 37
19 PLOSS and BARTELS, i, 890, 893, 905, 906

X

1 HARTLAND, i, 233–4
2 PLOSS and BARTELS, i, 784
3 HARTLAND, i, 105–6
4 TEIT, p. 363
5 *Life of St. Hilarion*
6 *Hammurabi,* § 144
7 *Manu,* ix, 59

8   *Dabistán*, p. 253. Washington and London, 1901
9   EGEDE, H. *A Description of Greenland*, p. 142. London, 1818
10   WESTERMARCK, *Marriage*, p. 524
*11 ROSCOE, *Further Notes*, etc., p. 38
12   WESTERMARCK, *Marriage*, p. 524
13   *Ib.*
14   *Nârada*, xii, 94

XI

1   FRAZER, *The Golden Bough*, i, 207-8
2   NELSON, E. W. "The Eskimo about Behring Strait."
     XVIII (1899) Annual Report Bureau American Ethnology, pt. i, 291
3   CRAWLEY, p. 9
4   *Ib.*, p. 55
5   *Ib.*, pp. 55, 165
6   FRAZER, *The Golden Bough*, iii, 223
7   *Ib.*, iii, 225
8   CRAWLEY, pp. 55, 166
9   TEIT, p. 326
10   iv, 41-2
11   FRAZER, *The Golden Bough*, iii, 223
12   *Ib.*, iii, 222
13   WESTERMARCK, EDWARD. *The Origin and Development of the Moral Ideas*, ii, 538, n. 2. London, 1908
14   FRAZER, *The Golden Bough*, iii, 225
15   CRAWLEY, p. 166
16   ELLIS, *The Tshi-Speaking Peoples*, p. 95
17   CRAWLEY, p. 114
18   TEIT, p. 326
19   SPENCER and GILLEN, *Northern Tribes*, etc., p. 615
20   CRAWLEY, pp. 165-6
21   *Ib.*, pp. 11, 166
22   SPIETH, p. 475
23   *Dabistán*, p. 168
24   *Vaśishtha*, v, 6. *Sacred Books of the East*, xix
25   PLINY, Bk. VII, ch. xv
26   FRAZER, *The Golden Bough*, iii, 232

27 FRAZER, *The Golden Bough*, iii, 222–3, 226–7

28 ELLIS, *The Tshi-Speaking Peoples*, pp. 94–5

29 SPIETH, p. 454

30 GRANVILLE, R. K., and ROTH, H. LING. "Notes on the Jekris, Sobos, and Ibos of the Warri District of the Niger Coast Protectorate," *Journal Anthropological Institute*, xxvii (1898–9), 110

31 DUPUIS, J. *Journal of a Residence in Ashantee*, p. 116. London, 1824

32 BASTIAN, i, 217

33 RIVERS, W. H. R. *The Todas*, p. 106. London, 1906

34 *Âpastamba*, i, 3, 9; v, 13

35 Cp. *Leviticus*, xii, 4

36 *Dabistán*, p. 162

37 DUBOIS, J. A. *Hindu Manners, Customs, and Ceremonies*, p. 713. Oxford, 1899

38 ELLIS, *The Tshi-Speaking Peoples*, p. 95; SPIETH, p. 642; GRINNELL, G. B. "Cheyenne Woman Customs," *American Anthropologist*, New Ser. iv (1902), 13, 14; HERRERA, iii, 1, 4; KAEMPFER, ii, 17; *Nicene and Post-Nicene Fathers*, xiv, 600, 613

39 ELLIS, *Studies in the Psychology of Sex: Modesty, Sexual Periodicity, Auto-Erotism*, pp. 213–4; FRAZER, *The Golden Bough*, iii, 232, n. 2

40 ELLIS, *Studies*, etc.; *Modesty*, etc., p. 212

41 FRAZER, *The Golden Bough*, iii, 223

42 ELLIS, *Studies*, etc. *Modesty*, etc., p. 206

43 *Ib.*, pp. 26–7

44 CRAWLEY, p. 192

45 HOFFMAN, W. J. "The Menomini Indians," *XIV* (*1892–3*) *Annual Report American Bureau of Ethnology*, p. 175

46 *Vašishtha*, v, 7

47 CRAWLEY, p. 194

48 *Reports Cambridge Anthropological Expedition to Torres Straits*, vi, 111

XII

1 CRUICKSHANK, B. *Eighteen Years on the Gold Coast of Africa*, ii, 219. London, 1853

2 HARTLAND, ii, 183
3 MACDONALD, D. *Africana*, i, 133–4. London, Edinburgh, Aberdeen, 1882; TOUT, C. HILL. *Salish and Déné. The Native Races of the British Empire*, i, 203. London, 1907
4 TURNER, L. M. "Ethnology of the Ungava District, Hudson Bay Territory," *XI (1889–90) Annual Report Bureau American Ethnology*, p. 199
5 DANKS, B. "Burial Customs of New Britain," *Journal Anthropological Institute*, xxi (1891–2), 355–6
6 DE GROOT, ii, 761
7 SPENCER and GILLEN, *Northern Tribes*, etc., p. 507
8 *Reports Cambridge Anthropological Expedition to Torres Straits*, vi, 252
9 SPIETH, p. 754
10 CALLAWAY, pp. 161, 316–18
11 MACDONALD, J. "Manners, Customs, Superstitions, and Religions of South African Tribes," *Journal Anthropological Institute*, xix (1889–90), 114
12 CAMPBELL, J. M. "Notes on the Spirit Basis of Belief and Custom," *The Indian Antiquary*, xxvii (1898), 138
13 SPENCER and GILLEN, *Native Tribes*, etc., p. 502
14 POWERS, STEPHEN. "Tribes of California," *Contributions to North American Ethnology*, iii (1877), 328
15 SPENCER and GILLEN, *Native Tribes*, etc., p. 500; SMYTH, R. BROUGH. *The Aborigines of Victoria*, i, 104–5. Melbourne and New York, 1878
16 DUBOIS, pp. 356
17 SIBREE, JAMES, JR. *The Great African Island*, p. 255. London 1880; DENNETT, R. E. *Notes of the Folklore of the Fjort*, p. 24. London, 1898; KOHLER, J. "Neue Beitrage zum Islamrechte," *Zt. f. Vergleichende Rechtswissenschaft*, xii (1897), 94–5
18 KIDD, DUDLEY. *The Essential Kafir*, p. 250. London, 1904
19 LEONARD, p. 174
20 DIXON, R. B. "The Northern Maidu," *Bull. American Museum Natural History*, XVII, pt. iii (1905), 242; TOUT, *Salish and Déné*, p. 201

21 WEEKS, p. 445; CHALMERS, p. 330
22 BOSE, S. C. *The Hindoos as they Are*, p. 250. Calcutta, 1883
23 KRIEGER, M. *Neu-Guinea*, p. 180. Berlin, 1889; CIEZA DE LEON, PEDRO DE. *Chronicle of Peru*, Pt. 1, chs. xli, lxxxiii, C. Pub. Hakluyt Society
24 SPENCER and GILLEN, *Native Tribes*, etc., pp. 50–7
25 SMYTH, i, 104–5
26 *Reports Cambridge Anthropological Expedition to Torres Straits*, v, 262
27 CODRINGTON, p. 198
28 KRIEGER, p. 305
29 YARROW, H. C. "A Further Contribution to the Study of the Mortuary Customs of the North American Indians," I (1879–80), *Annual Report Bureau American Ethnology*, p. 109
30 KINGSLEY, MARY H. *Travels in West Africa*, p. 516. London and New York, 1897
31 ELLIS, *The Ewe-Speaking Peoples*, p. 160
32 DIXON, p. 242
33 RUSSELL, FRANK. "The Pima Indians," *XXVI* (*1904–5*) *Annual Report Bureau American Ethnology*, p. 195
34 RIVERS, p. 370
35 DUBOIS, p. 356
36 SIMPSON, G. *An Overland Journey Round the World*, pp. 114–5. Philadelphia, 1847
37 DUBOIS, p. 356
38 SIBREE, p. 255
39 POWERS, p. 327
40 SPENCER and GILLEN, *Northern Tribes*, etc., p. 508; *Native Tribes*, etc., p. 500
41 SMYTH, i, 106
42 HOLLIS, C. "People of Taveta," *Journal African Society* (1901–2), 121
43 MARINER, WM. *Tonga Islands*, i, 409 n. London, 1817
44 DE GROOT, ii, 466
45 COX, ROSS. *Adventures on the Columbian River*, pp. 329–30. New York, 1832
46 TAYLOR, R. *New Zealand and its Inhabitants*, p. 218. London and Wanganui, 1870

47 Simpson, pp. 114–15; Bancroft, H. H. *The Native Races of the Pacific States*, i, 126. New York, 1874
48 *Ib.*, i, 744
49 Howitt, A. W. *The Native Tribes of South-East Australia*, p. 456. London and New York, 1904
50 *Reports Cambridge Anthropological Expedition to Torres Straits*, vi, 138, 157–8; Chalmers, p. 330; Krieger, p. 180
51 Mariner, i, 437–9
52 Cameron, V. L. *Across Africa*, ii, 66. London, 1877
53 Parker, K. L. *The Euahlayi Tribe*, p. 93. London, 1905
54 Kingsley, p. 516
55 Cavazzi, i, 404–8
56 *The First Book to His Wife*, i, ch. xi

XIII

1 Webster, Hutton. *Primitive Secret Societies*, 21. New York, 1908; Crawley, 296; Spencer and Gillen, *Native Tribes*, etc., p. 259
2 *Ib.*, 215
3 Webster, p. 22
4 Crawley, pp. 216–17
5 Codrington, p. 232
6 Frazer, *Totemism and Exogamy*, iv, 286
7 Crawley, p. 164
8 Howitt, A. W. "The Jeraeil, or Initiation Ceremonies of the Kurnai Tribe," *Journal Anthropological Institute*, xiv (1884–5), 306, 316; *The Native Tribes of South-East Australia*, p. 402
9 Beveridge, P. "The Aborigines of the Lower Murray, Lower Murrumbidgee, Lower Lachlan, and Lower Darling," *Jour. and Proc. Royal Society New South Wales*, xvii (1883), 27
10 Meyer, A. N. *Woman's Work in America*, p. 26. New York, 1891
11 Webster, p. 23
12 Hartland, ii, 24
13 Webster, p. 56
14 Frazer, *Totemism and Exogamy*, ii, 60

15 THOMSON, B. *The Fijians*, p. 154. London, 1908
16 FRAZER, *Totemism and Exogamy*, iii, 160
17 CODRINGTON, p. 87
18 KRAPF, J. L., *Travels*, etc., *in Eastern Africa*, p. 58. London, 1860
19 WEBSTER, p. 12
20 CRAWLEY, p. 38
21 TEIT, p. 324
22 SIGOURNEY, L. H., *Letters of Life*, p. 123. New York, 1866
23 *A Girl's Life Eighty Years Ago*, p. 90
24 WESTERMARCK, *Marriage*, 120
25 *Manu*, viii, 357; *Nârada*, xii, 66–8; *Brihaspati*, xxiii, 6
26 WESTERMARCK, *Marriage*, p. 120
27 ELLIS, *The Ewe-Speaking Peoples*, p. 204
28 FRAZER, *Totemism and Exogamy*, iv, 235
29 WESTERMARCK, *Marriage*, pp. 119, 120; HARTLAND, ii, 126
30 LEVER, CHARLES. *Charles O'Malley*, ch. xxvi. Cp. THACKERAY, *Vanity Fair*, ch. xliii
31 CRAWLEY, p. 173
32 *Ib.*, p. 168
33 *Ka Mooolelo Hawaii*, pp. 165, 167. Tr. JULES REMY. Paris and Leipzig, 1862
34 *Manu*, iv, 43
35 CRAWLEY, p. 37
36 *Ib.*
37 DENNETT, *At the Back of the Black Man's Mind*, p. 12
38 CRAWLEY, p. 37
39 JESSUP, pp. 14, 15
40 *Li Ki*, x, 14
41 ELLIS, HAVELOCK. *Studies in the Psychology of Sex; The Evolution of Modesty*, p. 25. Philadelphia, 1904
42 *Manu*, iv, 53
43 HOWITT, *Native Tribes*, etc., p. 354; SPENCER and GILLEN, *Northern Tribes*, etc., p. 498
44 *Reports Cambridge Anthropological Expedition to Torres Straits*, vi, 277, 278
45 CHAMBERLAIN, p. 372
46 WESTERMARCK, *Moral Development*, i, 665

47 WESTERMARCK, *Moral Development*, i., 665, 666
48 GARNETT, *The Women of Turkey: The Christian Women*, p. 106
49 McMASTER, JOHN BACH. *A History of the United States*, ii, 566. New York, 1885; MEYER, p. 18
50 LEONARD, p. 375
51 CODRINGTON, p. 233
52 BLACKWELL, ELIZABETH. *Pioneer Work in opening the Medical Profession to Women*, p. 89. London and New York, 1895
53 CRAWLEY, p. 40
54 CODRINGTON, p. 233
55 MOONEY, JAMES. "Sacred Formulas of the Cherokees," VII (1885-6) *Annual Report American Bureau of Ethnology*, pp. 330-1
56 DE GROOT, i, 7
57 DAWSON, pp. 31, 40
58 FRAZER, *Totemism and Exogamy*, iv, 233, 236
59 SIBREE, J. "Relationships and the Names Used for them among the Peoples of Madagascar," *Journal Anthropological Institute*, ix (1879-80), 48
60 ST. JOHN, SPENCER. *Life in the Forests of the Far East*, ii, 265. London, 1862
61 PUTNAM, p. 264
62 SPENCER and GILLEN, *Native Tribes*, etc., p. 463
63 STEINMETZ, S. R. *Ethnologische Studien zur ersten Entwicklung der Strafe*, ii, 96. Leiden and Leipzig, 1894

XIV

1 FRAZER, *The Golden Bough: Taboo*, p. 164
2 CRAWLEY, p. 51
3 *Narrative*, etc., of JOHN R. JEWITT, pp. 108, 111; FRAZER, *The Golden Bough: Taboo*, p. 191
4 WEEKS, pp. 458, 459
5 MURDOCK, J. "Ethnological Results of the Point Barrow Expedition," ix (1892) *Annual Report Bureau American Ethnology*, p. 414
6 RIVERS, pp. 27-8, 30
7 WESTERMARCK, *Moral Ideas*, i, 636

8 CRAWLEY, p. 49
9 WESTERMARCK, *Moral Ideas*, i, 637
10 CRAWLEY, p. 49
11 WESTERMARCK, *Moral Ideas*, i, 636
12 CRAWLEY, p. 49
13 *Ib.*, p. 50
14 *Ib.*
15 *Ib.*, p. 49
16 KIDD, *Savage Childhood*, pp. 11, 12, 17–18
17 MEYER, p. 160
18 *Ib.*, p. 224
19 MOLIÈRE, *Les Femmes Savantes*, Act ii, sc. vii
20 *Married Women*, p. 49. New York, 1871
21 HYADES, P. and DENIKER, J. *Mission Scientifique du Cap Horn*, p. 350. Paris, 1891
22 JOHNSTON, H. H. "The People of Eastern Equatorial Africa," *Journal Anthropological Institute*, xv (1885–6), 10
23 McDONALD, J. "East Central African Customs," *Journal Anthropological Institute*, xx (1892–3), 102, 109
24 CRAWLEY, pp. 168, 169, 173
25 WESTERMARCK, *Moral Ideas*, i, 636
26 Bk. II, ch. xxxv
27 *The Anatomy of Melancholy*, pt. 3, sec. 3, mem. 1, subs. 2
28 SPENCER and GILLEN, *Native Tribes*, etc., p. 220; MELVILLE, H. *The Marquesas Islands*, pp. 13, 245
29 KIDD, *Savage Childhood*, p. 39
30 CRAWLEY, pp. 50, 211
31 FRAZER, *Totemism and Exogamy*, iii, 416
32 HODSON, T. C. *The Nāga Tribes of Manipur*, pp. 45–6, 77. London, 1911
33 CRAWLEY, p. 208
34 ERASMUS, *Colloquies: The Abbot and Learned Woman*
35 RIVERS, p. 596
36 CULIN, STEWART. *Games of the North American Indians*, XXIV (1902–3), *Annual Report Bureau American Ethnology*, p. 421
37 *Ib.*, p. 647
38 *Ib.*, pp. 45, 183, 302; TEIT, pp. 272 ff.
39 CODRINGTON, p. 341

40 CULIN, pp. 267, 268
41 *Ib.*, p. 698
42 *Ib.*, p. 254
43 CHAMBERLAIN, p. 372
44 GREGORY, DR. *A Father's Legacy to his Daughters*, pp. 114–15. Annexed to Chesterfield, *Principles of Politeness*. Portsmouth, N. H., 1786
45 DAYTON, A. C. *Last Days of Knickerbocker Life in New York*, pp. 234, 246. New York and London, 1897
46 WILSON, C. T. and FELKIN, R. W. *Uganda and the Egyptian Soudan*, ii, 89. London, 1882
47 CULIN, pp. 576–7
48 ROUTLEDGE, p. 185
49 BESANT, WALTER. *Fifty Years Ago*, p. 91. New York, 1888
50 DAWSON, W. H. *The German Workman*, p. 31. New York and London, 1906

                        XV

 1 SPENCER and GILLEN, *Northern Tribes*, etc., pp. 498, 499
 2 HAGEN, p. 271
 3 WEBSTER, p. 42
 4 FRAZER, *The Golden Bough*, pt. ii, p. 399
 5 *Ib.*, pt. ii, p. 377
 6 *Manu*, ix, 18
 7 OBER, F. A. *Camps in the Caribees*, pp. 100–2. Boston, 1880; IM THURN, E. F. *Among the Indians of Guiana*, p. 186. London, 1883
 8 ERASMUS, *Colloquies: The Abbot and Learned Woman*
 9 HARVEY, GEORGE. *Women etc.*, p. 82. New York and London, 1908
10 JOHNSTON, H. H. *British Central Africa*, p. 452. London, 1897
11 MEYER, p. 173
12 *History of Woman Suffrage*, i, 81–2
13 SALEEBY, C. W. *Woman and Womanhood*, pp. 141–6. New York and London, 1911
14 BURGESS, GELETT. *Are you a Bromide*, pp. 24, 32. New York, 1910

References 351

15 *Decency in Conversation amongst Women*, p. 156
16 GARNETT, *The Women of Turkey; The Christian Women*, p. 62
17 JESSUP, p. 17
18 BURTON, pt. 3, sec. 2, mem. 3, subs. 4
19 KOURI-MOTO TEI-ZI-RO. "Sur la Condition de la Femme au Japan," *Revue Ethnographique*, i (1869–71), 239
20 ST. TERESA. *Conceptions of Divine Love*, pp. 225, 226. Tr. Dalton. London, 1860
21 ST. FRANCIS of SALES. *A Treatise on the Love of God*, pp. 23, 24. Dublin and London, 1860
22 Pp. 165–6
23 *Women and Men*, p. 3. New York, 1888
24 DAVIES, p. 71

XVI

1 EARLE, ALICE MORSE. *Customs and Fashions in Old New England*, p. 289. New York, 1896
2 SCHWEINFURTH, GEORG. *The Heart of Africa*, i, 152 ff. New York, 1874
3 WILSON and FELKIN, ii, 96
4 *History of Woman Suffrage*, i, 557
5 DUNNE, F. P. *Mr. Dooley in the Hearts of His Countrymen: The Divided Skirt*
6 CLAVIGERO, ii, 152
7 MALLET, *Northern Antiquities*, p. 348. London, 1890
8 ELLIS, *Studies*, etc.; *Modesty*, etc., p. 9
9 *Deuteronomy*, xx, 5
10 ELLIS, *Studies*, etc.: *Sexual Selection in Man*, p. 209 n. 2
11 ELLIS, *Studies*, etc.; *Modesty*, etc., p. 26
12 CRAWLEY, p. 210
13 HERODOTUS, i, 155
14 CRAWLEY, p. 93
15 WEBSTER, p. 23
16 LUCIAN, *Concerning the Syrian Goddess*, 51
17 DONALDSON, JAMES. *Woman*, p. 240. London, New York, Bombay and Calcutta, 1907
18 BLACKWELL, p. 203
19 *History of Woman Suffrage*, i, 127–8, 225, 375, 803

20 *History of Woman Suffrage*, i, 174
21 *Ib.*, i, 630
22 FRAZER, *Totemism and Exogamy*, iv, 73

XVII

1 CRAWLEY, p. 47
2 FRAZER, *The Golden Bough*, pt. ii, p. 336
3 *Ib.*, pt. ii, 339
4 CRAWLEY, pp. 47, 404, 434
5 JESSUP, p. 13
6 CRAWLEY, p. 434, BATCHELOR, p. 250; COLQUHOUN, i, 250
7 CHILD, p. 139
8 CRAWLEY, pp. 434, 435
9 *Ib.*, p. 48
10 JESSUP, p. 3
11 CRAWLEY, p. 48
12 *Âpastamba*, i, 4, 23–4
13 *Lî Kî*, Bk. i, sect. i, pt. iii, 36; Bk. XLI, 1
14 CRAWLEY, p. 433
15 *Lî Kî*, Bk. x, sect. ii, 37
16 WESTERMARCK, *Marriage*, p. 183
17 MACDONALD, J., p. 118
18 ANTIN, p. 54
19 P. 91
20 *On Female Dress*, Bk. ii, ch. i
21 ELLIS, *Studies*, etc.; *Sexual Selection in Man*, p. 167
22 *Ib.*, pp. 11, 15–16
23 PLOSS, ii, 333
24 SIGOURNEY, p. 224
25 *Lî Kî*, Bk. x, sect. iii, 32
26 Personal observation
27 TEIT, p. 300
28 HOWITT, *Native Tribes*, etc., p. 402
29 CHAMBERLAIN, pp. 371–2
30 *Judges*, xiii, 2–14
31 *Brihaspati*, xxiv, 7; *Vishnu*, xxxvii, 33; *Vasishtha*, xxi, 11
32 *Hammurabi*, § 110
33 PLINY, Bk. xiv, ch. xiii
34 WESTERMARCK, *Moral Ideas*, ii, 321

35 Dawson, J., p. 52
36 Crawley, J., p. 173
37 Westermarck, *Moral Ideas*, ii, 321-2
38 Roth, Walter E., p. 11
39 Westermarck, *Moral Ideas*, ii, 320, 321
40 Hodson, p. 182
41 Westermarck, *Moral Ideas*, ii, 320
42 Thomson, p. 104
43 Christian, p. 239

XVIII

1   Mathews, R. H. "The Origin, Organization and Cere-
    monies of the Australian Aborigines," *Proc. American
    Philosophical Society*, xxxix (1900), 560; Westermarck,
    Marriage, p. 390
2   *Ib.*
3   *Reports Anthropological Expedition to Torres Straits*, vi, 124
4   Westermarck, *Marriage*, pp. 392, 393-4, 397
5   *Ib.*, pp. 393, 394; Routledge, p. 125
6   Hodson, p. 90
7   Westermarck, *Marriage*, p. 394
8   Ellis, *The Tshi-Speaking Peoples*, p. 281
9   Westermarck, *Marriage*, p. 392
10 De Maulde la Clavière, p. 113
11 Hanoteau, A., and Letourneux, A. *La Kabylie et les
    coutumes Kabyles*, iii, 328. Paris, 1893; Westermarck,
    Marriage, pp. 392, 397
12 *Ib.*, p. 409
13 iii, 54
14 Westermarck, *Marriage*, p. 406
15 Ellis, *The Tshi-Speaking Peoples*, p. 281
16 Ellis, *The Yoruba-Speaking Peoples*, p. 182
17 Zache, p. 78
18 Hanoteau and Letourneux, iii, 427
19 Ellis, *Studies in the Psychology of Sex; Sex in Relation to
    Society*, p. 403
20 Roth, H. Ling. *The Natives of Sarawak and British
    North Borneo*, ii, clxxiv-v. London, 1896
21 Ellis, *The Ewe-Speaking Peoples*, p. 141

22 *The Social Evil in Chicago*, pp. 97 *ff.*
23 ADDAMS, pp. 76, 110–11
24 OLMSTEAD, F. L. *The Cotton Kingdom*, ii, 374. New York and London, 1862
25 SPEARS, JOHN R. *The American Slave Trade*, p. 210. New York, 1900
26 RHODES, J. F. *History of the United States*, i, 337, 338. New York, 1893; OLMSTEAD, i, 52
27 *A Girl's Life Eighty Years Ago*, p. 97
28 POST, ALBERT HERMANN. *Afrikanische Jurisprudenz*, i, 70. Oldenburg and Leipzig, 1887
29 PAULITSCHKE, i, 263
30 WESTERMARCK, *Moral Ideas*, i, 420–1
31 POST, i, 70
32 *Ib.*, i, 296
33 BROWN, p. 46
34 PLOSS and BARTELS, i, 391
35 *Ancient Laws and Institutes of England*, p. 311. 1840
36 HODSON, p. 134
37 PLOSS, i, 70
38 DAVIES, EMILY. *Thoughts on Some Questions Relating to Women*, 1860–1908, pp. 205–6. Cambridge, 1910

<h1 style="text-align:center">XIX</h1>

1 EURIPIDES. *Iphigenia at Aulis, l.* 1394
2 PLOSS and BARTELS, i, 390
3 LUMHOLZ, CARL. *Unknown Mexico*, i, 265. New York, 1902
4 BRIHASPATI, xxv, 11
5 *Clementine Homilies*, ii, 23; *Ante-Nicene Christian Library*, xvii
6 PHILO, *On the Virtuous being also Free*, xii–xiii
7 DÄHNHARDT, i, 116, 120
8 *Mahâbhârata*, in *The Indian Antiquary*, viii (1879), 321
9 WEBSTER, p. 62
10 DÄHNHARDT, i, 117
11 *The Questions of King Milinda*, iv, 1, 6
12 FÉNELON, ch. ix
13 *Vishnu*, xxiv, 16; *Manu*, iii, 8

References 355

14 WESTERMARCK, *Marriage*, pp. 524, 525
15 *Âpastamba*, Introd., xxix; *Journal Anthropological Society of Bombay*, ii (1890–92), 512
16 JESSUP, p. 18
17 BRACKETT, A. C. *The Education of American Girls*, p. 396. New York, 1874
18 HARVEY, pp. 3, 6
19 DAWSON, J., p. 52
20 *Qur'Ân*, xliii, 15
21 BRAND, JOHN. *Popular Antiquities of Great Britain*, iii, 102–8. London, 1849
22 CHAMBERLAIN, p. 374
23 BYRON. *Don Juan*, Canto i, st. 124
24 *Manu*, ix, 17
25 *Satapatha-Brâhmana*, xi, 5, 1, 9. *Sacred Books of the East*, xxxiv
26 SCHIRMACHER, p. 5
27 TEIT, p. 290
28 PLOSS, ii, 416
29 SHAKESPEAR, J. "The Kuki-Lushai Clans," *Journal Anthropological Institute*, xxxix (1909), 380–1
30 *Satapatha-Brâhmana*, xii, 7, 2, 11; xiii, 8, 3, 11
31 *The Questions of King Milinda*, iv, 1, 6
32 DONALDSON, p. 240
33 CHRISTIAN, p. 69
34 *Ib.*
35 SCHIRMACHER, p. 105 n. 2
36 *Hammurabi*, § 117
37 *Code Napoléon*, 373, 381
38 *Vishnu*, vii, 10; viii, 2
39 POST, i, 295–6
40 SCHIRMACHER, p. 202
41 POST, i, 295–6
42 *Nârada*, i, 313; vi, 9
43 PAULITSCHKE, ii, 153
44 DUNNE, F. P. "Rights and Privileges of Women," in *Observations by Mr. Dooley*, 254. New York, 1902
45 *On Women*
46 BLACKSTONE, Bk. i, ch. xv
47 *Manu*, viii, 112; *Vasishtha*, xvi, 35

48 FRAZER, *Totemism and Exogamy*, i, 147
49 *Sacred Books of the East*, xxxix, 104
50 CRAWLEY, p. 43
51 PARKER, p. 65
52 *Sacred Books of the East*, xvi, 293
53 *Lî Kî*, Bk. x, Sect. ii, 36
54 *The Whole Duty of a Woman*, pp. 33-4
55 *A Father's Legacy to his Daughters*, pp. 104-5
56 *Woman in the Nineteenth Century*, p. 120.   Boston, Cleveland, New York, 1855
57 MARTIN, E. S. *The Luxury of Children*, pp. 109-10. New York and London, 1905
58 *Sesame and Lilies: Of Queens' Gardens*
59 *The Rights of Woman*, p. 277. London, 1792
60 *History of Woman Suffrage*, i, 37 ff.
61 *Ib.*, i, 357. LUCRETIA MOTT makes this statement at the Pennsylvania Woman's Rights Convention in 1852
62 ELLIS, *Studies in the Psychology of Sex; Modesty*, p. 24
63 MEYER, pp. 10-11
64 *Ib.*, p. 143
65 *Ib.*, p. 144
66 ELLIS, *Studies*, etc.; *Sex in Relation to Society*, p. 45
67 DAWSON, J., p. 33
68 *Lî Kî*, x, ii, 36
69 ELLIS, *The Ewe-Speaking Peoples*, p. 215
70 CHAMBERLAIN, p. 373
71 HERRERA, iii, 318
72 *Hammurabi*, § 143
73 *Manu*, ix, 5; 13; *Brihaspati*, xxiv, 2; 7; *Vishnu*, xxv, ii
74 1 *Timothy*, ii, 12, 13
75 BLACKSTONE, Bk. III, ch. vii
76 SCHIRMACHER, p. 228
77 *Essays for Young Ladies*, pp. 145-6. London, 1777
78 *Vishnu*, xxv, 12
79 PETERSON, P. "Vatsyayana on the Duties of a Hindu Wife." *Journal Anthropological Soc. of Bombay*, ii (1890-2), 462
80 *Manu*, v, 147-8; ix, 2; 3
81 CHAMBERLAIN, p. 375

XX

1 SPENCER and GILLEN, *Northern Tribes*, etc., p. 499; HOWITT, *The Jeraeil*, p. 315; VETTER, J. "Aus der Märchenvelt der Papuas in Kaiser-Wilhelms-Land," *Mitt. der Geographischen Gesellschaft su Jena*, xi (1892), 105; ELLIS, *The Yoruba-Speaking Peoples*, pp. 110-11

2 *Ib.*

3 CHALMERS, J. "Note on the Natives of Kiwai Island, Fly River, British New Guinea." *Journal Anthropological Institute*, xxxiii (1903), 119; *Ib.*, *Toaripi*, p. 329

4 PARKER, p. 62

· 5 HOWITT, *The Jeraeil*, p. 310

6 THILENIUS, G. "Ethnographische Ergebnisse aus Melanesien," Pt. i, *Abhandlungen der Kaiserlichen Leopoldinisch-Carolinischen Deutschen Akademie der Naturforscher*, *LXXX* (1902), 68

7 BOAS, FRANZ. "The Central Eskimo," vi (1884-5), *Annual Report Bureau American Ethnology*, p. 636

8 STEINMETZ, ii, 351

9

10 ROTH, W. H., p. 152

11 ALLDRIDGE, p. 133

12 FRAZER, *Totemism and Exogamy*, ii, 57

13 STEINMETZ, ii, 351

14 SPENCER and GILLEN, *Native Tribes*, etc., p. 517; *Northern Tribes*, etc., pp. 496-7

15 DENNETT, *The Folklore of the Fjort*, p. 16

16 KIDD, *Savage Childhood*, pp. 136-7

17 RIEDEL, J. G. F. *De Sluik en Kroesharige Rassen tusschen Selebes en Papua*, pp. 271, 439. S-Gravenhage, 1886

18 *Reports Cambridge Anthropological Expedition to Torres Straits*, vi, 136

19 HOLMES, J. "Initiation Ceremonies of Natives of the Papuan Gulf," *Journal Anthropological Institute*, xxxii (1902), 420

20 HAGEN, B. *Unter den Papua's*, p. 237. Weisbaden, 1899

21 CODRINGTON, pp. 98, 99

22 PARKINSON, J. "Notes on the Asaba People (Ibos) of

the Niger." *Journal Anthropological Institute*, xxxvi (1906), 313

23 ELLIS, *The Yoruba-Speaking Peoples*, p. 108
24 KINGSLEY, *Travels in West Africa*, pp. 377–80. Also *West African Studies*, p. 448. London and New York, 1899
25 WEEKS, p. 118
26 CRAWLEY, p. 43
27 SPENCER and GILLEN, *Native Tribes*, etc., pp. 540, 549–50; *Northern Tribes*, etc., p. 466
28 BROWN, pp. 356–7
29 FURNESS, W. H. *The Home-Life of Borneo Head-Hunters*, p. 169. Philadelphia, 1902
30 STEINMETZ, ii, 351
31 DENNETT, *At the Back of the Black Man's Mind*, p. 89
32 *American Anthropologist*, ii (1900), New Ser., 195
33 *The Questions of King Milinda*, iv, 4, 43
34 *A Father's Legacy to his Daughters*, p. 101
35 SPENCER and GILLEN, *Northern Tribes*, etc., p. 507
36 CAVAZZI, i, 404–8
37 CHAMBERLAIN, p. 370
38 *Manu*, v, 154–5, 160, 164; WILKINS, W. J. *Modern Hinduism*, p. 333. New York, 1887; COLEBROOKE, H. T. *The Duties of a Faithful Hindu Widow. Miscellaneous Essays*, i, 134. London, 1873
39 JESSUP, pp. 11-12
40 *The Dabistán*, p. 166
41 WESTERMARCK, *Moral Ideas*, i, 652
42 *Genesis*, iii, 16
43 1 *Corinthians*, xi, 8–9
44 *The American Lady's Preceptor*, Baltimore. 1815
45 SCHIRMACHER, p. 24
46 *The Ancren Riwle*, p. 317. London, 1853

XXI

1 LEONARD, pp. 228–9; ROTH, H. LING, ii, cc
2 AYMONIER, E. *Les Tchames et leurs Religions*, pp. 44–5, 109. Paris, 1891
3 WALPOLE, F. *The Ansayrii*, iii, 377. London, 1851

4   LEO AFRICANUS. *The History and Description of Africa*,
    ii, 458–9. Pub. Hakluyt Society
5   SPIETH, p. 490
6   MARCHAIS, ii, 147–8; BOSMAN, pp. 375–6
7   DIODORUS SICULUS, i, ch. ii; PLUTARCH, *Concerning
    Isis and Osiris*, 2
8   BHATTACHARYA, J. N. *Hindu Castes and Sects*, p. 537.
    Calcutta, 1896
9   *Vishnu*, xxv, 15, 16
10 *Numbers*, xxxi, 3–12
11 1 *Corinthians*, xiv, 35
12 HOWELLS, *A Modern Instance*, ch. iv
13 *The Dabistán*, p. 166
14 WESTERMARCK, *Moral Ideas*, i, 667 n. 1; BATCHELOR,
    pp. 550–1
15 DAWSON, J., p. 55
16 BHATTACHARYA, pp. 485–6, 493
17 ROSCOE, *Further Notes*, etc., p. 46
18 BREHM, R. B. *Das Inka-Reich*, p. 74. Jena, 1885;
    BUTTLES, J. R. *The Queens of Egypt*, pp. 196–8. London,
    1908
19 CUTTS, E. L. *Scenes and Characters of the Middle Ages*,
    p. 130. London, 1872
20 ROSCOE, *Further Notes*, etc., p. 45
21 FRAZER, J. G. "The Pyrtaneum, The Temple of Vesta,
    The Vestals, Perpetual Fires," *The Journal of Philology*,
    xiv (1885), 159 n
22 *Luke*, ii, 36–7
23 DE GROOT, ii, 756
24 WILSON, H. H. "A Sketch of the Religious Sects of the
    Hindus," *Asiatic Researches*, xvi (1828), 96
25 *Nicene and Post-Nicene Fathers*, ix, 122, § 2
26 POWERS, p. 154
27 *Didaskalia*, ch. xiv
28 SPIETH, pp. 445, 448, 450
29 HEARN, LAFCADIO. *Japan*, p. 158. New York and
    London, 1904
30 SAHAGUN, pp. 14, 15, 459; ACOSTA, Bk. v, ch. xv
31 *Protevangelium of James*, ch. vii, ch. xv; *Pseudo-Matthew*,
    ch. vii, ch. viii

32 CUNNINGHAM, J. F. *Uganda and its Peoples*, p. 80. London, 1905

33 ATHENAEUS, xiii, 33

34 *Kullavagga*, x, 1, 4; 3, 1; 6; 7

35 LANSLOTS, D. I. *Handbook of Canon Law*, p. 277. Ratisbon, Rome, New York, Cincinnati, 1911

36 *Ib.*, pp. 131, 244, 245, 271

37 HEHN, J. "Hymen und Gebete an Marduk," *Beiträge zur Assyriologie*, v (1906), 286

38 GRAY, J. H. *China*, ii, 24. London, 1878

39 SOZOMEN, *Ecclesiastical History*, ii, 12. *Nicene and Post-Nicene Fathers*, ii

40 GRÉGOIRE DE TOURS, *Histoire Ecclésiastique des Francs*, vii

41 *Ancient Laws and Institutes of England*, pp. 292, 355

42 *Relation Historique de l'Ethiopie Occidentale*, i, 270

43 KIDD, *The Essential Kafir*, p. 190

44 *The Indian Antiquary*, xxiii (1894), 11

45 PLUTARCH, *Pythian Responses*, 22

46 *Theatre of the Hindus*, ii, 110-11. Ed. WILSON. London, 1835

47 LOWELL, PERCIVAL. *Occult Japan*, pp. 157, 162, 188. Boston and New York, 1895

48 TERTULLIAN, *Against Heretics*, ch. xxx; IRENÆUS, *Against Heresies*, I, xxv, 3, 6

49 SULPETIUS SEVERUS, ch. xlvi

50 ECKENSTEIN, LINA. *Woman under Monasticism*, p. 272. Cambridge, 1896

51 GASQUET, F. A. *Henry VIII and the English Monasteries*, i, 110-21. London, 1895

52 *The Letters of Saint Teresa*, p. 271. Ed. DALTON

53 *Kullavagga*, Tenth *Khandhaka*

54 STRABO, VII, iii, 4

55 *Sesame and Lilies: Of Queens' Gardens*, pp. 107, 108. New York, 1886

XXII

1 YUDELSON, S. "The Education and Professional Activities of Women," *Annals of the American Academy of Political and Social Science*, xxv (1905), 121

2 FRAZER, *Totemism and Exogamy*, iv, 330

3 CRAWLEY, pp. 93, 207

4 *Ib.*, p. 208; HOWITT, *Native Tribes*, etc., p. 402

5 BROWN, p. 409

6 CRAWLEY, p. 208

7 *Manu*, ii, 213; *Âpastamba*, i, 5, 14

8 *The Fo-Sho-Hing-Tsan-King*, iv, 22. *Sacred Books of the East*, xix

9 *The Book of the Great Decease*, ch. v, 23. *Sacred Books of the East*, xi

10 CLEMENT of Rome. *Two Epistles Concerning Virginity; Second Epistle*, ch. iii. *Ante-Nicene Christian Library*, xiv

11 BAIN, pp. 33–4

12 AULUS GELLIUS, *Attic Nights*, i, 6; DONALDSON, p. 9

13 *The Anatomy of Melancholy*, Pt. iii, sec. 2, mem. 6, subs. 5

14 CRAWLEY, pp. 325–6

15 *Ib.*, pp. 329–31; GARNETT, *The Women of Turkey: The Christian Women*, p. 235

16 DAWSON, J., p. 32

17 GARNETT, *The Women of Turkey: The Christian Women*, pp. 203, 235

18 CRAWLEY, pp. 338–9

19 *Reports Cambridge Anthropological Expedition to Torres Straits*, vi, 117

20 CHAMBERLAIN, p. 371

21 SHEANE, J. H. WEST. "Some Aspects of the Awemba Religion and Superstitious Observances," *Journal Anthropological Institute*, xxxvi (1907), 156

22 *Li Ki*, Bk. IX, sect. iii, 10

23 KOVALEVSKY, p. 45

24 *Ephesians*, v, 23; I *Corinthians*, vii, 4

25 SAINT TERESA, *The Way of Perfection*, p. 54. London, 1860

26 *Manu*, v, 154

27 WESTERMARCK, *Marriage*, p. 175 n. 6

28 *Ib.*

29 ERASMUS, *Colloquies: The Uneasy Wife*

30 TERTULLIAN, *On the Apparel of Women*, ch. xiii

31 *Ib.*, ch. iv

32 FRAZER, *Totemism and Exogamy*, iv, 234, 235
33 PLINY, *Letters*
34 JESSUP, p. 15
35 PLOSS and BARTELS, i, 904
36 *Ib.*, i, 924
37 *Brihaspati*, xxiv, 8, 9
38 CRAWLEY, p. 395
39 PAULITSCHKE, ii, 67
40 FRAZER, *The Golden Bough*, i, 28
41 *Decency in Conversation amongst Women*, p. 75
42 CHAMBERLAIN, p. 372
43 1 *Timothy*, ii, 9
44 *On the Apparel of Women*, ch. 1
45 *On the Veiling of Virgins*, ch. xii
46 DONALDSON, pp. 184-5
47 *On the Apparel of Women*, chs. ii, iii; *On the Veiling of Virgins*, ch. xv
48 *Letters to Young People*, pp. 90-1
49 JESSUP, p. 3
50 TERTULLIAN, *On the Apparel of Women*, ch. i
51 *Manu*, ii, 213-14
52 *Uttarâdhyayana*, viii, 18; *Âkârânga Sûtra*. Fourth Lesson in *Gaina Sûtras*. *Sacred Books of the East*, xxii

XXIII

1 HOWITT, A. W. "On Some Australian Ceremonies of Initiation," *Journal Anthropological Institute*, xiii (1883-4), 452 n.
2 WALLACE, A. R. *Travels on the Amazon and Rio Negro*, p. 348. London, 1889
3 *Reports Cambridge Anthropological Expedition to Torres Straits*, vi, 140, 145, 146
4 Cp. *Satapatha-Brâhmana*, xiv Kânda, 1 Adhyâya, 1 Brâhmana, 31
5 KINGSLEY, *Travels in West Africa*, p. 377
6 DENNETT, *At the Back of the Black Man's Mind*, p. 229
7 WESTERMARCK, *Moral Ideas*, i, 665
8 GARNETT, *The Women of Turkey: The Christian Women*, p. 106
9 RUSSELL, FRANK. "The Pima Indians," XXVI (1908) *Annual Report American Bureau of Ethnology*, p. 206

10 HODSON, p. 117
11 MACDONALD, D., i, 152
12 SUMNER, HELEN L. *Equal Suffrage*, p. 131. New York and London, 1909
13 *History of Woman Suffrage*, i, 81
14 *Ib.*, i, 53
15 *Ib.*, i, 144
16 *Ib.*, i, 515
17 *Ib.*, i, 555
18 *Memoirs of Margaret Fuller Ossoli*, ii, 205. Boston, 1852
19 MEYER, p. 10
20 *Ib.*, p. 9
21 *Ib.*, p. 26
22 SCHIRMACHER, p. 184
23 HIGGINSON, *Common Sense About Women*, p. 200
24 DAVIES, p. 159
25 DE MAULDE, p. 98
26 *Memoirs of Margaret Fuller Ossoli*, i, 321-2
27 POWERS, p. 150
28 DE MAULDE, p. 93 n. 1
29 Ch. VII
30 DE MAULDE, p. 93
31 *Ib.*, p. 134
32 PUTNAM, p. 186
33 MEYER, p. 27
34 EARLE, p. 269
35 DONALDSON, pp. 125-6
36 MEYER, pp. 222 *ff*.
37 *Ib.*, p. 227
38 SCHIRMACHER, p. 185
39 BARTELS, MAX. *Die Medicin der Naturvölker*, p. 53. Leipzig, 1893
40 GARNETT, *The Women of Turkey: The Christian Women*, p. 338
41 CAVAZZI, ii, 267
42 *Acts of Paul and Thecla*
43 *Ecclesiastical History*, viii, 23
44 PEARSON, ii, 38
45 ECKENSTEIN, p. 221
46 ELLIS, *Studies*, etc.; *Modesty*, etc., p. 242

47   EARLE, p. 357
48   *Vishnu*, xxv, 7; PETERSON, P.   "On the Duties of a Hindu Wife," *Journal Anthropological Society of Bombay*, ii (1890-2), 461
49   *Life*, Pt. iii, ch. v.   New York, 1820
50   BLACKWELL, p. 80
51   NEARING, SCOTT, and NELLIE, M. S.   *Woman and Social Progress*, p. 115.   New York, 1912
52   MEYER, p. 148 n., 160, 171
53   BLACKWELL, pp. 70, 190, 208-9
54   DENNETT, *At the Back of the Black Man's Mind*, p. 130
55   RIVERS, pp. 420-1
56   FRAZER, *The Golden Bough*, i, 223
57   EARLE, p. 81
58   *Woman in the Nineteenth Century*, pp. 150-1

XXIV

1   HOWITT, *The Jeraeil*, p. 315; Ib., *Native Tribes*, etc., p. 354
2   *Reports Cambridge Anthropological Expedition to Torres Straits*, v, 256
3   CODRINGTON, p. 83
4   POWERS, p. 194
5   *Untrodden Fields of Anthropology*, i, 69
6   *The Exemplary Life of the Pious Lady Guion*, pt. II, chs. xii, xiii.   Philadelphia, 1804
7   *Life of Saint Teresa*, p. 252.   Ed. Archbishop of Westminster.   London, 1865
8   SUMNER, ch. iv
9   SCHIRMACHER, pp. 164, 185, 224
10   BLACKWELL, p. 52
11   CHESTERTON, G. K.   *What's Wrong with the World*, p. 134.   London, New York, Toronto, and Melbourne, 1910
12   DUNNE, F. P.   *Mr. Dooley in Peace and in War: On the New Woman*
13   BLACKWELL, pp. 117-18
14   MEYER, p. 165
15   *Ib.*, p. 223
16   *History of Woman Suffrage*, i, 629

XXV

1 CODRINGTON, p. 262
2 *Reports Cambridge Anthropological Expedition to Torres Straits*, vi, 159
3 HOWITT, *Native Tribes*, etc., pp. 456, 459
4 COX, pp. 329-30
5 *Eddas*, p. 202. London, Stockholm, Copenhagen, Berlin, New York, 1906; GRÉGOIRE DE TOURS, i, 273
6 CRAWFURD, JOHN. *History of the Indian Archipelago*, ii, 244-9. Edinburgh, 1820
7 EARLE, p. 373
8 WOOD, *Survivals in Christianity*, p. 263. New York and London, 1893. His authority is a newspaper
9 SHAKESPEAR, p. 379
10 FELKIN, R. W. "Notes on the For Tribes of Central Africa," *Proc. Roy. Soc. Edinburgh*, xiii (1884-6), 218-19
11 CURTISS, p. 74 n. 3
12 WESTERMARCK, *Moral Ideas*, ii, 673
13 *Jour. Anthropological Soc. Bombay*, ii (1890-2), 512
14 *Reports Cambridge Anthropological Expedition to Torres Straits*, vi, 140
15 WIEDEMANN, A. *The Realms of the Egyptian Dead*, p. 30. London, 1902
16 OTWAY, THOMAS. *Venice Preserved*, Act I, sc. i
17 *On the Apparel of Women*, ch. ii
18 HARTLAND, i, 173
19 *Woman in the Nineteenth Century*, p. 41
20 *Description of Sukhâvatî, The Land of Bliss*, § 8, 34. *Sacred Books of the East*, xlix
21 *Nârada*, i, 204-5
22 *Timæus*
23 *Manu*, xii, 62-9
24 PLOSS, ii, 263
25 DE GROOT, i, 65

INDEX

Abyssinians, 34, 41, 133, 136, 264
Acting, 64, 124, 141
Addams, Jane, 147 n., 197, 199 n.
Africa, West Coast of, 13, 18, 22, 26, 28, 29, 38, 45, 60, 62, 63, 71, 82, 86, 93, 94, 96, 101, 102, 104, 106, 111, 117, 121, 123, 125, 131, 173, 190, 193, 195, 197, 220, 226, 228, 230–1, 233, 234, 240, 241, 242, 246, 247, 253, 274, 288, 292, 297
Agnodice, 173, 289, 291 n.
Ainu, 177, 178, 179, 181, 243
Akikuyus, 29 n., 60, 142, 193
Amazons, 23, 131, 312
Andaman Islanders, 181
Arabs, 2, 8, 22, 34, 104, 135, 179, 204, 241, 272, 318, 320
Armenians, 9, 41, 264
Aru Islands, 94
Assam, 207–8, 317
Australians, 9, 11, 13–14, 31, 32, 42, 55, 56, 57, 60, 70–1, 73, 76, 86, 91–2, 93–4, 95, 98, 99, 102, 103, 104, 105, 107, 109, 111, 114, 116, 124, 128, 129, 137, 149–50, 172–3, 188, 189, 190, 192, 205, 206, 207, 215, 220, 226, 227, 228, 232, 234, 243, 260, 264, 274, 296–7, 314, 318
Awemba, 265

Babylonians, 39, 44, 72, 87, 189, 212, 220, 252
Baganda, 21, 45, 60, 88, 193, 243, 244, 248

Bageshu, 56
Bahima, 60
Bakongo, 133
Bali, 38
Bangala, 60, 104, 132, 190, 231–2
Barea, 260
Bari, 142, 168
Barrenness, 75, 85 ff., 123, 177, 246, 304
Bashkirs, 193
Basques, 58
Basuto, 71, 80, 88, 91
Bedui, 41
Beni-Mzab, 121
Biography of women, vi, 135, 165
Blackwell, Elizabeth, 126, 173, 290–1, 291–2, 302, 305–6
Blue-Stocking, 47, 128, 214 ff., 311
Bogos, 212
Bondo, 193
Bongos, 137, 168
Borneo, 14, 33, 61–2, 106, 115, 128, 150, 178, 190, 197, 233, 240
Bornu, 267
Bororo, 117
Brahmans, 61, 73, 74, 87, 96–7, 99, 124, 204, 207, 208, 248, 272 n., 290, 320
Bride, qualifications of, 14–17, 43
Bride-price, 6, 34, 37, 38, 43, 192 ff., 247. *See* Marriage by Purchase
Buddhists, 20, 60, 73, 204, 205, 244, 245, 249–50, 253–4, 256–7, 261, 262, 275, 320

24

CPSIA information can be obtained at www.ICGtesting.com
Printed in the USA
BVOW06s1421100915

417468BV00005B/15/P